PENGUIN BOOKS

AWAY OFF SHORE

Nathaniel Philbrick is the author of the *New York Times* bestsellers *In the Heart of the Sea*, which won the National Book Award; *Sea of Glory: America's Voyage of Discovery, the U.S. Exploring Expedition*, winner of the Theodore and Franklin D. Roosevelt Naval History Prize; *Mayflower*, a finalist for the Pulitzer Prize; and *The Last Stand: Custer, Sitting Bull, and the Battle of the Little Bighorn*. He has lived on Nantucket Island since 1986.

Away Off Shore

Nantucket Island and Its People, 1602–1890

Nathaniel Philbrick

PENGUIN BOOKS

Published in association with Mill Hill Press of Nantucket

PENGUIN BOOKS

Published by the Penguin Group

Penguin Group (USA) Inc., 375 Hudson Street, New York, New York 10014, U.S.A.

Penguin Group (Canada), 90 Eglinton Avenue East, Suite 700, Toronto,
Ontario, Canada M4P 2Y3 (a division of Pearson Penguin Canada Inc.)

Penguin Books Ltd, 80 Strand, London WC2R 0RL, England

Penguin Ireland, 25 St Stephen's Green, Dublin 2, Ireland (a division of Penguin Books Ltd)

Penguin Group (Australia), 250 Camberwell Road, Camberwell,
Victoria 3124, Australia (a division of Pearson Australia Group Pty Ltd)

Penguin Books India Pvt Ltd, 11 Community Centre,
Panchsheel Park, New Delhi – 110 017, India

Penguin Group (NZ), 67 Apollo Drive, Rosedale, Auckland 0632,
New Zealand (a division of Pearson New Zealand Ltd)

Penguin Books (South Africa) (Pty) Ltd, 24 Sturdee Avenue,
Rosebank, Johannesburg 2196, South Africa

Penguin Books Ltd, Registered Offices:
80 Strand, London WC2R 0RL, England

First published in the United States of America by Mill Hill Press 1994
This edition with a new preface published in Penguin Books 2011

1 3 5 7 9 10 8 6 4 2

LIBRARY OF CONGRESS CATALOGING IN PUBLICATION DATA
Philbrick, Nathaniel.
Away off shore : Nantucket Island and its people, 1602–1890 / Nathaniel Philbrick.
p. cm.
"First published in the United States of America by Mill Hill Press, 1994"—T.p. verso.
Includes bibliographical references and index.
ISBN 978-0-14-312012-4
1. Nantucket Island (Mass.)—History. 2. Nantucket Island (Mass.)—Biography. I. Title.
F72.N2P47 2011
974.4'97—dc22   2010053110

Printed in the United States of America

For Melissa

Contents

Preface to the Penguin Edition

IN SEPTEMBER OF 1986, I moved to Nantucket with my wife Melissa and our two children. It was Melissa's job as an attorney that brought us to the island, a sandy crescent almost thirty miles out to sea about which I knew almost nothing—except, of course, for what I'd read in Herman Melville's *Moby-Dick*. Not surprisingly, in retrospect, I was immediately taken with Nantucket's whaling past. At that time I was a freelance sailing journalist, but with each passing year I delved ever deeper into the island's history, eventually publishing a handful of articles in academic journals such as the *New England Quarterly*. Then, in the spring of 1992, I got my first big break.

In those days any Nantucketer with literary aspirations looked for guidance from Mimi Beman, proprietress of Mitchell's Book Corner on Main Street. As it so happened, Mimi had been contacted by Albert "Bud" Egan, Jr., owner of the Marine Home Center, a highly successful lumberyard and home furnishings business on Lower Orange Street. Bud had a long-standing interest in the island's history, which he attributed to his mother who'd come from one of Nantucket's founding families, the Coffins. Just a few years before, Bud had started the Mill Hill Press and was now in search of an author to write a history of the island through the end of whaling in the late nineteenth century. Based on the articles I'd shown her, Mimi recommended me.

I'll never forget my first meeting with Bud in his second-floor office overlooking the sheds of the lumberyard and beyond that the marshy convolutions of Nantucket Harbor. Bud was a no non-sense kind of guy. I should submit an outline and sample preface to Mimi, who was acting as his informal consultant, and we'd take it from there. It was my first commission to write history.

Over the course of the next few weeks, I found myself writing and rewriting that preface. I didn't know it at the time, but I was establishing what was to become my method for starting a book. By working my way through draft after draft of the opening overview, I slowly came to understand what it was I wanted to say. I also began to find my own voice as an historian. Most important, I was able to move from a disparate pile of notes and ideas to a firm structure for the book. I would devote each chapter to a specific character whose story would move the overall history of the island forward to the next character until I had finally made my way to the end of Nantucket's whaling era.

Mimi gave me the green light, and in the fall of 1992, at the age of thirty-six, I embarked on the path I've been following ever since. By going directly to the sources—whether they be in the archives or out there in the landscape—I hoped to hunt out the stories and the characters that brought the past to life.

First I went to the Nantucket Town Building, an undistinguished brick edifice containing a warren of little rooms stuffed to overflowing with records and documents, many of them dating back to the mid-seventeenth century. Then it was on to the Nantucket Historical Association. This was the pre-Internet era, so instead of calling up archives on my laptop at home, I spent weeks in their library, reading almost a century's worth of island newspapers on microfilm. I was so new to it all that I didn't fully appreciate at that time the extraordinary richness of the association's collection: journals, logs, daybooks, and letters that revealed the history and culture of both an island and the industry that made it famous. It was in the archives of yet another island repository, the Nantucket Atheneum (which also happened to be the town's public library), that I found my favorite artifact: the journal of Peleg Folger, a young whaleman in the middle of the eighteenth century with an eye for the telling detail and a wicked sense of humor.

Since my children, then seven and ten, could be counted on to return home from school every afternoon at precisely two thirty (and I was the one responsible for meeting them), I decided to enlist them in the enterprise. After school we'd all pile into the car and search out the places about which I'd been reading, places like the Hidden Forest in the eastern portion of the island, near where the Wampanoag leader King Philip seized the "praying Indian" John Gibbs, and Capaum Pond, the kettle hole to the west that had once been at the center of the first English settlement. What became known as "Daddy's wild goose chases" often left us muddy and itchy with poison ivy, but these escapades proved immensely helpful when it came to understanding the importance of place to the past. On a tiny sea-swept island, geography matters, and I was lucky to have the past right there, under my feet.

By the end of December I was about a quarter of the way through a first draft. During a New Year's Day visit to Lake Winnipesaukee, my good friend Peter Gow provided crucial input and encouragement and became the book's editor. By Memorial Day weekend I'd finished a first draft, and with the help of Peter, my father (a retired English professor who doubled as our copy editor), and my mother-in-law (a retired librarian who created the index), I rethought, rewrote, and revised, another process I've followed in every book since. The manuscript was done by the fall of 1993 and published in the spring of 1994.

In the almost twenty years since, much has changed on the island. Sadly, Bud Egan and Mimi Beman have both passed away. However, Bud's love of Nantucket history has been memorialized in the form of the Egan Maritime Institute, an organization that celebrates Nantucket's seafaring heritage and continues to publish books through the Mill Hill Press, while the store Mimi turned into a Nantucket institution, Mitchell's Book Corner, is still operating on Main Street. This book honors both Nantucket's past and its future. With the reissuing of *Away Off Shore* as a Penguin paperback, it's my hope that the book with which I found a calling will now find a new audience.

—Nathaniel Philbrick
Nantucket, January 2011

Preface

"Nantucket! Take out your map and look at it.
See what a real corner of the world it occupies:
how it stands there, away off shore . . ."
—*Herman Melville*

I T IS A CURIOUS DESIGN: the arm of Cape Cod bent north-
ward over the irregular shapes of Martha's Vineyard and
Nantucket Island. If the Vineyard hovers beside the Cape
like a clinging child, Nantucket stands out defiantly to the east,
straining to put even more distance between itself and the continent behind it. It is a curling crescent of sand that wants to be
left alone.

Given the island's place on the map, you might expect Nantucketers to be an independent bunch, and you would be right.
After crossing Nantucket Sound more than 300 years ago, the
first white settlers were not about to follow in the footsteps of
the New Englanders they sailed all that distance to escape.
Instead, they went their own way in a truly spectacular fashion.
By 1775 this tiny island had become the foremost whaling port
in the world, prompting the British statesman Edmund Burke to
look to its inhabitants as the leaders of a new American breed: a
"recent people . . . who are still, as it were, but in the gristle, and
not yet hardened into the bone of manhood."

Although the Nantucketers undoubtedly enjoyed Burke's
praise, they were reluctant to identify themselves with the
colonies to their west. When America went to war, Nantucket
wanted no part of it, steadfastly avoiding all involvement in the
Revolution and even negotiating its own private peace treaty
during the War of 1812. It is true that many of the Nantucketers

were Quaker pacifists, but there were other motives influencing their determination to go it alone. Living on an island that already enjoyed world-wide recognition and respect, Nantucketers were not about to defer to another and (in their eyes) less esteemed country. As far as they were concerned, Nantucket was a commonwealth of its own. During a visit in 1847, the essayist and poet Ralph Waldo Emerson recognized "a strong national feeling" on the island and commented in his journal, "Nation of Nantucket makes its own war & peace."

As a nation beside a nation, Nantucket was (and is) both a microcosm of America and an exception to the rule: a tightly knit community that took its special brand of provincialism all across the world, becoming, in the process, one of the most cosmopolitan places in America. On an island of paradoxes, the Quaker whalemen were perhaps the most paradoxical. At once pacifist whalehunters, plain-dressed millionaires, abolitionist floggers of common seamen, and devoted family men who were never home, these "Quakers with a vengeance" embodied a truly mind-boggling array of contradictions.

But the whalemen are only part of the story. Since their husbands were often on the other side of the planet, the women of Nantucket developed their own kind of independence, enjoying freedoms and responsibilities that were literally centuries ahead of their time. Nantucket also had vital and well-defined African-American and Portuguese communities that contributed significantly to the island's whaling prosperity. Before a horrifying plague decimated their population in 1763, Native Americans exerted a strong and lasting influence on the island, to be followed by yet another native culture in the nineteenth century when increasing numbers of Pacific islanders came to Nantucket on the decks of whaleships.

Ultimately, the history of Nantucket is as much about the interaction of different cultures as it is the story of what Obed

Macy, the island's first historian, described as "the peaceable settlement of a few enterprising families, and their slow progress in wealth and numbers." Just as it has become increasingly difficult to insist that the West was actually "won" by the American cowboy, so is it time to recognize that the island was something more than a spawning ground for Quaker whalemen. If in the pages that follow many heroes of old are portrayed in a less than flattering light, I am by no means the first to claim that Nantucket's past was hardly as "peaceable" as Obed Macy would have had us believe. In 1877 the Nantucketer Alexander Starbuck began his *History of the American Whale Fishery* with this statement: "If in the search for facts the historical idols of others have been shattered, it may be a source of satisfaction to them to learn that the writer has been equally iconoclastic with many that he too has reverenced."

But the main aim of this book is not to discredit the mythic men of Nantucket's heyday; instead, it is to bring to life the island's history by focusing on the individual men and women—in all their flawed and fascinating glory—who helped to make Nantucket the whaling capital of the world. The dates referred to in the book's subtitle (1602–1890) span two events: Bartholomew Gosnold's first exploratory voyage to the Cape and islands and the death of Frederick C. Sanford, the man who not only lived through the final rise and fall of the Nantucket whale fishery but also helped to record (and romanticize) it for future generations. While the story of the island's subsequent rise as a summer colony is an important one that needs to be told, it is beyond the scope of this work.

In an effort to make the Nantucketers of the seventeenth, eighteenth, and nineteenth centuries more accessible to a modern-day audience, the spelling and punctuation of quotations have been modernized. Although the text contains no footnotes, an extensive "Notes" section at the end of the book includes references as well as additional information and anecdotes.

In a book about Nantucketers, it is only appropriate, I think, that we begin with the island they all shared and helped to shape. No matter how much it has changed over the years, Nantucket still occupies the same place on the map. More than anything else, it is this place, "away off shore," that has determined who the Nantucketer is.

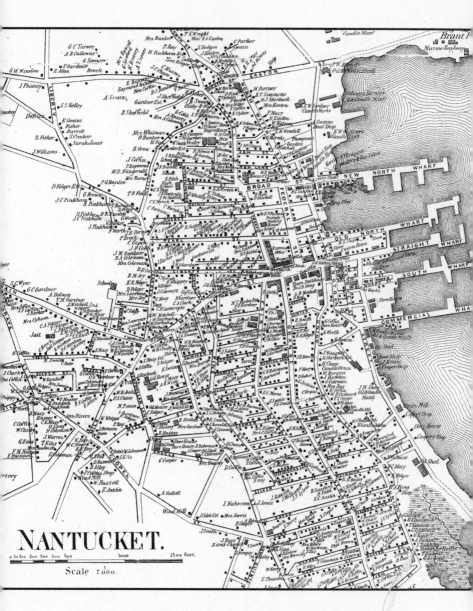

NANTUCKET.

0 50 100 200 300 400 500   1000   1500 feet.

Scale $\frac{1}{7000}$.

Map of the Town of Nantucket, surveyed under Henry F. Walling,
Superintendent of State Maps, 1858.

Reproduced by permission of the Nantucket Historical Association.

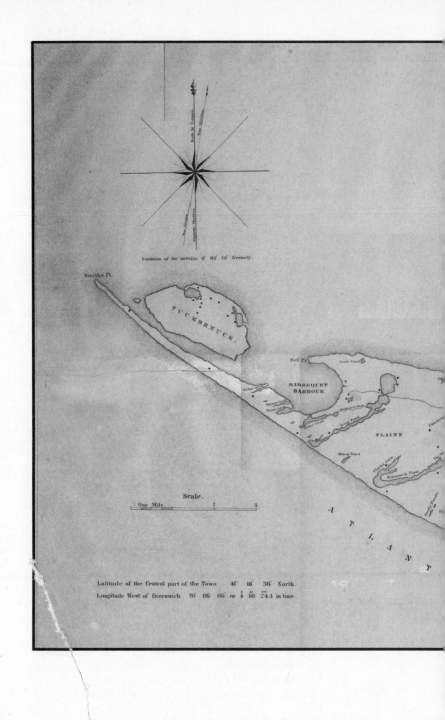

Variation of the needle 9° 02' 19" Westerly.

Smiths Pt.

T U C K E R N U C K.

Eel Pt.

MADDEQUET
HARBOUR

North Pond

Barber Creek

Warren Creek

Round Swamp

Miller Swamp

McKesson Ditch

Long Pond

PLAINS

Cambridge

Sheep Pond

Clarks Cove

Romawack Pond

A T L A N T I C

Scale.

One Mile.   2   3

Latitude of the Central part of the Town   41° 16' 36" North.
Longitude West of Greenwich 70° 06' 06" or 4ʰ 40ᵐ 24.4ˢ in time

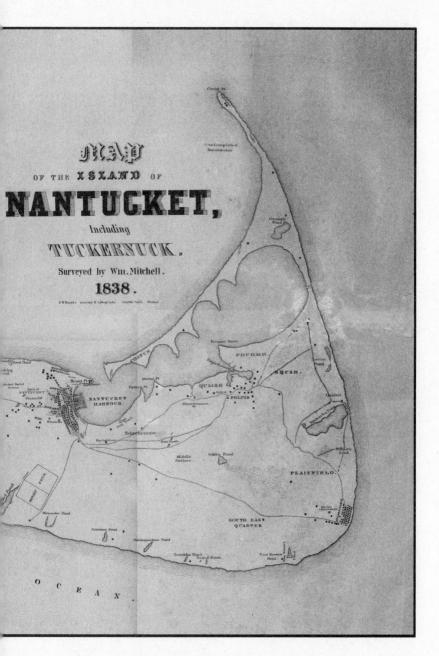

William Mitchell's map of Nantucket, 1838.

Reproduced by permission of the Nantucket Historical Association.

Away Off Shore

CHAPTER I

An Island and Its Altar

I<small>T IS A FARAWAY PLACE</small> on a faraway island but well worth the trip: Altar Rock set atop Saul's Hills, one of the highest points on Nantucket. Tradition has it that this glacier-scored boulder was once sacred to the island's Native Americans. Certainly it is hard to resist a religious sense of awe when standing beside it.

The view is breath-taking, particularly in fall when the gently rolling heathlands that stretch out in all directions (known locally as the Moors) are tinged with red and yellow. Although the hill is not high enough to enable one to see Nantucket in its entirety, Altar Rock is the best seat in the house when it comes to imagining how the island originally came into being. Between 22,000 and 16,000 years ago, a giant glacier stretching across what is now Nantucket Sound bulldozed Saul's Hills into a rough approximation of their present form. This is where the icy shovel of the bulldozer stopped, dumping the boulder we see beside us.

As global warming (by no means a new phenomenon) caused the glacier to melt, water began to run to the south, leaving behind a relatively smooth terrain of lighter sands and gravel known as an outwash plain. This is why the beach sand on the southern shore of the island is so much finer than that to the north, prompting one old-timer to observe, "I never saw a stone along the [south] shore bigger than a man's head." Fifteen thousand years ago, however, what is now a beach was a long way from the ocean; instead of being an island, Nantucket was a low range of hills more than forty miles inland.

As the climate continued to warm (and the ocean continued to rise), plant life inevitably began to spring up among these hills, providing the basis for an ever-improving soil. Thirteen thousand years ago, jack pines and spruce trees began to grow; a few thousand years later, oaks appeared. What is now Nantucket Sound was then a valley of ponds, lakes, and forests. It was not until just 5,000 years ago—a drop in the bucket of geological time—that the ever-encroaching ocean flooded this valley and Nantucket became an island. Then the ocean's waves and currents went to work, sculpting the "glacier's gift" into the shape we all recognize today, most notably creating Great Point at the northeastern extremity of the island as well as the barrier beach known as Coatue (pronounced "Koe-TOO") along the outer rim of Nantucket Harbor.

Whether or not Nantucket was ever thickly forested after it became an island is a debated point. Certainly the newly risen ocean would have had a stunting effect on shore-side tree growth. But this did not keep an exposed area such as Coatue from becoming so heavily wooded that as late as 1711 the town selectmen commented on "the great benefit" of this neck of land "to the succor of our sheep in hard seasons," while passing a provision against the cutting of "cedars, pines, or any other growths" on Coatue. According to the early historian Obed Macy, oak trees "of an uncommonly hard and firm texture" once flourished throughout the island and provided the timbers for many of the old homes that are still standing today; a particularly "good growth of white oak trees" apparently shaded the area around what is now Cliff Road on the north side of the island.

Instead of salt spray, it was probably fires—either naturally occurring or man-made—that limited the growth of trees on the island. And, in fact, the forests that are specifically mentioned in seventeenth-century town records were all surrounded (and protected from spreading fires) by either water or swamps: the Longwoods within the embrace of Hummock Pond, the Broadwoods in Coskata (pronounced "Kos-KAY-ta"), and the Beechwoods near the cranberry bogs in Polpis. The remnants of this last area of tree growth are now known as the Hidden Forest. This is yet another sacred place. Standing within the sun-dappled quietude of these ancient beech trees, it is difficult to believe that you are on an island thirty miles out to sea.

Nantucket's original human residents first came to the area approximately 8,000 years ago, long before it was an island. At this time America's native inhabitants were a hunting culture, pursuing the caribou and other large game that followed in the wake of the glacier. As the climate continued to warm and the caribou moved north, early Nantucketers began to rely increasingly on seeds, fruits, and roots for nourishment. Archeological digs on the eastern end of the island in Quidnet indicate that deer were an important part of the Indians' diet in the first century A.D., by which time Nantucket had been an island for more than 3,000 years. At some point, however, over-hunting must have led to the animals' extirpation (the deer that now exist on Nantucket were introduced in the 1920s). Other game animals, such as the raccoon and fox, were also killed off by the Indians. In fact, when the naturalist John James Audubon came to Nantucket, he reported that "the largest quadruped found in a wild state is the Norway rat." There were cases, however, in which the island seems to have provided a refuge for species that had disappeared elsewhere in the region. Much to the chagrin of some modern-day developers, Nantucket is one of the few places in Massachusetts that still offers a habitat for the short-eared owl. In his day, Audubon found species of jumping mice, shrews, and bats on Nantucket which were so unusual that he preserved them in jars of rum for further study.

Although Nantucket has developed a reputation as an infertile and unforgiving land (one eighteenth-century observer described it as a "barren sandbank fertilized with whale-oil only"), this is not the way the island's native population would have perceived it. Indians throughout the Northeast commonly sought out sandy soils (of which Nantucket, of course, has plenty) that could be easily worked with hand tools made from wood, stone, and quahog shells. It is true that archeologists have found no evidence of the mounds and storage pits associated with Indian corn crops on Martha's Vineyard and Cape Cod, but this does not necessarily mean that Nantucket's Indians failed to cultivate the island. As we shall see, given the extreme abuse any arable plot would ultimately receive at the hands of the English, it is not surprising that few signs remain of the Native Nantucketers' agricultural activity. In fact, without any game animals on the island, farming must have been especially important to Nantucket's Indians, who also enjoyed the benefit of a long, frost-free growing season due to the warming influence of the nearby Gulf Stream. Today, autumn and winter temperatures on the island are as much as five degrees above those experienced in the nearby Boston area.

As its first human inhabitants, Nantucket's Native Americans had a major impact on the island's ecology. Besides ridding the island of game animals, they also may have been responsible for the relative scarcity of trees. Prior to spring planting, they cleared the land through burning, and as we have seen, when the English first arrived on Nantucket, tree growth was limited to a few swampy and water-enclosed sections of the island. The Indians also had no qualms about abandoning their traditional, less invasive methods of working the land when the English arrived in the 1660s. According to one account, they "would with delight, for whole days together, follow the path of the plowshares; and they would earnestly entreat the English to plow their land for them."

It was not just a new technology the English introduced to Nantucket; they also applied a whole new set of priorities to their environment. Whereas the Indians had kept on the move, changing their village sites on a seasonal basis, the English appointed a delegation of "lot-layers" who divided up the land into a permanent settlement. Soon the footpaths of the Indians were replaced by cart paths, which in turn evolved into deeply rutted roads as increasing numbers of horses and oxen were brought to the island.

As farming and sheep-raising developed, the English set out to reduce the number of dogs (not to mention crows and rats) on Nantucket. These small, fox-like creatures had been highly prized by the Indians for their assistance in hunting waterfowl. The English sheepherders, however, had no place for native dogs, which delighted in scattering and occasionally attacking their flocks. As early as 1663 the town determined that a "warning shall be given to all the Indians to kill the dogs among them." In 1670 a kind of canine Moby Dick seems to have afflicted the island; the record states, "whosoever shall kill the wild dog—a white dog having been seen several times about the town, shall be paid 30 shillings."

The English were also less than enamored of Nantucket's snakes, particularly in the eastern end of the island, where a snake was reportedly sighted "as big round as a gallon keg" and eleven or twelve feet long! Jethro Swain, a third-generation Nantucketer, recalled how one sunny day in the early spring, a huge number of snakes, groggy with cold, were discovered near a natural spring still known today as Snake Spring. According to Swain, the English "mustered a company . . . that dug two holes, and with hay rakes they raked as many of them into the holes as they could—about two cartsfull." The English then set huge bonfires over the pits and "as the heat caused the snakes to attempt to escape, they were driven back . . . until they were all subdued." Today snakes are no more common on Nantucket than they are anywhere else in New England.

The English also took the bull by the horns when it came to managing the island's many ponds, an approach they seem to have inherited from the Indians. In 1665 the town decided to "dig a trench to drain the Long Pond . . . with regard to a weir for taking fish. . . . The work is to be carried on thus: the one half of the work is to be done by the Indians, the other half by the English inhabitants or owners, the Indians to have half the fish so long as they attend the weir carefully." To this day the "Madaket Ditch" connects Long Pond to the tidal waters of Hither Creek.

Just how fragile these ponds were (and are) is demonstrated by the history of Lily Pond, which once lapped the base of what is now called Sunset Hill, site of the Oldest House. In the pond's center was Gull Island, where the first settlers had built a fort in case of Indian attack. One afternoon in the early eighteenth century, an eleven-year-old girl by the name of Love Paddack stopped to play along the water's edge, not far from where Center and Westchester Streets now intersect. Taking up a handy clam shell, she dug a small trench so that a rivulet of water began to run out of the pond. By the time she had finished playing, the rivulet was a running stream. Thinking nothing of it, Love returned home, ate her supper, and went to bed. The next morning she was awakened by the shouts of her father, who announced that "some evil-minded person has let the Lily Pond out." Love's trench had grown into a "great gully" through which the rush of water had washed away the town's fulling mill—a disastrous occurrence for Love's father, a weaver. Since there was nothing she could do to bring back the pond, Love quite sensibly decided to keep her secret to herself; it was not until seventy years later, while on her deathbed, that she finally revealed her role in the demise of Lily Pond.

Due to the porosity of its sandy soil, there are very few

streams on Nantucket, a fact that made the loss of Lily Pond all the more painful to an island economy desperately in need of water power to run grist and fulling mills. In fact, the lack of rivers and streams meant that no matter how many sheep might thrive on this island without natural predators, Nantucketers were without adequate means to process the wool, thus severely limiting their ability to turn a significant profit. Indeed, the argument can be made that it was the lack of water power instead of the infertility of Nantucket's soil that ultimately forced the English to turn to whaling.

Lily Pond was not the only thing to vanish from the Nantucket landscape in the eighteenth century. As the growing population ravaged the existing forests for timber and firewood, lumber was soon in short supply all across Nantucket, forcing many islanders to dig peat for fuel during the Revolutionary War. Even after the war had ended, peat remained popular as a wood substitute. Burrowing down as much as six to eight feet, the peat-diggers created what the local paper described in 1822 as a network of "vast subterranean vaults" throughout the swamps of the island. Many of Nantucket's present-day wetlands may have been artificially created by the peat-diggers. According to a Nantucketer writing in 1922, "The old [peat] beds are now low, wet swamps."

This peat-digging, when combined with the absence of trees and the overuse of farmland (not to mention the effects of grazing animals), had a disastrous impact on the island's topsoil. By 1773 an acre of Nantucket farmland that fifty years earlier had reportedly produced 250 bushels of corn (husks included), now produced only 20 bushels. At this time, Hector St. John de Crèvecoeur, a Frenchman then living the life of an American farmer, visited the island and observed an interesting fertilizing technique. After gathering their sheep in a field where they wanted to grow crops, the Nantucketers waited until dark:

"Three times during a night it is permissible to terrify their sheep with burning coals; each time terror forces them to depose their manure; during one night a flock of these animals fertilize and enrich to a great extent the field in which they are enclosed."

When they were not being subjected to these nocturnal torture sessions, Nantucket's sheep (which numbered in the thousands) roamed freely throughout the island, keeping its landscape almost altogether treeless. After the annual "Shearing Festival" in June, during which all the island's flocks were collected in the vicinity of Miacomet Pond, the sheep would immediately disperse, rushing as fast as they could to their "accustomed haunts." Given the remarkable sameness of the Nantucket landscape, one wonders how they were able to find their way. According to Ralph Waldo Emerson, writing to his daughter in 1847:

> *As soon as you have walked out of the town or village of Nantucket (in which there are a few little gardens and a few trees) you come on a wide bare common stretching as far as you can see on every side, with nothing upon it but here & there a few nibbling sheep. And if you walk on till you have lost sight of the town, and a fog rises, which is very common here, you will have no guide to show you the way, no houses, no trees, no hills, no stones, so that it has many times happened here that people have been lost, & when they did not come back, the whole town came out & hunted for them.*

Emerson's naturalist friend Henry David Thoreau visited Nantucket in December of 1854 and described it in much the same terms: "This island must look exactly like a prairie, except that the view in clear weather is bounded by the sea." Thoreau traveled to Siasconset (referred to as "Sconset" by Nantucketers) on the eastern end of the island with a Captain Gardner, whose experimentation with tree-growing would ultimately have a profound impact on the island. Gardner showed Thoreau several tracts of land where he had grown fields of Norway and pitch pines—both of which were then new to Nantucket. Thoreau prophetically commented, "These plantations must very soon change the aspect of the island."

The real point of interest on Nantucket Island in the eighteenth and nineteenth centuries was not, however, its outlying areas; instead, it was the town, which had grown to become the third largest port in New England. Located at a place the Indians called Wesco (meaning "white rock"—a feature that was buried beneath Straight Wharf in 1723), the town did not spring up overnight. In a process that would continue for more than a century, the shoreline's naturally occurring marshes were buried beneath successive layers of fill as the town's waterfront crept gradually out into the harbor from its original high-water mark along what is now South Water Street. In 1730 a major portion of "Quanaty Hill" (along which runs Orange Street) was dug out to create the low, flat area that now exists between Union and Washington Streets. In 1743 sand dunes in the vicinity of the Nantucket Atheneum were leveled to create the "Bocochico" Lots. By the late eighteenth century, the town seemed an organic part of the surrounding landscape: "pleasantly situated upon a gentle slope, . . . surmounted by a row of windmills, and flanked to the right and left, by extensive ropewalks; . . . the stores and houses being mostly painted red, or white, and crowned by the steeples, or rather towers, of two Presbyterian [actually Congregational] meeting houses."

At this time, the commercial center of Nantucket was not the quaint tourist mecca it is today. For one thing, the whaling business had an unfortunate side-effect. According to Crèvecoeur, "At my first landing, I was much surprised at the disagreeable smell which struck me in many parts of the town; it was caused by the whale oil and is unavoidable." Instead of the tinkertoy docks of a modern-day pleasure-boat marina, huge solid-fill wharves reached out into the harbor to receive whaleships and their malodorous cargo. Crèvecoeur has left us an excellent description of the waterfront:

> *They have three docks, each 300 feet long and extremely convenient, at the head of which there are ten feet of water. . . . Between these docks and the town there is room sufficient for the landing of goods and for the passage of their numerous carts; for almost every man here has one. When their fleets have been successful, the bustle and hurry of business on this spot for some days after their arrival would make you imagine that this is the capital of a very opulent and large province.*

The carts referred to by Crèvecoeur were known locally as "calashes": springless, two-wheeled, horse-drawn contraptions that moved relatively easily through the heaping sand of the town's unpaved streets (the cobblestones on Main Street were not laid until the 1830s). As late as 1840, Audubon wrote, "You would be surprised to see the people riding through the streets in carts standing up like draymen, the females seated in chairs and trotting along merrily."

Whereas the hectic commercial activity of the waterfront focused on the Rotch "Counting House" at the foot of Straight Wharf, the Town Hall only a half mile up Main Street (just across from today's Civil War monument) presided over a very different scene: a quiet, almost rural community of Quakers on a hill. According to a visitor in the early nineteenth century, "The tranquility of a convent pervades the streets, except when the bell rings for dinner, and droves of cows go out and come in [through the town gate] under a herdsman grotesquely accoutered." Sheep were also a regular part of town life. Although some homeowners complained about the animals' habit of leaping over fences (even as high as four feet) and plundering gardens, other townspeople praised them for keeping the grass trimmed and eating "the vegetable matter that is thrown into the street."

In 1797 the twenty-six-year-old Phebe Folger painted an extremely detailed watercolor of the view from her house on Pleasant Street. Looking to the north toward Main Street, we see a barn, a manure pile, and a bed of lettuce, while a network of board and rail fences divides up a field of green grass running from east to west. Instead of gray, almost every house is a dark red, casting doubt on the authenticity of today's weathered-shingle look. Even though their ships now ventured to the other side of the globe, many eighteenth-century Nantucketers never strayed beyond the boundaries of this quiet and intimate world. In 1793 a resident wrote to an acquaintance in Virginia: "As small as [the island] is, I was never at the extreme east or west and for some years I dare say have not been one mile from town." In September of 1827 two four-year-old boys remained lost for more than forty-eight hours even though they lay languishing on a road just outside the town gate. Although a thorough search of town and the waterfront was made, it apparently never occurred to the children's parents (or anyone else) that they might have strayed beyond the fences of town.

By the 1830s and '40s, Nantucket had entered into its most heady days of commercial activity, becoming what the lawyer and statesman Daniel Webster (who came to the island several times on business) described as that "Unknown City in the Ocean." By 1832 Nantucket possessed a shipyard on Brant Point, five boat shops, seventeen oil factories, nineteen candle factories, ten ropewalks, twenty-two cooperages (barrel-making shops), one brass foundry, three tanneries, ten blacksmith shops, four spar shops, two bakeries, two block factories, four sail lofts, three rigging lofts, two candle-box factories, clothing stores, food provisioners, ship chandleries, brickyards, a rum distillery, four banks, and several insurance companies. Besides whaling-associated enterprises, there were bookstores, clock and jewelry shops, and ice cream stores. In a single afternoon in the 1840s you could buy a fur coat, get your hair cut, or hang out at a local bowling alley (even the little fishing village of Siasconset had one). At this time the town of Nantucket had several well-defined sections: "Chicken Hill," centered around Milk and Prospect (then known as Copper) Streets; "North Shore" and "Egypt" to the north of Main Street; "New Town," to the south of Main Street; "New Guinea," the black section centered around the African Meeting House at Five Corners; "Downtown," around Main Square; and "Upper Town," west of the head of Main Street.

But as Nantucket grew, its expenditures for capital improvements did not keep pace. Even though their wharves were piled high with casks of the world's best illuminant, the tight-fisted townspeople resolutely refused to light their own streets. According to the local paper, "When oil will not sell, the people cannot afford to light the streets; and when it will sell, it cannot be expected that they who have it will illumine the common pathway of the community." As a result, walking the streets of town on a foggy summer night was an extremely hazardous undertaking as more than a few Nantucketers bumped into parked calashes or fell into open cesspools.

Without a municipal sewer system, this highly concentrated urban center of 10,000 people (very close to Nantucket's current year-round population) suffered from the stench of more than just whale oil as the mucky swamp that had once been Lily Pond degenerated into an open sewer. The town's growth also threatened its squeaky clean moral reputation. According to an account published in 1846, sailors frequented a section known as "Nantucket hill" (which seems to have been in the vicinity of today's Cliff Road), where "vice knows no bounds, and crime has no stopping place, . . . the days and nights being spent in drunkenness and debauchery." Before a rabid temperance movement began to take hold in the 1830s and '40s, no less than sixty grog shops existed between New North and Commercial wharves.

But Nantucket's prosperity—both ill-gotten and whale-gotten—was not to last. On one terrible night in 1846 fire destroyed more than one-third of the town. Today, all that survives of Nantucket's original waterfront is a partly submerged pile of rubble off the stunted remnants of Old North Wharf. While the many historic homes on the island are fascinating in their own right, they do little to evoke a sense of Nantucket as the tremendously active (and fairly seedy) commercial center it once was.

Nantucket's fall as a whaling port was only partly a result of the Great Fire of 1846. Even though they had found a way to pay for the food and lumber they could no longer grow on the island, Nantucketers were ultimately unable to overcome yet another challenge presented by their environment: the sandy shoals that surrounded them. As early as 1760, the itinerant Quaker preacher John Woolman remarked on the "great shoal, which encloses their harbor [and] prevents them going in with sloops, except when the tide is up; waiting without which, for the rising of the tide, is sometimes hazardous in storms; waiting within, they sometimes miss a fair wind." Extensive clay deposits under the sand meant that the Nantucket Bar was not about to wash away. Even if there had never been a fire, the inaccessibility of the town's harbor to deep-draft ships had sealed (quite literally) Nantucket's fate as a whaling has-been.

During the second half of the nineteenth century, the sheep gradually disappeared and Captain Gardner's pitch pines began to spread across the island as Nantucket evolved into the scrubby, tree-dotted summer community it is today. In 1851 two leading whaling merchants, Charles and Henry Coffin, planted the first elm trees on Main Street. In 1875 one visitor commented on the "scraggly, weird-looking pitch-pines that are slowly replacing" the once unencumbered vistas. Today, a century after the end of island-wide sheep grazing on Nantucket, a program of brush-cutting and controlled burning has been instituted in an effort to preserve the remaining heathlands.

Just as it had helped lure the Indians centuries before, Nantucket's climate played a key role in bringing tourists to the island at the end of the nineteenth century. But instead of the mildness of the winters, it was the cool sea breezes of summer that attracted the city-dweller to Nantucket. There were, however, some major impediments to the establishment of a tourist industry. The town's sanitation problems could no longer be ignored. A report written in 1891 commented on "the dumping place where we invite our visitors to land from steamers where fish offal, slaughterhouse filth, and decayed fruit are deposited in quantities, filling the air with foul gasses." What is now known as Easy Street (and the site of a much-heralded scenic view) was then simply called "The Dump." Gradually and inevitably, Nantucket began to clean itself up until it is now, some would say, an overly tidy restoration of the nineteenth-century whaling port it once was.

Although two jetties now keep a channel open across the Nantucket Bar, there are bigger problems facing the island. Dramatic beach erosion, particularly on the southeastern side of Nantucket, continues to whittle away at its sandy shores. It is estimated that the rising sea levels that created the island 5,000 years ago will ultimately lead to its demise in a fraction of that time. Some estimates put it at 2,000 years; others say that in as few as 400 years waves will be lapping over Altar Rock, the boulder that the glacier deposited high atop what was then a sandy hill.

If Nantucket is destined to become another Atlantis, we can only hope that its inhabitants will not be forgotten. With this in mind, let us now turn to the island's first people, the Indians.

CHAPTER 2

Native Origins: Maushop, Roqua, Wonoma, and Autopscot

INSTEAD OF A GLACIER, the Indians credited Nantucket's formation to Maushop, the Native American forefather of Paul Bunyan. According to legend, Maushop was so big that the only place he could comfortably sleep was along the southern shore of Cape Cod. Unfortunately, he did not like getting sand in his moccasins—a difficult thing to avoid when your bed is a beach. One night, after many hours of tossing and turning, Maushop finally kicked off one of his moccasins in exasperation. It only went a short way and became Martha's Vineyard. Growing increasingly restless and annoyed with the sand in his other moccasin, he kicked it even farther. It became known as Nantucket, meaning "the faraway land."

Although there is archeological evidence that Native Americans had been coming to Nantucket when it was still an inland hillside, the myths that have been passed down to us come from a culture that knew it only as an island. These were the Wampanoag (often referred to as the Pokanokets in the seventeenth century), a subset of the Algonquians who settled throughout southern New England. It was the Wampanoag who greeted the Pilgrims at Plymouth, and their sachem (or leader) Massasoit seems to have had jurisdiction over Indians throughout Cape Cod and the islands.

There were two distinct groups of Wampanoag on Nantucket. Those on the eastern end of the island originally came from Cape Cod and brought with them the legend of Maushop's moccasin. The Indians to the west, however, came from Martha's Vineyard and, as might be expected, had a different view of Nantucket's origin. According to these Indians, Maushop originally lived on the Vineyard, known then as Noepe, where he spent his time feasting on whales and smoking his pipe while his people prospered. Then one day a young couple, Nanina and Waposset, came to him with a problem. Nanina's father refused to let her marry Waposset because of his humble birth. Maushop, who had always favored Waposset, told them to fetch Nanina's father and meet him at the eastern end of the island. Soon everyone was assembled, and in truly glacier-like fashion Maushop began to dig a deep hole into the sea, which he then filled up with many stones. After lighting his giant pipe with a thunderbolt, he knocked out the ashes into the sea, causing a great hissing cloud of steam to rise up into the air. Eventually the fog cleared and a new island appeared before them. This, Maushop declared, was to be Nanina and Waposset's home. With his future son-in-law's new real estate holdings more than compensating for what he lacked in social standing, Nanina's father readily agreed to the marriage. It is this legend of the island's spectacular birth that has led certain jealous parties from the Vineyard to refer to Nantucket as the "Devil's Ash Heap."

There is a third legend about Maushop and Nantucket that may give us some indication as to why these two groups of Indians originally came to Nantucket. According to this story, there was once a huge bird that would swoop down over the villages of Cape Cod, grab a child in its talons, and fly off across the sea. Finally the mothers banded together to ask Maushop to find out where the bird was taking their children. Always willing to help, Maushop waded far out into the sea until he sighted an island he had never seen before. After a thorough investigation, he found a pile of small whitened bones beneath a tree. His search now ended, Maushop sat down for a contemplative smoke and soon the island was blanketed by a thick gray cloud. For years to come Nantucket's Native Americans would greet the appearance of fog by saying, "Here comes old Maushop's smoke."

By linking the island's discovery with sudden and inexplicable death, this legend may point to how the European-spawned plagues that decimated New England's Native Americans from 1616 to 1619 contributed to the growth of Nantucket's Indian population. While huge numbers of Indians died up and down the coast (more than half the total population, according to some estimates), Nantucket appears to have been left relatively untouched by disease in the first half of the seventeenth century. The many shoals surrounding the island discouraged sailors from approaching Nantucket, thus minimizing early English-Indian contact. Testifying to the dangers of these shoals were the names left by the crew of Bartholomew Gosnold's ship in 1602: "Tucker's Terror" and "Point Care." In fact, if it had not been for the shoals off Monomoy that caused them to double back in panic around Cape Cod in 1620, the Pilgrims might very well have first stepped on Wesco instead of Plymouth Rock.

As increasing numbers of white settlers arrived in New England, the shoal-guarded remoteness of Maushop's sandy moccasin or ash heap, depending on your point of view, may have become increasingly attractive to Indians on the Cape and Martha's Vineyard. Indeed, as the Native American population dramatically shrank throughout the rest of the region, Nantucket's Indian population seems to have, if anything, increased. It is estimated that by the middle of the seventeenth century there were as many as 3,000 Indians on Nantucket (equivalent to almost a third of the island's current year-round population). This would have meant that the island possessed an Indian population that was more than *ten times* what the concentration on the mainland had been before the plagues, placing tremendous demands on Nantucket's natural resources. No wonder there were no deer left on the island.

According to tradition, the eastern and western Indians developed noticeably different cultures, partly as a result of the different natural features and wildlife the two portions of the island had to offer. The western group, known as the Taumkhods, relied primarily on shellfishing and driftwhaling (even today dead whales most commonly wash up along the southwestern shore of the island), while the eastern Indians, known as the Khauds (which may have referred to the codfish that frequent the shoals off Siasconset), were bird hunters and fishermen, using tree bark to fashion fishing lines.

Tradition has it that the Indian depicted on the Massachusetts Bay seal of 1629 was based on a Khaud sachem who was taken to England. The seal depicts a slender yet muscular dark-skinned man with long black hair tied behind; except for a cluster of leaves around his mid-section, he is naked; in his right hand is a feather; in his left is a bow. As far as clothing, James Freeman reported in 1807 that prior to the arrival of the English the Indians wore "sometimes skins, but for the most part coarse mats, made of grass." He also claimed that Nantucket Indians knew how to roast but did not know how to boil their food. Unlike those on the mainland, Nantucket Indians did not manufacture wampum. According to Crèvecoeur, "The only ancient custom of these people that is remembered is that in their mutual exchanges, forty sun-dried clams, strung on a string, passed for the value of what might be called a copper." While most Native Americans in New England smoked tobacco, those on Nantucket smoked pokeweed in "stone" pipes made from the rich clay deposits along the north shore of the island. In the swamps near Siasconset in the eastern end of the island grew groundnuts, a white, potato-like tuber that the Indians relied upon for food.

For shelter, they built wigwams: low, rounded dwellings made from bent saplings covered with mats to keep the weather out. These structures were easily taken down and rebuilt as the Indians moved throughout their territories to take advantage of seasonal changes, a process that Obed Macy attributed to "a restless disposition inherent in their nature." In winter, a central fire kept the wigwams surprisingly warm, "albeit very smoky," according to a contemporary account, with only an opening in the roof serving as a chimney.

Nantucket Indians also built "sweat houses," temporary, cave-like structures dug into shore-side hills, that functioned much in the same way as the modern-day sauna. In 1724 Paul Dudley gave this description of such a house, provided to him by "a gentleman of the island of Nantucket where the Indians sometimes practice it even at this day":

> *Near the cave they make a good large fire, and heat a parcel of stones . . . and roll them in hot, piling them up in the middle of it; when this is done, the Indians go in naked, and sit-round the heated stones; as soon as they begin to grow faint, which may be in a quarter of an hour, they come out and plunge themselves all over in the water for a minute or two. . . . The Indians often used it before and after long journeys, hunting, or voyages to strengthen and refresh themselves.*

While the men sweated, hunted, and fished, the Indian women shouldered the brunt of the day-to-day labor of village life—tending crops, grinding corn, cooking meals, weaving baskets and reed mats, making clay pottery—not to mention raising the children. Indeed, even the English, who were far from being feminists, remarked on the lopsided division of labor among the Indians throughout New England: "[The men] bestow their times in fishing, hunting, wars and such man-like exercises, without the doors, scorning to be seen in any effeminate labor, which is the cause that women be very painful."

Before we begin to think that the Indian men had it easy, we must realize that hunting, fishing, and fighting were not idle amusements in Native American culture; they were, quite literally, matters of life and death, requiring great skill and endurance. When a state of war existed between the two factions on the island, surveillance and communication were vital to avoiding surprise attack. A single Indian runner was capable of covering as many as 100 miles a day (roughly equivalent to two circumnavigations of the island), demonstrating that even before the horse, car, and telephone, news traveled fast on Nantucket.

If the legends that have been passed down to us are any indication, the early seventeenth century was a time of bitter fighting between the Khauds and Taumkhods—their territorial rivalries exacerbated, no doubt, by competition for food on this overcrowded island. One legend tells of a titanic battle in Madequecham (pronounced "MAD-a-ka-sham") Valley, a glacier-induced crease across the center of the island that also provided a boundary between the two factions. Another legend tells of several massacres in Madaket on the western end of the island. But it is the story of Roqua that provides the best example of just how claustrophobically brutal life could be when there were two warring peoples on an island only fourteen miles in length.

The son of an old Khaud sachem on the eastern end of the island, Roqua lived with his father, wife, and daughter in their village near what is today the cranberry bogs. At one point, war broke out between the Khauds and the Taumkhods. Although Roqua led his men heroically in battle, it was a lost cause. By the time the fighting had ended, Roqua was one of the few easterners left alive. Meanwhile, as this terrible struggle was reaching its conclusion in Madequecham Valley, yet another party of Taumkhods launched an attack on Roqua's undefended village.

When the defeated eastern warriors returned home, they found ruins.

The wigwams were ashes; the bodies of his people—including his father, wife, and daughter—lay scattered amid the embers. After binding his wounds, Roqua spent most of the day burying the bodies of his loved ones. Then, with a war club in one hand and a spear in the other, he waited for darkness.

Moving swiftly along the narrow, hard-packed Indian trails that crisscrossed the island, Roqua approached the western Indian stronghold in Miacomet (which means "at the meeting place") situated beside a narrow, centrally located pond. Assuming their victory had been total, all in the village now lay asleep. Roqua noiselessly entered the enemy sachem's wigwam and, without hesitation, buried his club in the leader's head. By the time the warriors of the village had been alerted, Roqua had set most of the wigwams on fire.

Back-lit by the burning village, Roqua stared defiantly at his enemies until an arrow pierced his chest. Falling to his knees, he looked up and spoke this prophecy: "I see a storm approaching from the north. The canoes of the white men with white sails will come to this island. All will die and be buried in a single grave." With these words, Roqua fell down dead to the ground.

As with any legend, it is difficult to determine the degree to which hindsight helped shape what would prove to be a chillingly accurate prophecy. For now at least, let us look to how peace finally came to the island around 1630 (thirty years before the first English settlers arrived), when—according to legend—Wonoma, the beautiful daughter of sachem Wauwinet in the east, fell in love with Autopscot, the young sachem of the west. Since she was the daughter of a sachem, Wonoma had a relatively easy life. Instead of being subjected to the drudgery that was usually required of a squaw, Wonoma was taught the art of healing—using cranberry poultices and water lilies for skin sores; blackberries for sore throats; not to mention skunk cabbage, pokeberries, milkweed, cherry bark, and a whole assortment of plants and herbs to treat almost every conceivable complaint. (These medicines were so effective that even as late as the early 1800s, the three white doctors on the island still made up their own "prescriptions" based on Indian remedies.) Soon Wonoma—who would search throughout the eastern end of the island for the necessary plants, dry them in the sun, then grind them with a mortar and pestle—gained a reputation as the island's foremost healer.

One day a strange disease broke out in the Taumkhod village at Miacomet. In a short while the situation had grown so desperate that sachem Autopscot took the extraordinary step of sending a messenger to his avowed enemy, Wauwinet, requesting the help of his daughter Wonoma. After discussing the matter with another Khaud sachem, Wauwinet finally allowed his daughter, accompanied by an escort, to help the western Indians.

Soon Wonoma began to work her magic in Miacomet—not only curing the sick but winning the affections of sachem Autopscot. When it finally came time for her to return to her village in Squam, she and Autopscot had fallen deeply in love. However, given the history of bloodshed between their two peoples, both decided it was best to keep their affections a secret.

It was not long before relations between the eastern and western Indians began to deteriorate once again. Braves loyal to Autopscot were seen hunting to the east of Madequecham Valley, prompting Wauwinet to plot a surprise attack. Wonoma overheard his plans, however, and determined to warn her lover. That night she stole a canoe and paddled several miles up the harbor until she came to a place known as Monomoy, where she landed and followed the trails to Miacomet.

After Wonoma told him of her father's plans, Autopscot

immediately decided to talk it out with his enemy, promising to punish the offending braves while also declaring his love for Wauwinet's daughter. Although it took a while for the Khaud sachem to reconcile himself to this startling turn of events, Wonoma and Autopscot were married, and Nantucket's Indian wars finally came to an end.

According to the Nantucket Indian expert Elizabeth Little, there is historic evidence that this Romeo-and-Juliet scenario did in fact occur, but instead of Wonoma and Autopscot, it was Askammapoo and Spotso; and instead of Wauwinet, the old sachem's name was Nickanoose. In any event, the good times among Nantucket's native population were not to last long. The diseases that had helped to make possible this reconciliation in 1630 by bringing Wonoma and Autopscot together would inevitably contribute to the Indians' catastrophic decline once the first English settlers arrived in 1659. In only twenty years, the Indian population had shrunk to half its former size. In 1763, almost exactly a century after the arrival of the whites, one final epidemic in the village site of Miacomet, where Roqua had issued his dying prophecy and where Wonoma and Autopscot had first met, virtually removed the Indians as a cultural presence on the island.

Today, bikers passing Miacomet on their way to Surfside Beach may notice a simple rail fence that marks the roughly circular site of what Roqua predicted would be his race's "single grave": the Indian burial ground where the more than 200 victims of the 1763 epidemic are buried. In the end, not even the wondrous medicines of Wonoma's descendants were enough to counteract the white man's poisons. And, as Roqua had predicted, it would all begin with a storm . . .

CHAPTER 3

Thomas Macy's Great Escape

I T I S A C R I S P October morning in 1659 as a small open boat, filled to the gunwales with people and provisions, sails down the Merrimack River. Most of the boat's passengers belong to the Thomas Macy family from Salisbury on the north side of the river, a place so dedicated to lumber that barrel staves are accepted for taxes. As the river approaches the ocean, the heavily wooded riverbank to the south gives way to a sandy, shell-scattered shore beyond which stretches a wide tidal marsh. This, Thomas Macy tells his wife and children, is what their new home—an island known as Nantucket—will look like. To Sarah Macy and her five children, it might as well be the surface of the moon.

Leaving the river behind, they head down the coast, never losing sight of land as they sail past Cape Anne, Boston Harbor, and Plymouth, then veer east along the northern shore of Cape Cod. At some point along the way, they probably pull into a small cove for the night. Throughout the voyage, bluefish and striped bass are theirs for the taking—abounding in numbers that would astound someone from the twenty-first century. Thousands of right and Atlantic gray whales are just beginning to arrive from the north, and it would not be surprising if at some point the Macys find themselves surrounded by a pod of these curious and companionable leviathans.

Not long after passing Barnstable Harbor on the north side

of Cape Cod, the Macys begin to look for Boatmeadow Creek in the vicinity of Eastham. This narrow, naturally occurring passageway across the Cape (closed by a storm in 1770) enables them to avoid the potentially dangerous waters off Province-town. Once on the south side of the Cape, they do not imme-diately head for Nantucket; instead they sail for Great Harbor (now Edgartown) on Martha's Vineyard, where they are greeted by Macy's cousin, Governor Thomas Mayhew.

Although he is related by blood to the Puritan magistrate, Macy's Baptist religious beliefs have added an inevitable element of tension between the two men, especially since it is a mat-ter of religion that has prompted Macy's hurried sail for Nan-tucket. Earlier that year, during a brief shower of rain, Macy made the mistake of giving shelter to four Quakers on their way to the nearby town of Hampton. The Puritan authorities were not pleased and demanded that he answer to the charge. In a letter of explanation Macy claimed to "have been for some weeks past very ill" and could therefore not appear before the General Court. It was not long, however, before Macy and his family were sailing down the New England coast. Now, after resting themselves and gathering a final store of provisions, they have only a few more miles to go before they are home free.

To this day, the passage from Martha's Vineyard to Nan-tucket is no easy matter; the shoals that line the waters between the two islands are notoriously dangerous. So Macy seeks the assistance of a Vineyarder by the name of Daggett, who agrees to serve as pilot for the last leg of the journey to Nantucket. His family has recently gotten into trouble with Governor May-hew for purchasing a tract of land directly from the Indians, and Daggett is looking forward to spending the entire winter on Nantucket, far away from the turmoil on the Vineyard.

Unfortunately, the fall is not the safest time for sea travel in New England. The months of October and November are known for sudden and dangerous storms. And, true to form, almost as soon as Macy's little boat leaves Great Harbor, the weather takes a turn for the worse. Storm clouds appear on the horizon as the wind and waves begin to build. Soon all on board are soaked and miserable, with several miles still left to go against a stiff easterly head wind. Above the cries of her children, Sarah Macy suggests that tomorrow might be a better day to sail for Nantucket. Her husband, however, tells Daggett to continue on.

As the weather worsens, it all becomes a little more than Sarah Macy can stand. In no uncertain terms she suggests that there is something downright diabolical about the storm; the work of witchcraft perhaps? Thomas Macy will have none of it. In words destined to become a Nantucket legend, he shouts: "Woman, go below and seek thy God. I fear not the witches on earth nor the devils in hell!" Thus, in the storm that the Indian Roqua had predicted would bring the white man to Nantucket, Thomas Macy sails into Madaket Harbor.

∽

He was fifty-one years old, a self-described "merchant and clothier" and had been living in New England for close to a quarter of a century. Only a few years earlier, he had become part owner of a sawmill in the "new" section of Salisbury on the other side of the Powow River. And as his reputed words to his wife suggest, there was also a bit of the orator in Thomas Macy, who is elsewhere described as both a planter and "withal a preacher."

In the fall of 1659, he and Sarah had five children—Sarah, thirteen; Mary, eleven; Bethia, nine; Thomas, six; and John, four. Uprooting a brood of this size from a town that he had helped carve out of the wilderness was not something to be entered into lightly. But life in Salisbury was not what it had once been. The town had been polarized by a squabble over the payment of a minister; those in the new section of town (now Amesbury) resented the fact that they were still supporting a minister in the old section of town. The combination of these local tensions with the General Court's new repressive measures against religious dissent had turned neighbor against neighbor; it had been a fellow townsman, after all, who had told the Puritan authorities about Macy's kindness to the Quakers. Given this atmosphere of treachery and deceit, an island twenty-four miles off the south coast of Cape Cod must have seemed like a beckoning refuge.

Macy, however, was careful not to burn any bridges by his sudden removal to Nantucket. The fine levied against him by the General Court was promptly paid, and, contrary to a myth popular among Nantucketers, his property in Salisbury was never confiscated. In fact, in 1664 Macy would return there for the apparent purpose of selling his home and land. The town record for that year states: "Thomas Macy sold unto Anthony Colby, the house in which he, Thomas Macy, dwelleth at present. . . ."

Although we do not know the exact date on which Macy left for Nantucket, there is indirect evidence that it was in late October. His letter to the General Court is dated October 27, 1659. As town clerk, Macy (who was by one account a "good penman") kept the Salisbury town records, and on the first of November, 1659, the record book shifts to a different, less careful hand. Also of interest is the fact that Peter Folger, a Vineyarder who would ultimately move to Nantucket in 1663, chose to state publicly his Baptist beliefs at a Great Harbor town meeting that October. Was Folger's "Laying Down of his Creed" connected in any way with Macy's sail for Nantucket? Accompanying Macy on this historic voyage was Edward Starbuck, a fifty-five-year-old lumber trader from Dover who had been fined for professing his Baptist beliefs more than ten years earlier.

In any event, Macy's decision to relocate was not altogether spontaneous. For the previous year or so, he and several friends and neighbors in the Merrimack River Valley had been examining the possibility of purchasing Nantucket Island, with the expectation of beginning a new community outside the realm of Puritan control. In June of that year, Macy as well as Tristram Coffin and John Coleman had all traveled to the island where they witnessed the sale of the "plain at the West end of Nantucket" to Thomas Mayhew by the Indian sachems Nickanoose and Nanahuma. Then on July 2nd, Macy and Coffin negotiated the purchase of the island from Mayhew for the sum of thirty pounds and two beaver hats. Until Macy's hospitality toward the Quakers prompted him to pack up and leave Salisbury that fall, the original and more sensible plan appears to have been to begin settlement during the following spring.

While it was religious beliefs that may have spurred Macy and Starbuck to sail for Nantucket, there were two other crew members who came to Nantucket for different reasons. The nineteen-year-old James Coffin (son of Tristram Coffin) probably went along to protect his father's business investment. With control over not only his own share in the island but also those of his three sons and a son-in-law, Tristram Coffin had more reason than most to be concerned that nothing happened to endanger the future of the settlement during that first winter. And clearly Macy and Starbuck (no longer young men, particularly by seventeenth-century standards) could use all the help they could get. Also along for this historic ride was a twelve-year-old boy by the name of Isaac Coleman.

But if this assortment of four men, one woman, and six children might seem like an unlikely group of pioneers, Nantucket in 1659 was not exactly a howling wilderness. For many years now, Mayhew and others had been visiting the island on a regular basis for the purpose of converting the Indians to Christianity. The Vineyarders had also been grazing their sheep and cattle on the western end of the island, and Macy and company undoubtedly sailed for some kind of dock or boat landing upon their arrival at Madaket.

According to Obed Macy, Nantucket's first English resident ultimately "chose a spot for settlement on the southeast side of Madaket harbor, where he found a rich soil and an excellent spring of water"—not far from what is now known as Warren's Landing. According to another account, Starbuck chose to live "near two miles apart" from the Macy family, a tradition that is born out by the town records from 1670 in which there is mention of "the meadows lying between Long Pond by the old cellar built by Edward Starbuck." The colonial architecture expert Henry Chandlee Forman hypothesizes that along with wigwams, Nantucket's Indians also built "dugouts" to escape the winter winds, describing them as "crude abodes half inside the ground," the rough equivalent of what the English would call a cellar. Given the time of year of their arrival, a dugout based on the Indian model certainly seems like a quick and sensible housing option, the remains of which apparently provided a lasting memorial to that first winter.

By all accounts the Indians greeted Macy and Starbuck "with kindness and hospitality," otherwise it is difficult to believe that the two men would have chosen to live so far apart. At one point, however, Macy seems to have gotten quite a scare. According to one tradition, a large number of Indians assembled near Macy's dwelling and "worked themselves up into a great fury, singing and dancing with all their might." Fearful that this was the prelude to an attack, Macy sent "a boy" (probably Isaac Coleman) to Starbuck's house. "Being a bold man," Starbuck immediately put on his hat, picked up his cane, and charged over to Macy's. After studying the Indians for a few minutes, Starbuck is reputed to have shouted, "Is not the Lord on our side? Of whom shall we be afraid? One shall chase a thousand, and two put ten thousand to flight!" Then, brandishing his cane as if it were a sword, he "sallied forth upon the astonished natives," who quickly dispersed. Later, once they had become better acquainted with local Indian customs, Starbuck and Macy realized that the gathering had been nothing more than a "grand Pow-wow."

Starbuck (which in Norse means "great" or "grand") was apparently a man of considerable force and determination, and the Indians—despite his histrionics with the cane—seem to have been especially fond of him. He was one of the few settlers who took the time to learn the Wampanoag language, and on the fifth of January, 1660, the sachem Nickanoose was moved to deed to Starbuck all of Coatue "out of my free voluntary love."

Daggett, the Vineyarder, also deeply impressed the Indians, but in a different way. Daggett spent most of that first winter "gunning" for birds. According to one source, the Native Nantucketers "were astonished at the effect of the firearms, by which more birds could be killed in a day, than they could destroy with their arrows in a month." In all probability, Sarah Macy served a lot of duck during that first winter on the island.

Thus was established the foothold that would open the way for the arrival of ten more families that summer. Edward Starbuck would be joined by his children (there is no evidence, however, that his wife Katherine ever emigrated to Nantucket). Although Daggetts eventually settled on the island in the following century, this first Daggett would return to the Vineyard. James Coffin would return to the Merrimack Valley area, get married, and then eventually return to become Nantucket's first Judge of Probate. The Macys would become an important part of the community that soon sprang up around them, although Thomas, Jr., would die tragically in 1675 at the age of twenty-two, leaving only John (who would die at thirty-six) to carry on the Macy name. And what about Isaac Coleman, the twelve-year-old boy?

Isaac is something of a mystery. According to popular tradition, he was an orphan, but the record shows that he was the son of Thomas Coleman, who ultimately moved from Hampton to Nantucket with several of Isaac's siblings. Why Isaac accompanied the Macys to Nantucket in 1659 is unknown. Perhaps he was apprenticed to Macy, who was a skilled weaver. In any event, if the anecdote about the Indian pow-wow is any indication, the boy seems to have been a genuine help to his caretakers during that first winter.

When only nineteen Coleman was appointed to a committee to collect fines from Indian and English Nantucketers who refused to kill their dogs, demonstrating that he was already a respected member of the community. Except for this one reference, he disappears from the record until two years later in June of 1669, when we know that he sailed to the Vineyard in a canoe. Accompanying him were four others—Eleazer Folger and his sister Bethiah with her new husband John Barnard, plus an Indian. In Great Harbor they purchased, among other things, an iron plowshare, and soon they were on their way back to Nantucket, a southwesterly sea breeze hurrying them on their way.

Although it was under very different circumstances, the sail back to Nantucket must have reminded Isaac of that first voyage so long ago, particularly as the sea breeze built to the point of becoming dangerous. But instead of Mr. and Mrs. Macy's tense exchanges, these young people showed little concern; sailing between the two islands had become old hat.

Then the fate that the Macys had been lucky enough to avoid suddenly struck: the boat capsized. Although they tried to cling to the canoe, it was not long before Isaac and the Barnards, as well as the Indian, were dragged under by their heavy clothes and drowned. Just as Eleazer was about to go down for the last time, his feet struck the sand of a shoal. It took all his strength, but he was able to right the canoe and pull himself into it. A swamped canoe, however, is more than likely to capsize once again, so it was imperative that Eleazer bail it out as quickly as possible—but with what? Lashed inside the canoe was the plowshare, and so with its heavy iron scoop he gradually emptied the boat of water. Exhausted, and without oars or a sail with which to guide the canoe, he put down the plowshare and collapsed. Ultimately he would drift all the way to Cape Cod, where two Indians fishing off Morris Island near Chatham were surprised to find a man lying inside what they had assumed was an empty canoe.

In the next several days, the English community on Nantucket went into mourning when it was realized that the canoe was never coming back. And then, after all had been given up for lost, Eleazer arrived on a sloop from Cape Cod and told his terrible story. Although not related by blood, Edward Starbuck, James Coffin, and particularly the Macy family must have felt a special bond to their former shipmate, Isaac Coleman. On a cold fall day almost a decade before, it could have just as easily happened to all of them.

CHAPTER 4

Tristram Coffin, Country Squire

TRISTRAM COFFIN appears to have been a more worldly man than either Thomas Macy or Edward Starbuck. There is no record of his religious affiliation, and when he and his wife ran into trouble with the Puritan government back in Newbury (just down the river from Macy's Salisbury), it was not for lay-preaching but for beer-making. According to a law written in 1645, only four bushels of malt were to be used in brewing a beer that was to cost no more than two pence a quart. But at his inn in Newbury, Tristram charged an extra pence a quart, and in 1653 this put him afoul of the authorities. When it was disclosed that his wife Dionis had been using two extra bushels of malt to brew what was apparently a higher quality— and thus premium priced—beer, the case against her husband was dropped.

Even though they were exonerated in this instance, the Coffins did not take well to such governmental regulation, and thus they had a difficult time settling down in Puritan New England. After leaving behind a considerable estate in Brixton on the southeastern coast of Devonshire, the Coffins (who came to America with five young children, Tristram's mother, and his two sisters) lived for a short time in Salisbury only to move to Haverhill, then on to Newbury, and then back to Salisbury in 1654, where Tristram and Dionis soon began to make plans for moving to Nantucket. Besides an inn, Coffin ran a ferry on the

Newbury side of Carrs Island on the Merrimack River, but he never seems to have been very content with his position in Puritan New England. This sort of restlessness was not uncommon, particularly among those from the West Country of England. The power structure of Puritan New England was made up, for the most part, of people from the opposite side of the country in East Anglia, and "Westcountrymen" such as Coffin, from Devonshire, and Macy, from Wiltshire, often felt compelled to move elsewhere.

Unable to carve out a comfortable niche on the mainland, Coffin and his fellow "first purchasers" looked to Nantucket, an island under no colonial jurisdiction where they might create a community free from the religious and economic restrictions they had experienced in New England. Although it may have been Macy's blood tie to Thomas Mayhew that initially got the ball rolling, it was Coffin who carried forward the actual negotiations that resulted in the purchase of the island in 1659. From the first, the Nantucket proprietary was structured differently from its counterparts on the mainland, where an individual's wealth and rank usually had a direct relationship to the amount of land he received. On Nantucket, equal grants were given to the first purchasers and their partners, who included not only Tristram Coffin, Thomas Macy, Edward Starbuck, and Thomas Mayhew from the Vineyard (who maintained an interest in the island) but also Richard Swain, Thomas Barnard, Christopher Hussey, John Swain, William Pile, Thomas Coleman, Robert Barnard, Robert Pike, John Smith, Thomas Look, and a total of four Coffin sons and sons-in-law—Peter Coffin, James Coffin, Tristram Coffin, Jr., and Stephen Greenleaf. With control over five out of twenty initial shares in the proprietary, Coffin was clearly in the driver's seat from the beginning.

But why Nantucket? Why did Tristram Coffin, at the age of fifty-four, with three children still living at home, decide to pin his hopes on an island almost thirty miles out to sea? First and foremost, it gave him a degree of control over his own and, most important, his children's destinies that had been unavailable to him on the mainland. And yet, Coffin did not look to Nantucket out of a desperate need to escape Puritan New England; instead it marked the fulfillment of a carefully calculated plan to consolidate the gains he and particularly his eldest son Peter, a leading sawmill owner and lumber trader from Dover, New Hampshire, had already made in the Merrimack Valley region.

Although an island off the New England coast, Nantucket in the seventeenth century was far less remote than it would ultimately become in the nineteenth century when a burgeoning railroad system would knit together the interior of the country, isolating many hitherto prosperous island communities along the Atlantic coast. In 1660, and for the next century and a half, overland travel was extremely slow and difficult, with water travel being the preferred mode of transportation. Given this reality, the fact that Nantucket was surrounded by water actually worked to its advantage. But even more important than its relative ease of access was its lack of trees, providing a ready-made market for Peter Coffin's lumber business. And sure enough, only a few years after Tristram's arrival on the island, the town "agreed to allow Peter Coffin liberty to trade on [the] island at present and to prohibit all others." Indeed, the town's many early measures against the use of on-island trees may have been motivated by something more than a seventeenth-century concern for the island's ecology.

Although Coffin was clearly in a position to exert control over the island proprietary, there was something of a wild card present on Nantucket in the form of a large Indian population. If Coffin was to build a community to his own specifications, he could only do it if the Indians allowed him to. So, in keeping with established practice in Massachusetts, Coffin and company were careful to purchase the land not only from Mayhew but also from the Indians. In the first deed signed by the sachems Wanackmamack (pronounced "Wan-ACK-ma-MACK") and Nickanoose in May, 1660, the English land is described as "lying from the west end of the Island of Nantucket unto the pond called by the Indians Waqutaquaib [pronounced "Wa-KU-ta-kabe"] and from the head of that pond upon a straight line unto the pond situated by the Monomoy harbor or creek now called Wherfore Creek and so from the northeast corner to the said pond to the sea. . . ." Today, Waqutaquaib is the first, lily-choked pond visible on the left as you begin a walk through the conservation land at Sanford Farm; although it is difficult to see the pond referred to in Monomoy from a public road, it still exists at the head of the Creeks not far from Our Island Home.

To a remarkable extent, these boundaries circumscribe what still is today the island's population center. But whereas the modern-day town is oriented toward the harbor to the east, Nantucket's first settlers looked to Cappamet Harbor at Capaum (pronounced "Ka-PAWM") along the northern side of the island to the west. Before it was cut off from Nantucket Sound by a sandbar in the early eighteenth century (and became Capaum Pond), Cappamet Harbor provided the first settlers with a ready-made, relatively deep anchorage without the sandy beaches and mucky marshes that inhibited access to the larger harbor to the east. Wonderfully protected by the rolling hills that surround it, Cappamet also had the benefit of being situated in the geographic center (east to west) of the new settlement.

From the first, Coffin was careful to insure that he and his children were positioned here, at the center of the new community. While most proprietors were assigned their land "by casting lots," Coffin laid claim to a prime spot at Capaum, where he built a house that he would later describe in a deed "as under the hill by the herb garden" on the western side of the harbor where it was well protected from the prevailing winds. With his eldest son Peter owning the land on the other side of the harbor, the Coffins were strategically located with regard to what would inevitably become the early commercial hub of the island.

The layout of house lots also worked to the Coffins' advantage. Unlike the standard Puritan community on the mainland, in which relatively small plots of land were clustered around a centrally located green, the first house-lot division of July, 1661, contained plots of approximately twenty-one acres—four or five times the average lot size found in Massachusetts. The large size of these lots enabled Coffin to monopolize the area surrounding the harbor as the rest of the community settled in two lines curving out from Capaum. The first ran to the south toward the western arm of U-shaped Hummock Pond; the second ran eastward toward the "Great Harbor" at Wesco. While this layout gave each family plenty of elbow room—thus diffusing the meddling-neighbor syndrome of the usual, closely packed New England village—all roads along these two wings of settlement led to the Coffins at Capaum.

But if Nantucket was to remain a market for Peter Coffin's lumber, there had to be a way for its inhabitants to make an adequate living, and here again, father Tristram did his best to give the English settlers every possible advantage. Throughout New England in the seventeenth century, islands were favored for sheep-raising since they were free of the wolves and other natural predators that ravaged flocks on the mainland. And in the first deed with the Indians in the spring of 1660, Coffin was careful to secure "free liberty for the feeding of all sorts of cattle on any part of the island after the Indian harvest is ended until planting time." In other words, even though they initially owned only a small portion of the island, the English were free to use the entire island as common land for grazing from October until May.

As sheepherding emerged as the driving force behind the island's economy, it quickly became apparent that this small, water-bound community had some gaps to fill. This led to the designation of fourteen additional "half-shares" in the proprietary to attract specific tradespeople to the island. As early as 1662 William Worth was brought on to be "employed in sea affairs"; in 1663 Peter Folger became the town's Indian interpreter, surveyor, and miller; and in 1664 Thomas Macy, already a full-share man, took up the "trade of weaving" in exchange for an additional half-share accommodation. Although Worth was given a part in all future divisions of land, the proprietors were not so generous when it came to subsequent half-share men, limiting their future opportunities to acquire real estate to what was called the "first plantation." As we shall see, the creation of what amounted to a form of second-class citizenship would come back to haunt Coffin and company in the years ahead.

As Nantucket's population grew, so did the number of grazing animals, and the English quickly began to feel that the island was overstocked. In June of 1667 the "Vineyard men" were told to take their "horses, mares, and colts" off the island, and soon after, "finding by experience that horses are likely to be the ruin of the neat cattle," Nantucketers limited themselves to one horse per household while prohibiting altogether the sale of horses to Indians. In 1668 the town established rules for the number of animals each shareholder was permitted to graze, with forty cattle and forty sheep designated for each full-share. Such rules, known as stinting rights, required the policing of the herd by the proprietors, and each shareholder was assigned his own earmark (Tristram Coffin's was "a half-fork under the right ear and a half-penny under the left") so that his livestock could be identified. If it was found that a shareholder was overstocking the common, his extra animals were confiscated, for which purpose the town ordered the building of an eighty-foot-square "pound" or pen "about Cappamet" with "sufficient good strong posts and five rails ten feet long and a cap on the top."

Here at Capaum, Coffin did his best to re-create a New World version of his ancestral home in England where he had been a card-carrying member of the landed gentry. He soon named the pebbly beach beside his home "Northam" for a coastal village in his native Devon while the beach to the west of Capaum still bears the name of Coffin's wife, Dionis. Without a church or town hall, public meetings were held in private homes, with Tristram Coffin's large house beside the harbor commonly being used for court sessions and town meetings. Around 1677 he built a "new dwelling house upon the hill" overlooking his original home near the water's edge.

Beyond the anchorage at Capaum, Wesco (later called Lily) Pond and its grist mill served as another important focal point, with the miller receiving two quarts for every bushel of milled grain as payment. Providing a glimpse into what this mill entailed is a reference in the town records to maintenance of the "water wheel" as well as "the running gears, the hollow tree at the pond, and the sluice at the head of the mill." And when the management of the mill ran into problems, it was Tristram Coffin who took over its operation in 1672.

By that time, prices had been established on Indian corn (two shillings and eight pence per bushel), wheat (four shillings per bushel), barley (three shillings), and rye (three shillings). In 1678 twenty acres in the center of what is today's town were subdivided into twenty very narrow strips (20 by 2 rods) known as the Wesco division. Rather than heralding the town's eventual movement to the larger harbor to the east, the narrowness of the lots suggests that the division was intended for farming purposes only.

Along with farming and raising livestock, Nantucketers were kept busy raising large families—a process that eventually helped to fulfill Coffin's early hopes for an island dynasty. The record (begun in 1662) shows that in the first fifteen years, there were only six deaths and seventy-four births on Nantucket. Among the first families on the island, Coffins contributed more than their share to the future generations. At his death in 1681, Tristram had seven children, sixty grandchildren, and several great-grandchildren. By 1728, 1,582 descendants had been born, of whom 1,128 were still alive throughout New England, a staggering number when we consider that in 1726 there were only 917 English people on all of Nantucket. No wonder, then, that in 1792 Zaccheus Macy referred to Tristram Coffin as "the old grandfather to almost all of us."

If as patriarch of the island's leading family Coffin sought to mold the future destiny of the community, there was one aspect of life on Nantucket that he apparently did not seek to control. Having experienced the intrusive influence of a Puritan-run government (from both a spiritual and an economic point of view), Coffin and company chose to avoid the issue of religion altogether. It would not be until the following century that an organized faith established a foothold in the English community, meaning that for close to fifty years the only churches on Nantucket were to be found among the Indians!

This is not to suggest that religion was unimportant to many English Nantucketers. Throughout the seventeenth century, islanders of similar beliefs conducted meetings in private homes, with people such as Thomas Macy, Edward Starbuck, and Peter Folger functioning as lay-preachers. However, virtually nowhere else in New England were people left to do as they pleased on Sunday, and this apparently left some Nantucketers with a little too much time on their hands. In 1680 a law was passed, "For the prevention of such misdemeanors which some take occasion to practice on the Lord's Day by reason of absence of most people from their habitations and such temptations as vagrant persons are exposed to, thereby the court orders that no person present in Lord's Day to be absent from their houses or usual places of abode. . . ."

Here, in this reference to "vagrant persons," we may recognize the genesis of an ancient Nantucket term known as the "rantom scoot," meaning a day's "cruise" about the island with no definite purpose or destination. Without laws requiring them to attend a local Congregational church, Nantucketers seem to have created a less structured tradition of their own, in which it was common for people to wander freely about the island on a Sunday. And with laws severely limiting the number of horses on the island, seventeenth-century Nantucket was a place where everybody walked. (Indeed, it was no accident that three of the tradesmen who were invited to settle on the island listed shoe-making as one of their trades.) On Nantucket, even if you were not in the peak of health, you traveled by foot. According to one account of Peter Folger's wife Mary, "she was a large fleshy woman, and . . . when she went to visit a neighbor . . . she had a chair carried for her to rest herself on the way."

Apparently, however, by 1680 (if the above-quoted law is any indication), this island of rantom scooters was experiencing some social problems. As was common in towns throughout New England, Nantucketers had been careful to guard against undesirables. An ordinance from 1672 reads: "no person shall receive any person into the town as a tenant in house or land, but he shall give security to the town to free the town from public charge." There were even instances when the town went to the trouble of footing the bill for a person's deportation, particularly if the person were a single, unattached woman. In 1679 it was determined that "Sarah Neeffeld shall be sent away to her home . . . in Plymouth Colony at the charge of the Town."

Instead of a medieval drawbridge or stockade fence, the Nantucketers had the surrounding waters of Nantucket Sound to assist them in the control of their island community. It was also the sea, however, that required regular contact with probably the most difficult-to-control element in colonial America: sailors. Court records indicate that in December of 1673, a group of ten seamen attempted "to deliver a man from out of the hands of authority." John Glover, the leader in the "insurrection," was sentenced to "pay four pounds or be securely whipped and also to be confined to the vessel and not to depart from the vessel without order of the master." That Coffins were closely involved in all goings-on about the waterfront is suggested by the sentence given to Edward Bennett who was ordered to "pay ten pounds and be whipped and to remain in charges unless he can prevail with Mr. James Coffin to take him aboard and to be bound to him."

Nantucket officially came under the control of a specific mainland authority in 1664, giving Coffin and company plenty of opportunity to begin the settlement on their own terms. Significantly, it was not nearby Massachusetts but relatively distant New York to which Nantucket reported, and it was not until seven years later, in 1671, that Governor Lovelace established a direct relationship with the island by appointing Tristram Coffin as chief magistrate. From the beginning, Coffin and subsequent officials consulted off-island authority only when it suited their own purposes, paying the annual tribute of two barrels of "merchantable codfish" to New York on a somewhat irregular basis.

It may have been to help pay this tribute that in 1672 the island offered John Gardner "of Salem, Mariner, a seaman's accommodation . . . to set up the trade of fishing with a sufficient vessel fit for the taking of codfish. . . ." Already on island were Gardner's brother Richard (a seaman) and Richard's son Joseph (a shoemaker), who had come to Nantucket five years earlier. From an established family in Salem, the Gardners brought with them economic ambitions and a political savvy that inevitably placed them on a crash course with Coffin's vision of the island's future.

Recognizing the advantages of the much larger harbor to the east, John Gardner established a home site "upon the highway at Wesco going down to the Landing Place" where he could operate his codfishing business far away (relatively speaking) from the nodal point established by Coffin at Capaum. Already in this general area was his brother Richard, who had built his home on what is now known as Sunset Hill. Thus was established a rival family enclave, but whereas Coffin represented the island's original purchasers or full-share men, the Gardners were half-share men, a group of tradespeople that with John's arrival had grown to the point that it almost exactly equalled the number of full-share men living on Nantucket.

So quickly did Gardner win the acceptance and trust of the community that in February 1673, he and his brother Richard were asked to represent the island in New York. Perhaps some of the townspeople, particularly the tradesmen whose half-share accommodations gave them no stake in the future distribution of land on the island, had grown weary of Coffin's role as Nantucket's self-appointed country squire. Inevitably, Coffin, who represented the interests of several full-share men who did not even live on Nantucket (most notably his son Peter), had a view of the island's destiny that differed dramatically from that of the new arrivals.

Certainly there are indications that Coffin did not always see eye-to-eye with his fellow townspeople. In 1672 he protested the town's determination that some Indians accused of having "cast away . . . Mr. Price's vessel" be acquitted. The following year the wife of Edward Cottle was sanctioned by the court for "reproachful words" directed against Coffin. Mrs. Cottle felt that ever since the "death of her daughter's child," Coffin had encouraged "persons to speak more against her [daughter] than they know."

For those such as Mrs. Cottle, for whom Coffin's control over the island had become intrusive, the town was in need of a new order. And, to a certain extent, by so carefully orchestrating the original settlement of the town, Coffin had laid a trap for himself. Although the town would prove remarkably slow in reorienting itself to the larger harbor, the island's future clearly lay to the east, and it was Gardner, a late-coming fisherman, who was in the best position (both geographically and occupationally) to take advantage of the shift.

Before we see how Coffin and Gardner would come to personify the forces of conservatism and change on early Nantucket, we must turn to its native inhabitants. No matter what ambitions the English might have for their community, it was still very much the Indians' island.

CHAPTER 5

"An Island Full of Indians": King Philip, John Gibbs, and Peter Folger

Almost by definition, things were different on Nantucket. Instead of a Native American ghost town—which is what the Pilgrims had found at Plymouth—Coffin and his first purchasers bought "an island full of Indians," at least according to Massachusetts Governor John Winthrop. If they were to make a go of this Nantucket enterprise, the English would have to deal with something the Puritans had never known: a Native American society at full, preplague strength.

Whether it was wishful thinking or a pragmatic solution of the quick-and-dirty variety, the English purchased the western end of the island from the two "Head Sachems of Nantucket"—Wanackmamack and Nickanoose. The problem was that although they may have been Nantucket's two most powerful Indians, these two "Khaud" sachems lived on the eastern end of the island. Over the next eighteen years, western "Taumkhods" would demand (and receive) restitution for land that had been sold out from underneath them by Wanackmamack and Nickanoose.

Part of the problem was that English and Native Nantucketers had only a partial understanding of each other's culture. Indeed, the entire notion of ownership, as assumed by the English, was foreign to the Native Americans. As Henry Barnard Worth has said,

*Land was to [the Indian] as free as the water or the air.
Nobody could have exclusive right to it. So when the white
men came and obtained deeds from the sachems it was merely
the admission of the new settlers on equal terms with themselves. It was not that the Indian had ceased to have the right
to enjoy the land but that another had become his co-occupant.
Hence the idea that an Indian could be guilty of trespass was
a strange innovation.*

For their part, the English only gradually began to appreciate the complexity of Native American society on Nantucket.
While there were two distinct groups of Indians on the island,
both the easterners and the westerners looked to Wampanoag
headquarters on the mainland to settle any major disputes
between them, especially if they involved bloodshed.

But no matter what higher Indian authority the Khauds and
Taumkhods appealed to, on-island English–Native American
relations had to be governed by a mutually agreed upon set of
rules. And since the English were not about to adopt the Indians'
ways, it was only a matter of time before they began to subject
their Native American neighbors to what they considered to be
"established law." In order to formalize this process, the English
requested that the governor of New York grant them "power to
summon [the Indians] to our courts with respect to matters of
trespass, debt, and other miscarriages, and to try and judge them
according to town laws." Having seen how poorly the indiscrim-
inate use of such power had worked in eastern Long Island, the
New York authorities recognized the potential perils of applying
a completely foreign group of laws to another culture. Governor
Lovelace warned the English "that they be careful to use such
moderation amongst them, that they be not exasperated, but by
degrees may be brought to be conformable to the laws." As we

shall see later, it was here, in the courts, that Native Nantucketers would become not only acquainted with English law but also increasingly victimized by it.

At the outset, however, the Indians had one undeniable advantage: their numbers. If they became sufficiently "exasperated," the English would be the ones to suffer the consequences since they were outnumbered by more than twenty-five to one. And as the legends from the pre-English era made clear, in times of war there was no place to hide on this sandy island thirty miles out to sea. As a consequence, a remarkable degree of cooperation seems to have existed between the two cultures, particularly when compared to the rest of New England. When the town decided to dig the Madaket Ditch referred to in the first chapter, it was designated a joint Indian-English project. As we have seen, genuine efforts were made to appease those Indians who claimed that their land had been illegally sold. Complaints against English cattle interfering with native crops also seem to have been conscientiously attended to during the first decade of the settlement. But there was yet another factor contributing to the complexity (and potential danger) of English–Native American relations on Nantucket, one that many of the English had come to this island hoping to escape: the matter of religion.

Even before Thomas Macy first arrived in Madaket, the Mayhews of Martha's Vineyard had converted a significant number of Nantucket's Native Americans to the Christian faith. According to the missionary Daniel Gookin, these Indians were quite "poor," which tended to make them "more readily receive the gospel and become religious." As Gookin suggests, Indians generally adopted Christianity not from a position of strength but out of desperation. As might be expected, those who maintained their traditional beliefs tended to view the Christianized or "praying Indians" as sell-outs.

Less than five years after the arrival of the English, an event occurred that pointed not only to the divide between traditional and Christian Native Americans but also to the fact that no matter how hard both the English and Indians might try to work with each other, Nantucket was not immune to violence. The leading "praying Indian" on Martha's Vineyard was Hiacoomes, and in 1664 his son Joel was on the verge of receiving a degree from Harvard. After sailing to the Vineyard to visit his family, Joel was on his way back to Cambridge for the commencement when he and "other passengers and mariners" were shipwrecked on Coatue. According to Gookin, "the bark was found put on shore; and in all probability the people in it came on shore alive, but afterwards were murdered by some wicked Indians of that place; who, for lucre or the spoil in the vessel, which was laden with goods, thus cruelly destroyed the people in it."

As to be expected, these murders threw both the English and Indians on the island into a panic. Since the killings had occurred in his territory, sachem Nickanoose was immediately under pressure to prove that he had had nothing to do with the incident. According to testimony entered into the Nantucket town records by William Worth, "Nickanoose being accused of being privy to a murder committed by the Indians on English men at Coatue and being in great fear he hired or otherwise got Quaquachwinnit to go with him to Plymouth in the winter to ask council of Nickanoose's head Sachem." Notice that it was not the death of Joel, despite his status as a leading Christian Indian, that put Nickanoose in such "great fear"; rather it was the murder of the white men.

At this time the head of the Wampanoag was Metacom (better known in popular history as King Philip) who had just recently attained the sachemship after the death of his brother Wamsutta (called Alexander by the English). Philip apparently passed sentence on the offenders, and, according to another reference in town records, "Indians were hanged on Nantucket . . .

in the year 1665." This, however, was just the beginning of a community psychodrama that would help determine the future course of English–Native American relations on Nantucket.

Whether or not it was the execution of Nickanoose's men that originally brought him to the island, Philip himself appeared on Nantucket in the fall of 1665. By the time of his arrival, his intentions had apparently shifted to the apprehension of yet another Native Nantucketer—Assassamoogh (also called John Gibbs), a leading Christian Indian who, according to one traditional reference, had, like Joel, spent some time at Harvard. Gibbs's crime was that of speaking the name of Philip's deceased father, Massasoit. According to Obed Macy, "Rehearsing the name of the dead, if it should be that of a distinguished person, was decreed by the natives a very high crime, for which nothing but the life of the culprit would atone." For Philip, who resolutely refused to adopt Christianity, it was an inspired test case: the life of a praying Indian who had broken a sacred Indian law for the lives of several traditional Indians who had broken English law.

Philip and his party of war canoes are said to have arrived at Low Beach on the southeastern end of the island. Although he was only twenty-five years old, Philip was every inch a Native American king. Two years before his appearance on Nantucket, he was spotted by the English travel writer John Josselyn as he strutted through the streets of Boston: "[He] had a coat on and buckskins set thick with these beads in pleasant wild works and a broad belt of the same. His accoutrements were valued at twenty pounds." This was clearly a man to be reckoned with.

It did not take Philip long to find his quarry near a pond in the eastern part of the island that still bears the Indian's name— Gibbs. By this time the English had been alerted to the sachem's presence and at least some of them rode out across the Moors to find Philip preparing for the execution amid a crowd of local Indians. At this point the English "commiserated [Gibbs's] condition" and, according to Obed Macy, "made offers of money to ransom his life." Displaying a very kingly willingness to compromise his principles at the right price, the young sachem named a figure. Unfortunately, it was well beyond the Nantucketers' means. In an effort to postpone the inevitable, the English proposed that they return to the settlement to collect as much money as possible. It also appears that Philip, his entourage, and their prisoner returned to town with them.

After passing around the hat, the English came up with the paltry sum of eleven pounds. Philip was not impressed and threatened drastic action if the amount he had originally demanded was not quickly raised. By this point he and his men had, according to Macy, "surrounded and taken possession of one or two houses, to the great terror of the inmates." Throwing caution to the wind, the English decided to call Philip's bluff. If he did not leave the island immediately, they would "rally the inhabitants" and annihilate Philip and his warriors.

With the eleven pounds in hand and no way of knowing exactly how many whites were actually on the island (in fact fewer than thirty families, or about 100 men, women, and children), Philip took to his heels, beating a hasty retreat to his canoes on the other side of the island. John Gibbs was once again a free man.

That Philip was indeed on the island is indicated by an entry in the town records dated October 10, 1665: "At a public meeting of the town, Attapehat signified that himself with all the Tomokommoth [Taumkhod] Indians doth subject to the English government of Nantucket. Do own themselves subject to King Charles the Second. This was done in the presence of Metacom alias Philip Sachem of Mount Hope." There is no way of knowing if this town meeting occurred at the same time as King Philip's attempted execution of John Gibbs. It is difficult to believe that the tense sequence of events Obed Macy described would have allowed for an impromptu town meeting. In fact, Philip may have made two different appearances on the island during the 1660s. Whatever the case may be, the incident involving John Gibbs may have helped to bolster Indian-English relations on the island. Many of Nantucket's Indians, despite their traditional ties to King Philip, were undoubtedly more than a little impressed by the fact that the English were willing to endanger their own lives to protect the life of a local Indian.

Although Macy speaks of the English collectively in his account of the incident, there was only one man on the island fluent enough in the Wampanoag language to undertake what must have been extremely tense and complicated negotiations, and who by his own testimony in 1677 had been "interpreter here from the beginning of the plantation, when no English man but myself could speak scarce a word of Indian." His name was Peter Folger, and ever since his arrival on the island as a permanent resident in 1663 (after almost twenty years on Martha's Vineyard as an instructor to the Indians), he had been the one who had overseen relations with the Native Americans. As he wrote to New York Governor Andros, "I am sure some of these men . . . had felt arrows in their sides . . . had I not stepped in between them and made peace."

Folger's personal ties to Philip's intended victim may have been especially close. Assassamoogh's English name of John Gibbs was also that of Folger's maternal grandfather—the result, according to tradition, of a Folger-officiated baptism in the waters of Gibbs Pond. Folger's relationship to Gibbs helps to explain the resolution of the English in the face of Philip. As the Indian's mentor, he was not about to let him die for a sin that from the English perspective seemed relatively inconsequential, especially given Philip's evident willingness to take money in exchange for Gibbs's life.

Just how important the standoff with Philip was both to Folger as an individual and to Nantucket as a community is made plain by a ballad the interpreter wrote more than a decade later in 1676. By the time Folger wrote "A Looking Glass for the Times," much had changed since that tension-filled confrontation beside Gibbs Pond. Philip was now in the midst of what would become known as King Philip's War—a bloody and desperate series of uprisings against what the historian Francis Jennings called the Puritans' "righteous zeal and unrighteous covetousness" that would only accelerate the mainland Indians' slide into "subjugation and debauchery." But while New England burned, the view from Nantucket was relatively serene. Despite having the highest concentration of Indians in the region, the island had experienced none of the violence with which Philip had threatened them a decade earlier. In fact the town record from 1675 reads, "Old Merchant, Skipper, Miaskpo, George Haye, Cross Herry, Pottoser, Sapachaset, and Maosaaquat did come to court and did disown Philip and did freely subject themselves to King Charles the Second."

For Folger, whose Baptist beliefs meant that he was no friend to the religious intolerance of Puritan New England, there was a lesson in this. New England was suffering the consequences of forty years of religious persecution, and it was time the Puritans changed their ways. Rather than killing Indians, the New Englanders should become more tolerant of others, for "to scorn and domineer/To pride it out as if there were/Not God to make us fear" was conduct hardly becoming a Christian. At one point in the poem, which Folger's more famous grandson Benjamin Franklin praised for its "decent plainness and manly freedom," there is a reference that brings to mind that tense scene of 1665:

> When Jonathan is called to court
> Shall we as standers by
> Be still and have no words to say
> To suffer him to die?

All possible local references aside, this is also an allusion to the Bible's Book of Samuel, in which King Saul gathers "all the chief of the people" together so that he can determine who has sinned against him. Saul soon decides that Jonathan of Gibeah (who has just led the Hebrews against the Philistines) must die for breaking Saul's proclamation against eating during the battle. As to be expected, the Hebrews immediately voice their objections: "And the people said unto Saul, Shall Jonathan die, who hath wrought this great salvation in Israel? God forbid. . . . So the people rescued Jonathan, that he died not."

Adding to the possible similarity between this scene and what occurred on Nantucket in 1665 is that prior to the trial of Jonathan, Saul orders his people to "roll a great stone unto me this day." The stone is later described as "the first altar that he built unto the LORD," and it is here that Saul conducts the trial. Not far from where we know John Gibbs was initially apprehended is the boulder-topped hillside upon which this book began—Saul's Hills and Altar Rock. Was this dramatic setting the staging ground for Philip's Saul-like encounter with the English Nantucketers, and did Folger and his Bible-bred compatriots name the hill and rock accordingly? Even Assassamoogh's English name of John Gibbs (which may have been awarded after the incident) may have first been inspired by the similarity between his situation and that of Saul's son *Jon*athan of *Gib*eah.

There are other intriguing parallels between the biblical Saul and what we know of Philip on Nantucket, none of which are very flattering to the Indian sachem. When Saul is first chosen to be king of the Hebrews, Samuel leads the people in a loyalty oath: "And all the people shouted, and said, God save the king." Of course, Philip also witnessed a loyalty oath while on Nantucket, during which a local Indian sachem proclaimed himself "subject to King Charles the Second." The biblical portrait of

Saul as a pathetic and tormented outcast king who ultimately dies ignominiously in battle—while it may not conform to our current tendency to see Philip as a doomed and valiant hero— probably corresponded very closely to the Nantucketers' view of the man. Rather than stand up to a group of no more than thirty-five English men and boys, Philip had chosen—quite literally—to take the money and run. And, in point of fact, a stream flowing near where Philip's war canoes are supposed to have landed is still referred to as "Philip's Run," a name that, according to island tradition, is a pun, once again, at Philip's expense.

Clearly, then, the standoff with Philip in 1665 left an indelible mark on the island, but not only in terms of its place names. In "A Looking Glass" we see how it may have helped shape the islanders' collective identity, contributing to a somewhat self-righteous sense of Nantucket's being above the fray that was then engulfing the mainland. Philip—the supposed instrument of divine retribution according to many a Puritan sermon of the day—had been shown to be nothing more than a haughty and indecisive bully by Folger and his fellow Nantucketers. Indeed, behind his pleas for Christian charity and love, Folger displays a certain hubris in "A Looking Glass," implying that his moral ground atop Altar Rock on Nantucket is higher than that of all New England's Puritan divines put together.

But was this self-righteousness truly justified? Was Nantucket better than anywhere else when it came to English– Native American relations? To a certain extent, Nantucket in the seventeenth century had all the makings of an exemplary bi-cultural community: an isolated island with a tiny group of English surrounded by a large Native American population. But what might first seem like a veritable laboratory experiment for the advancement of interracial cooperation would ultimately create a community of an altogether different stamp.

⌒

The evidence reveals that once the English began to feel at least a measure of safety on Nantucket (a confidence that Folger's poem exudes), a new dynamic started to operate. It was not just survival the English were after; they also wanted to prosper, and for that they needed workers. While their counterparts on the mainland imported African slaves and indentured servants from England, the Nantucketers had, potentially at least, an indigenous solution to their labor needs: the Indians.

In addition to the "innovation" of conveying land, the English judicial system began to educate the Native Americans in the consequences of certain "miscarriages," in particular theft. And it was here that the English found a surprisingly efficient method for securing a cheap, long-term labor supply. If an Indian was found guilty of an offense and did not have the goods or money with which to pay the court-determined fine, he or she was condemned to work it off—not over a matter of weeks or months but over years. For example, after being convicted of stealing some beer, molasses, and rum, the Indian Alewife discovered that for "the time of six whole years" he would be the servant of Nathaniel Starbuck and Peter Coffin. Moab stole a sheep from John Macy and, unable to pay the fine, found himself at Macy's beck and call for the next three years. For stealing eighteen pieces of whalebone, another Native Nantucketer was sentenced to serve Thomas Macy for seven years.

Here was a form of economic slavery, commonly referred to as "peonage," that the Spanish conquistadors had perfected in their dealings with the Indians in Mexico. As the historian Daniel Vickers has observed, Indian debt servitude on Nantucket amounted to "a type of communal labor control," in which the English first secured an Indian worker through the courts, then found a "Master" for him. Coottas, for example, was sentenced to pay "a fine of four pounds and ten shillings or to lie in prison till the court do find a way to sell him for payment." The sentence of the Native American Kessasume included this condition: "and if he run away from his master then he is to be whipped every time he so runs away."

It was not just a question of the Indians serving the English; other Indians, such as the sachem Wauwinet (son of Nickanoose), sometimes paid the fine and secured the condemned as a servant. In fact, the Native Nantucketers had their own court system that often seems to have been dominated by the personalities of the justices rather than adherence to any law. Zaccheus Macy tells of Corduda: "He was justice of the peace, and very sharp with [the Indians] if they did not behave well. He would fetch them up, when they did not tend their corn well, and order them to have ten stripes on their backs. . . ."

And, in fact, this same principle (or lack thereof) also applied to the English courts. As Vickers says, "The local courts were . . . dominated by magistrates who understood the need for strictly enforcing native obligations." In other words, in an English community in which everyone had an interest in securing cheap labor, it was virtually impossible for an Indian to get a fair trial. According to Matthew Mayhew on the Vineyard, "the Indians cannot expect any justice" on Nantucket.

Given the relatively large size of the Native American population throughout the seventeenth century (the English would not begin to outnumber Native Nantucketers until the 1720s), what is truly astonishing is how early the English began to enlist the Indians as servants. In 1670, only a decade after the beginning of the English settlement, it was resolved that "if any person English or Indian shall at any time carry in any vessel any Indian servant . . . off the Island without orders from his master he shall be fined twenty shillings." Here we see yet another reason why debt servitude (which was not officially institutionalized

in island courts until the early 1700s) flourished on Nantucket.
Since they lived on an island, it was relatively easy for the English to round up and keep their servants. Unless the Indian
was able to escape by boat, he was at the mercy of the English.
Some Indians appear to have sought refuge on the neighboring
island of Tuckernuck, where Nantucket courts had no jurisdiction throughout the seventeenth century. According to a 1711
petition, the Indians "run over to Tuckernuck in the winter to
avoid the payment of the just debts." Since the court records
reveal that some Indians were not only fined and whipped but
also branded "on the forehead with the letter B" (for "burglarly"),
one can appreciate Tuckernuck's attractions.

Given this state of affairs, made all the worse by the combined effects of liquor and disease on the native population,
English-Indian relations had nowhere to go but down. When
a French privateer plundered Nantucket in 1695, the island's
Indians showed none of the loyalty to the English they had displayed in the face of King Philip. Indeed, the governor of Acadia's report to the French government offers a sad and telling
commentary on the Native Nantucketers' decline: "Our freeboo-
ters made a raid this spring on an island off Cape Cod called
Nantaquet. The more than 200 savages there were very friendly
to them while they pillaged the English and moreover [the En-
glish] have turned them into peasants by selling them no weapons and requiring them to fish and farm the land. . . ."

Certainly there is a danger in relying upon the testimony of
privateers and court records in assembling a portrait of English–
Native American relations on Nantucket. In that it emphasizes
those instances when things go wrong, a police blotter can never
provide a fully balanced account of a community. In spite of the
numerous and unconscionable injustices suffered as a result of
their contact with the English, not all Native Americans were
reduced to a state of slavery. According to Zaccheus Macy,

"many of them . . . lived in a very good fashion. Some of them were weavers, some good carpenters." And as we shall see in Chapter 7, others were to make more than a decent income as whalemen.

The fact of the matter remains that for more than 100 years Indians and whites lived and worked side-by-side on this fourteen-mile-long island. Although they were doomed, in the words of one nineteenth-century commentator, to "melt away like ice in the blaze of sunshine," the Native Nantucketers inevitably left their mark. Decades after the Plague of 1763, the whale fishery was still using terminology first coined by the Indians. Instead of crying, "Thar she blows!" when a whale was sighted from the masthead, a Nantucketer in the eighteenth century— no matter what color he was—shouted, "Awaite Pawana," which means, "Here is a whale." Even today when we mention not only the name of this island but almost every place on it, we are still speaking the Wampanoag language.

And what about Philip's intended victim? John Gibbs lived on to lead a thirty-person congregation at the island's first Indian church at Okorwaw, or Occawaw, not far from the pond that still bears his name. Although he owed so much to the Baptist Peter Folger, Gibbs (true to the Puritan beliefs of the missionaries from Martha's Vineyard) insisted on baptizing the newborns in his congregation. According to John Cotton on the Vineyard, the English Baptists on Nantucket "did at first seek to hinder them from administering baptism to infants; but now they are quiet, and meddle not with them." Gibbs appears to have been a man of principle, unwilling to compromise his actions in the face of not only Philip but the English as well.

It is here, in this early split between English Baptists and Native American Congregationalists, that we see how conditions unique to Nantucket would enable the Indians to maintain at least a portion of their cultural identity in the years ahead.

Anywhere else in New England (with the exception of Rhode Island), Congregationalism was the religion of the state. But on Nantucket, where no English churches existed, such was not the case. Rather than knuckling under to the English, "praying Indians" on Nantucket established their own, increasingly distinctive spiritual identity—an assertion of independence that was not always appreciated by white Nantucketers, especially in the century to come.

On Nantucket a minister was called a "cooutaumuchary," and he conducted a service that would have probably made both King Philip and your average Puritan minister equally uncomfortable, but for entirely different reasons. According to Zaccheus Macy, services were conducted in Wampanoag and followed the form of a Congregational meeting except that they convened twice a week as was practiced by the Quakers. He adds:

> *And when the meeting was done, they would take their tinder-box and strike fire and light their pipes, and, maybe, would draw three or four whiffs and swallow the smoke, and then blow it out of their noses, and so hand their pipes to their next neighbor. And one pipe of tobacco would serve ten or a dozen of them. And they would say "tawpoot," which is, "I thank ye." It seemed to be done in a way of kindness to each other.*

If it had not been for this form of cultural cross-pollination, Nantucket's Native Americans might have lost all touch with their traditional ways by the end of the seventeenth century. According to John Gardner writing in 1694, "I may now say there is not known a powaw [medicine man] among them; . . . yet amongst the now praying Indians, there is an increase. God raising up even of themselves preachers. . . ."

In that he helped save the life of the Native American who

established the first Indian church on Nantucket, Peter Folger was an important part of this legacy—a legacy that developed amid the wreckage of what had once been a thriving and multi-faceted Native American culture. Whether or not it could have been otherwise, Folger seems to have done everything in his power to insure that English–Native American relations began, at least, in a positive way. Certainly the murders on Coatue and the appearance of Philip must have demanded extraordinary diplomatic skills on Folger's part, skills that the more authoritarian Tristram Coffin did not necessarily possess. And as we shall see, less than a year after writing his rousing and self-assured ballad, "A Looking Glass for the Times," Folger would need every bit of diplomatic skill he could muster. This time it was not the Indians who were disturbing the island's peace; this time it was the English themselves.

CHAPTER 6

Gardner versus Coffin: The Revolt

I T IS THE WINTER OF 1677. The English settlement, which had displayed such admirable solidarity in the face of King Philip, is now riven by controversy. On one side are Tristram Coffin and the "full-share" men who cling jealously to their status as privileged landowners. If they have their way, all future distribution of land on Nantucket will be reserved to only fully vested members of the proprietary, leaving the new arrivals out in the cold. John Gardner and the "half-share men," on the other hand, feel that it is time to stop managing the island as if it were simply an investment for the original proprietors. In their view, the town should be a community of relative equals in which all resident landowners have a say in the future of the island. But instead of Tristram Coffin and John Gardner, it is Peter Folger who gets caught in the middle of this war of principles and personalities.

The date is February tenth; a light snow is on the ground, and Folger, a local hero a decade ago, is now on the run from the law. Twice that day the town constable, William Bunker, his stave with "the King's Arms upon it" firmly in hand, has come knocking on Folger's door. Representing the full-share men who are in search of documentation to back up their claims, Bunker demands that Folger, who besides being an Indian interpreter is also the town clerk, hand over his court book containing the town's records. Unsure of what to do, Folger stuffs the book beneath his coat and rushes past Bunker for the home of John Gardner.

It was not much of a jog from Folger's house on a hill in Roger's Field (just off Madaket Road where a monument now stands) to Gardner's place near "the Cliff" in the vicinity of what is now North Street. We have no way of knowing what exact route he took, but he probably traveled along cart paths that still exist today as roads: Madaket Road (then known as Main Street) to Crooked Lane and then down either Grove Lane or Westchester and on to the "Cap's House."

Bunker seems to have had a pretty good idea of where Folger was headed, and on his way to Gardner's house he rounded up some reinforcements. By the time the constable arrived, Folger and Gardner had safely stashed away the court book, and they apparently greeted Bunker and his henchmen with surly contempt. According to Folger, the constable, with the "help of other men hauled and dragged me out of the Cap's House" and carried him off to court.

Although Folger escaped incarceration that day, he was not so lucky four days later when he once again refused to hand over the court book. Folger was charged with contempt and ordered to pay a twenty-pound bond or go to jail. So the sixty-year-old Folger, who according to his own testimony was "a poor old man and not able to maintain my family," went to jail.

In those days, the prison was not far from Bunker's house on Grove Lane near No-Bottom Pond. It was not a heavily used facility. According to Folger, the "neighbor's hogs had laid but the night before" in the prison, and although Bunker was willing to sweep away "most of the dirt, hogs' dung, and snow," he was not about to roll out the red carpet. With only naked floorboards to sleep on and no food or heat, Folger pleaded with him to "fetch a little hay," which Bunker grudgingly provided. Finally a friend brought Folger some blankets and food.

According to Folger, his imprisonment "set a fire to the whole island, for I, having lived thirty years upon this island and the Vineyard, was so well known and so well beloved of English and Indians (whether deserved or not) that the Indians inquired what the cause was of my imprisonment." Although both the half- and full-share men were unwilling to reveal the details of the incident, the Indians apparently began to speak belligerently concerning their recent treatment in island courts. According to John Gardner, who quickly wrote to the governor in Folger's defense, "amongst the Indians there has been great disturbance of late." What had happened in the last ten years since Indian and English Nantucketers had stood shoulder-to-shoulder against an off-island threat?

It all dated to the Gardner brothers' initial visit to New York back in the spring of 1673. It had been then that Richard and John engineered the beginnings of a coup d'état when they convinced the governor that all previous deeds and land grants "shall be esteemed of no force and validity," with only those "who live upon the place and make improvements thereof" able to lay claim to their land. This, of course, incensed many of the full-share men, especially Coffin, whose dominant role in the proprietary was based on the presence of nonresident shareholders. Throwing salt onto an already open wound, the Gardners had the audacity to out-Coffin Coffin when it came to assigning ancestral place names to the new island, securing the official title of "Sherburne" (their family's village in Dorset) for the town.

The Gardners were able to pull it off (for the moment, at least) because even though they did not have control over the proprietary (the body of full-share men who supervised the distribution and use of land), they did have control over the town meeting, where all resident landowners were given a vote. This meant that town meetings became a battleground as the Gardners did everything within their power to loosen the full-shareholders' grip on the island's resources. As to be expected, Tristram Coffin and his cohorts fought them every inch of the way, and in 1675 a measure was passed against anyone who "turbulently and disorderly behaves himself in the time of meeting." Coffin's dream of a harmonious manor by the sea was looking more remote by the minute.

Stoking the fires of controversy on Nantucket was a series of extremely traumatic events in New York and New England that not only increased the tensions felt by both factions but also made an appeal to off-island authority next to impossible. Just a few months after the Gardners' visit to the governor, the Dutch recaptured New York, and it was not until October of the following year that the English retook the city and installed Edmund Andros as the new governor. Then in June of 1675 came the outbreak of King Philip's War. Even though a portion of Nantucket's Indians had reaffirmed their allegiance to the English and even handed over some of their weapons, there was always the chance that off-island Indians might once again travel to Nantucket and stir up trouble. In September of 1675, Governor Andros dispatched a sloop to Nantucket with "one barrel of powder, ten muskets, and three skeins of match." The vessel's captain was instructed "not to stay . . . above one tide unless it may happen that the Indians should flock over from the main [land], and the chief magistrate or officer desire your assistance for obstructing the same by water." Certainly the prospect of fighting off the Indians from the tiny fort on Gull Island was terrifying to consider.

But it was not just off-island Indians that concerned the Nantucketers. Local Native Americans had become increasingly dissatisfied with their treatment by the English, the result of a controversy that had been brewing ever since Coffin and company first negotiated a deed for island-wide grass rights. As far as the English were concerned, they had purchased exclusive right to all grass on Nantucket from October to May. This was fine with the Indians as long as it did not conflict with their own use of the land. Problems developed, however, when their culture and economy inevitably began to change through contact with the English. What they increasingly coveted were horses. But when the Indians attempted to graze their newly acquired horses on their own land, the English felt justified in confiscating the animals since, in their view, they owned the grazing rights. To be barred from using their own land was inconceivable to the Indians, and they soon began to maintain that they had been illegally denied use of their own land. (Although English Nantucketers would continue to defend their right to winter grass, in 1700 the Earl of Bellomont corroborated the Indians' point of view when he bluntly informed James Coffin that the deeds were a "circumvention and fraud.")

But horses were not the only thing the Indians wanted as a result of their exposure to the English. They also wanted rum. And as Obed Macy would observe, this had a corrosive, even lethal effect on their health and culture. At this time, Obed's great-great-grandfather, Thomas Macy, was the town's chief magistrate; he was also one of the few full-share men to back the Gardner cause. However, as the pressures mounted during King Philip's War, a fault line began to develop between himself and Gardner over the issue of supplying liquor to the Indians.

In Thomas Macy's view, rum was the chief culprit when it came to degrading and agitating Nantucket's native population. In a letter to the governor, he maintained that "they have been by the drunken trade kept all the while like wild bears and wolves in the wilderness." Although "some that dwell elsewhere" were originally responsible for supplying drink to the Indians, they were now getting their liquor, according to Macy, from none other than Captain John Gardner, who recruited Indian fishermen by promising "each man a dram before they go out to fishing in the morning." At some point Macy and Gardner had a falling-out, causing the town's chief magistrate to shift his alliances to the more conservative Coffin group, who supported the enforcement of laws against selling liquor to the Indians.

By the fall of 1676, the defection of Macy and others, when combined with the arrival of Peter and James Coffin (who temporarily moved to Nantucket seeking refuge from the war), had made the full-share faction "the bigger party" at town meeting. Just as Gardner and the half-share men had attempted to reshape the island's government in their own image, now Coffin and company proceeded to "mold all things after their pleasure," according to Gardner. With the threat of Indian war hovering over the island, a weirdly giddy, almost carnival atmosphere began to characterize town meetings as the full-share men made no attempt to disguise the glee with which they attended to their own interests.

Leading the way was Stephen Hussey, a paradoxically bellicose Quaker who would gain a reputation for litigiousness. The son of Christopher Hussey, one of the first purchasers, Stephen was a little younger and a little more animated than many of his fellow full-share men and had spent some time in Barbados before removing to Nantucket. According to Folger, it was Hussey who carried out the "design in such a rude manner" at town meeting, flippantly proposing that Peter Coffin be voted into office so that the town could collect a ten-pound fine from him when he returned to the mainland after the war. Hussey also proposed the election of "two young men more" for the simple reason that he had "cattle at their houses to winter" and wanted to make sure that the potential officeholders took good care of his livestock. Folger finally erupted in anger, scolding Hussey and the others "not to make a May game of choosing men for such employment." But Folger's words had little effect. "As they began," he ruefully commented in his letter to the governor, "so they ended."

It was only a matter of time before the new full-share administration directed its attention to the problem of Peter Folger, the town clerk who refused to give them access to the court book that contained documents vital to the claims of both factions. Convinced that Macy and Coffin planned to alter the official records in their own favor, Folger refused to hand the book over, and, as we have already seen, in February he was thrown in jail.

Things soon went from bad to worse. In March the town issued an order forbidding "Captain Gardner and Peter Folger . . . to meddle at all . . . in any of the town's concerns." Then in June, after two attempts, Constable Bunker forcibly brought Gardner to court for reportedly spreading the rumor among the Indians "that there was no government on Nantucket." Gardner was in no mood to cooperate, and according to the sentence written by Matthew Mayhew, he "demeaned himself most irreverently, sitting down with his hat on [and] taking no notice of the court." At this same court session, both Gardner and Folger were officially disenfranchised.

Although there were some fairly complex issues involved in what has become known as the "Half-Share Revolt," it all came down to two men—John Gardner and Tristram Coffin—who had grown to hate each other. Perhaps they were too much alike. Both were forceful men who had come to the island so that they might do as they wished. But even though Coffin staked out a claim at Capaum and Gardner went east to Wesco, the island was not big enough for the two of them. Coffin saw the island in truly medieval terms, with the tradespeople at the bottom of the pyramid and the landowners at the top. But Gardner was not about to submit to this pigeon-holing, no matter how the laws of the proprietary might read.

It was also a generational conflict. In 1677 Coffin was seventy-two years old and already beginning to hand over the management of his properties to his children; Gardner was a still vital fifty-three, unwilling to show Coffin and the other graybeards what they considered to be the proper degree of respect. Perhaps no document better illustrates the animosity between these two men than Coffin's recorded testimony concerning Gardner's conduct during the General Court session on June 6, 1677. When Gardner came into the room, he made a point of taking a seat beside Coffin "on a chest where I sat." According to Coffin, "I spoke to him and told him that I was very sorry that he did behave himself [in this way. He] said: 'I know my business and it may be that some of those that have meddled with me had better have eaten fire.'"

In August, Governor Andros, after receiving a flurry of contradictory letters from both factions, issued his long-awaited decision. Offering his official support of Macy as chief magistrate (who would be replaced by Tristram Coffin in September), Andros also insisted that all charges against Folger and Gardner be dropped. The full-share men, however, chose to ignore the second half of the decision. Under the pretense that the governor was "without knowledge of the facts," they continued to sell off Gardner's cattle to pay his fine. In March of 1678, Thomas Mayhew, a staunch supporter of Coffin and the full-share cause, smugly informed Gardner "that if the governor did unwind then he would wind; and that he would make my fine and disenfranchisement to abide on me."

By June of 1678, almost a year and a half after Folger's initial imprisonment, most of the English on Nantucket had become sick and tired of the in-fighting. At this point a compromise was reached that paved the way for the gradual reconciliation of the two factions. As long as the half-share men agreed to transfer all their individual land purchases from the Indians to the "capacity of the whole," then the full-share men agreed that the half-share grants "shall not be confined to the first township . . . but shall, according to proportion, extend throughout the whole island." At long last, all those with a stake in the proprietary—full- and half-share men alike—were included in future divisions of land. Six months later the order against Folger and Gardner acting as agents of the town was rescinded.

Coffin, however, still held a grudge. In January of 1680, when John Gardner was elected to serve on the island's General Court, Coffin and Mayhew used their influence to oppose the town's nomination, declaring that Gardner was "incapacitated to bear such an office of trust." In clear defiance of Coffin, who seems to have been alienating an increasing number of once loyal supporters through his unreasonable bitterness toward Gardner, the town nominated John and Richard Gardner to be the island's chief magistrates.

By this point, Coffin's star was clearly on the decline. Two years before in September, 1678, he had supervised the salvage of a French ship wrecked on Nantucket shoals. Then in October, hearing that "portions of the cargo and rigging were being carried away," Governor Andros ordered Coffin to "prevent embezzlement and secure as much property as possible." Directing the operation in his typically authoritarian way, Coffin failed to follow established procedures and in 1680 was found guilty of numerous violations by the admiralty court.

Here, at long last, was an instance in which Coffin could not simply do as he pleased. Faced with a hefty fine and the possibility of serving time in jail, Coffin appealed to his hated foe, John Gardner (who had sat on the admiralty court), for help. Eating a large slice of humble pie, Coffin admitted to Governor Andros that he had acted "contrary to the law . . . through ignorance in regard of not being acquainted with the maritime laws," then made what must have been a painful reference to "my loving neighbor, Captain John Gardner," who had apparently spoken in his behalf. That November Andros discharged Coffin on the matter; a year later Coffin was dead.

With Coffin's aggressively conservative voice forever silenced, the town was now in a position to begin the work of reconciling its differences. Signaling the emergence of a new consensus was the renewal of negotiations with the Indians concerning grass rights in 1682. In exchange for what became known as "winter feed" rights throughout the island, the town granted the Indian sachems the right to graze a limited number of horses and cattle. Known as "horse commons," these deeds gave the Indians the opportunity to participate, albeit on a limited basis, in the proprietary, thus resolving (temporarily, at least) the Indians' side in the Half-Share Revolt.

The symbolic resolution of the conflict would not occur, however, until 1686 with the marriage of Peter Coffin's son Jethro and John Gardner's daughter Mary. Tradition tells us that Coffin provided the lumber and Gardner provided the land for the couple's new home, now known as the Oldest House on Sunset Hill. According to this same tradition, Coffin held up the wedding ceremony until Gardner registered the deed to the land, indicating that old suspicions died hard.

∽

From these and other intermarriages among the children of the first settlers would emerge a community in which the names remained remarkably the same, with the Coffins, Gardners, Macys, Starbucks, Folgers, Swains, Bunkers, Barnards, Colemans, and Husseys dominating island life for the next 100 years. Indeed, although Tristram Coffin may have died thinking that he had ultimately lost out to Gardner and the forces of change, in the end it was Coffin's conservatism that won out. Even as whaling and Quakerism transformed the island economically and religiously in the century to come, the community remained faithful to Coffin's conception of Nantucket as a familial strong-hold. Wrote one observer, "Before the Revolution, the people of Nantucket were like a band of brothers. They were an unmixed race, of English descent. They were all clad in homespun and minded their own business." According to Walter Folger writing in 1791, "The inhabitants live together like one great family, not in one house, but in friendship."

There was, however, a darker side to this intimacy. Given the limited number of families on Nantucket in the seventeenth century, it was inevitable that second- and third-generation Nan-tucketers would have to look dangerously close to home (from a genetic point of view) when it came to choosing marriage part-ners. In 1693, Matthew Mayhew on the Vineyard commented that the English on Nantucket, "having many years married in the relation of first and second cousins," were "so nearly related" that it was impossible to find an impartial jury to hear court cases. Although no medical records exist, one commentator has insisted that these marriage patterns meant that "mental defects, deaf mutism, insanity, feeble mindedness, and peculiar traits were common" on the island. One circumstance, however, miti-gated against a disastrous thinning of the Nantucketers' blood. Unlike some towns on Martha's Vineyard, whose original settlers moved in a group from England only to continue a longstand-ing tradition of inbreeding (with serious genetic consequences, which included deafness and hermaphroditism), Nantucketers began with a fresh gene pool collected from towns throughout the Merrimack Valley.

Whether or not they were too ingrown for their own genetic good, Nantucketers remained almost fanatically obsessed with maintaining close ancestral alliances. In fact, when an islander recognized a specific family resemblance, he or she proudly referred to it as "Seeing the Look." Many families kept detailed genealogical records (called a "census") so that they could determine who were and who were not their "cousins"—an increasingly important distinction on Nantucket around which many business relationships were based (see Chapter 9).

The inevitable result of this attitude, especially given what Crèvecoeur called "their secluded situation, which has prevented them from mixing with others," was that Nantucketers never strayed far from the ways of the first settlers. Indeed, more than a century after the Half-Share Revolt, an attorney by the name of Phineas Fanning wrote a piece of doggerel about the leading families on the island that rings remarkably true when we consider the players in this seventeenth-century power struggle: Tristram Coffin, autocratic and outspoken; John Gardner, who began his career on Nantucket by quietly undermining his predecessor's powerbase; Thomas Macy, who (no matter how righteous his intentions may have been) strategically shifted his alliances and as a consequence received more than his share in land grants and other benefits; Edward Starbuck, although not a major player in the Revolt was a man with a known ability to express himself; Stephen Hussey, the Quaker who delighted in questionable shenanigans during that notorious town meeting; and, finally, Peter Folger, undoubtedly the most intelligent man on the island but who was barely able to support his family:

> *The Coffins noisy, fractious, loud,*
> *The silent Gardners plotting,*
> *The Mitchells good, the Barkers proud,*
> *The Macys eat the pudding;*
> *The Swains are swinish, clownish called,*
> *The Barnards very civil,*
> *The Starbucks they are loud to bawl,*
> *The Pinkhams beat the devil;*
> *A learned Coleman very rare,*

And scarce an honest Hussey,
The Rays and Russells coopers are,
The knowing Folgers lazy.

No matter how much things changed on Nantucket in the next 100 years, its people would remain remarkably the same.

CHAPTER 7

The Whaling Legacy of Ichabod Paddock

MORE THAN ANY OTHER people in America and the world, Nantucketers would come to embody an attitude conducive to bloodshed on the high seas. Indeed, killing whales seems to have quickly become an almost reflex reaction on Nantucket. When, in 1744, three islanders came across a forty-foot whale stranded on the shore, they did what any self-respecting Nantucketer would have done— they attacked it with the only weapons they had available, their jackknives.

Where did it come from, this fierceness, this horrifying playfulness, especially once (as we will see in the next chapter) Quakerism began to exert its staid, rigidly nonviolent influence? Certainly, the first settlers, who were mainly landsmen, did not bring it with them. No, whaling was a learned activity on Nantucket, and to begin to understand how the island became the fabled fountainhead of this "most sanguinary" business, as Melville called it, we must look to its original practitioner: Ichabod Paddock, the island's first professional whaleman.

Unfortunately, we know precious little about the man. Although he came to Nantucket in 1690, he was back in his hometown, Yarmouth on Cape Cod, by 1710, when he was granted seven and a half shares of common land. His brothers, however, Nathaniel and Joseph, stayed on the island, and it would be Ichabod's niece, Love, who would let out the water from Lily Pond. Indeed, there seems to have been something mischievous and daring about the Paddocks, who had a difficult time maintaining the proper level of Quaker-required decorum throughout the eighteenth century. In 1730, Nathaniel Paddock was censored by the Monthly Meeting for having been "excessive in taking of strong liquor to [his] own scandal and shame." And then in 1781, a kinsman named for the illustrious father of all Nantucket whalemen, Ichabod Paddock, was "disowned" by the Quakers for having "sailed about in a vessel where dancing was performed and he a partaker therein."

When it comes to the original Ichabod Paddock, however, all we have is a legend that has been passed down to us involving a green-eyed mermaid. As was true with the Indian legends, this tale, if not historically correct, is an important indication of the emotional and cultural truth of what it was Ichabod Paddock started on Nantucket. But first a little background.

The sighting of mermaids and mermen was a fairly regular occurrence in the early eighteenth century, particularly in the neighborhood of Nantucket. In 1714, a sojourner by the name of Valentyn was on a ship in the vicinity of Nantucket when he and other members of the crew spotted "a creature of a grizzlish, or gray color, like that of a codfish skin" who "appeared like a sailor, or a man." Before Valentyn could take a closer look, the merman dove underwater, revealing to the man at the masthead "a monstrous long tail." About this same time the crew of yet another ship passing near Great Point spotted a mermaid cavorting in the sea. According to one account, she swam ashore and disappeared into the "strange forest" that then existed on what is now a treeless sand spit. Two hundred years later, the lighthouse keeper at Great Point determined that someone had been living in this forest, and there were many on Nantucket who claimed it had been the mermaid's hiding place.

As might be expected, Ichabod Paddock's connection with a

mermaid came as a consequence of a run-in with a whale, a big bull sperm whale by the name of Crook-Jaw. In the tradition of Moby Dick, Crook-Jaw confounded all of Ichabod's attempts to harpoon him. No matter how many harpoons he might heave, none of them succeeded in fastening to the tough-skinned whale. But Ichabod, who had a reputation to uphold, was not about to give up.

One warm, sunny day, after hours of unsuccessfully pursuing old Crook-Jaw, he decided it was time to discover what made this monster tick. With his knife clenched between his teeth, he leapt into the ocean. It was a fairly calm day, and as his crew looked on in horror, Ichabod swam up to the whale and waited for him to open his huge gnarled jaws. Growing bored with the proceedings, the whale yawned, and in swam Ichabod, a voluntary Jonah.

What he found inside amazed him. Instead of chewed-up squid and stomach lining, he found himself face-to-face with the door to a ship's cabin. Inside the lamp-lit room were two figures on opposite sides of a table playing cards. One was a gorgeous, emerald-eyed mermaid, with flaxen blond hair and not a stitch of clothing to conceal what was a very human and well-developed body above the glittering scales of her fishy tail; the other was the Devil. Suddenly the Devil threw down his cards and cursed, and eyeing Ichabod with bitter contempt, vanished in a puff of foul-smelling, tryhouse smoke.

Ichabod politely apologized to the bewitching mermaid for interrupting her card game, then asked what had been the stakes. The mermaid laughed coquettishly. "The stakes, Captain Paddock?" she asked. "Why, they were you!"

Meanwhile, back on Ichabod's whaleboat, his crew had given him up for lost, but being a loyal crew they waited out the night beside the weirdly passive Crook-Jaw. As they slept on their oars, the crew was suddenly awakened the next morning by the sound of a very weary but surprisingly content Captain Ichabod swimming toward them.

After returning to his ship for the day, Ichabod and crew were once again back out that evening; and once again he spent the night within the belly of the whale. This continued for several voyages until Ichabod's wife, hearing some of the wild rumors that had been told by the crew, began to grow suspicious.

The next time Ichabod came ashore, his wife—a beautiful woman in her own right and not yet thirty—presented him with a gift: a shiny, freshly forged harpoon. Whatever guilt Ichabod felt was not enough to keep him from setting out the next day, but this time his wife had a request: could he take her father along? Whaling with his father-in-law was not exactly what Ichabod had in mind, but he reluctantly agreed.

Soon old Crook-Jaw once again came in sight. By now the whale had become accustomed to Ichabod's appearances and rather than swimming away from the whaleboat, he waited patiently for its arrival. Confident that it would prove impossible to fasten to the whale, Ichabod watched his father-in-law take up the new harpoon and hurl it at Crook-Jaw. To his astonishment, the harpoon held, and it was not long before the whale was in its final flurry.

Back at the ship, Ichabod watched tensely as they cut into the whale. But where there had once been a ship's cabin all he found was a strand of yellow seaweed and two green, glittering shells. It was not until long after they had left Nantucket and returned to Yarmouth that Ichabod's wife confessed to what she had done. It had been no ordinary harpoon she had given him; instead of iron it had been fashioned out of silver—the only metal that will pierce the heart of a witch.

Ichabod Paddock introduced the Nantucketers to something more than a new occupation; he introduced them to a whole new way of life, that of the sea. Terrifyingly unpredictable, it could also be tantalizingly alluring, with Ichabod's mermaid finding her real-life embodiment in the South Sea maidens who would tempt future generations of islanders in the nineteenth century. And so, with this tall tale as a beginning, let us now examine the historical circumstances surrounding the rise of whaling on Nantucket.

⟳

According to Obed Macy, it all started when a "scrag" (otherwise known as an Atlantic gray) whale found its way into Nantucket Harbor perhaps a decade after the arrival of the English. In those days whales were a common sight throughout the Cape and islands; in fact, when the *Mayflower* sailed from Provincetown Harbor to Plymouth in 1620, the Pilgrims found themselves literally surrounded by whales "playing hard by us." Although dead or "drift" whales commonly washed up along the southwestern shore of the island, the Indians still exercised their traditional right of control over these whales. In typical fashion, however, the Gardners seem to have worked out their own deal with the Indians, for in 1668 Edward Starbuck and Peter Folger were appointed "to make a bargain with the Gardners concerning all the whales that shall come on shore on the island on the town's behalf."

This whale, however, was different. It was alive, and no one on this island of mostly farmers and sheepherders seems to have known what to do about it. As large numbers of townspeople lined the "high cliff" along which now runs Orange Street and watched the disoriented whale spout and churn the waters from Brant Point to Wauwinet, others in the town, no doubt supervised by the Gardners, "invented and caused to be wrought for them a harpoon." On the third day of the whale's captivity within the shielding arm of Coatue, an unnamed Nantucketer began what would become a 200-year tradition by successfully killing the sea mammal with the brand-new harpoon.

Since it had already become clear that they were not going to get rich by raising sheep, the Nantucketers were eager to exploit this new and potentially lucrative endeavor. So in 1672 the town looked to the eastern end of Long Island, where along-shore whaling had been going on since the 1640s, offering one James Lopar, a whaleman from Southampton, and John Savage, a cooper, the opportunity to set up a whaling business on Nantucket. Although Savage did decide to relocate, there is no evidence that Lopar ever left Long Island.

Then in 1690, with King Philip's War and the Half-Share Revolt safely behind them, the townspeople looked across the Sound to Cape Cod, where in Yarmouth there was a twenty-eight-year-old fisherman by the name of Ichabod Paddock with a reputation as one of the region's most proficient whalemen. Since his students would go on to become the foremost whalers in the world, he must have been, at the very least, a good teacher. Certainly Ichabod's timing was excellent. In 1692, two years after his arrival on Nantucket, the fledgling whale fishery received an important boost when the island came under the jurisdiction of Massachusetts. Unlike New York, the Bay Colony did not tax whale oil, placing the Nantucketers in a much more advantageous position relative to their predecessors on Long Island.

The Nantucketers also desperately needed whaling not only in an economic but also in an ecological sense. The town records throughout the 1680s and '90s are filled with measures to conserve and protect grass and farmlands as well as trees. With an ever-expanding population, the pressure was mounting on Nantucket as the English and Indians vied for an ever-diminishing supply of natural resources. In this respect, whaling was for Nantucket what the frontier would be for the nation, providing the island with an escape valve through which to vent the increasing pressures of a growing population. Here at last was a way for the islanders to make a living that did not depend on the productivity of Nantucket's not-so fertile land.

Almost immediately the town seized upon this new endeavor with a desperate and thankful excitement. When it came to whaling, the selectmen were willing to make an exception to the normally strict rules against cutting lumber. In an order against cutting cedar trees on Coatue made in April of 1695 is this caveat: "nevertheless any freeholder may cut timber for whaleboats or the like, anything in this order to the contrary notwithstanding." Whaling was where the money was, and nothing, not even the loss of almost every tree on the island, was going to get in the Nantucketers' way. They would come to regard this newfound occupation with an almost religious enthusiasm. In the same year Ichabod Paddock came to the island, some Nantucketers were on a high hill on the south side of the island watching "the whales spouting and sporting with each other, when one observed, 'There,' pointing to the sea, 'is a green pasture where our children's grandchildren will go for bread.'"

By 1700, anyone who could hold an oar—English and Indian alike—was involved in the whale fishery, which in those days lasted from November into late March and early April, dovetailing nicely with the seasonal demands of farming and sheep grazing. At this point, the fishery had the potential to have a positive effect on English-Indian relations, with approximately 60 English and 160 Indian shore whalers on Nantucket by the turn of the century. According to Obed Macy:

> When the English began to establish themselves in the whaling business, the Indians showed a readiness to join in and were preferred to the whites in some parts of the business. They were a stout, strong race of people and generally very industrious, never gave back but were always ready to go forward where they were sent by the captain. Some of them were capable men, and men of good judgment, so much so that they were often promoted to a station above a common

*hand, even to head a boat, and were as dextrous as the
whites. I have known instances of the whole crew on board to
be Indians except the Master.*

As Elizabeth Little has pointed out, shore whaling enabled
Nantucket's Native Americans to earn up to four times the
annual wage of a Boston seaman in the first half of the century.
However, as the Indian population shrank and the whale fishery
expanded, the English began to rely increasingly on the age-old
system of debt servitude to maintain a steady supply of Indian
crew members. According to the estimates of Daniel Vickers,
about three-fourths of the Native Americans that served on
Nantucket whaleboats between 1725 and 1733 were working not
for themselves but for their "masters."

In the early days whaling was conducted in small, twenty-
foot open boats that would in time evolve into the whaleboats
carried throughout the world from the davits of Nantucket
whaleships. Although their light, double-ended design may
have been influenced by the Indian canoe, Spanish and French
Basques had been whaling from boats of a similar appearance
since the Middle Ages.

The whale of choice at this time was the relatively mild-
mannered right whale, so named because it was "the right whale
to catch," in part because it did not sink after it was killed.
Crèvecoeur, writing several years after along-shore whaling had
ceased on Nantucket, describes how the islanders organized
themselves into whale stations:

*The south sides of the island, from east to west, were divided
into four equal parts, and each part was assigned to a company of six, which, though thus separated, still carried on
their business in common. In the middle of this distance, they
erected a mast ... and near it they built a temporary hut,*

where five of the associates lived, whilst the sixth from his
high station carefully looked toward the sea in order to observe
the spouting of the whales. As soon as they were discovered,
the sentinel descended, the whale-boat was launched, and the
company went forth in quest of their game.

In the first Proprietors' Book is a sketch from 1776 of a whale
station on the southeastern end of the island. On either side of a
two-sectioned spar are a row of tiny shacks, all of which feature
a chimney (this was, after all, a winter-time occupation). It was
shacks such as these, moved from whaling and fishing stations
throughout the island, that would ultimately make up the village
of Siasconset.

Ironically, given the modern-day slogan for putting a halt to
all whaling, the process of extracting oil from the dead sea mammal was known as "saving the whale." Obed Macy describes the
process: "After the whale had been killed and towed ashore, a
crab was used, an instrument similar to a capstan, to heave and
turn the blubber off as fast as it was cut. The blubber was then
put into their carts and carried to their tryhouses, which at that
early period, were placed near to their dwelling houses, where
the oil was boiled out and fitted for market."

The method of crew payment that developed on Nantucket,
which would ultimately become known as the American "lay
system," was entirely different from what was practiced on
European whalers, where crew members received wages. On
Nantucket, each member of the crew received a prearranged
share of the oil and bone taken in each voyage, thus providing
an incentive to all members of the crew to take risks that they
might not have been willing to endure if they had not had a
direct stake in the success of the voyage. Indeed, it is hard to
conceive of a more dangerous occupation: rowing around in tiny
boats, miles from shore in the dead of winter in the pursuit of

a whale that could flip over the entire boat with a flick of its tail. Tradition has it, however, that in the whole history of shore whaling on Nantucket, not a single white man was lost. (The Native Americans, apparently, were not so lucky.) According to Obed Macy, this safety record could be attributed in part to the weather in the first half of the eighteenth century, which was "not so windy and boisterous at that time as present." Taking advantage of calms that often lasted "a week or even a fortnight," the whalemen "sometimes . . . ventured off in their boats nearly out of sight of land."

The biggest year for along-shore whaling on Nantucket was 1726, when a total of eighty-six whales were taken, including eleven whales in a single day! Since a single sixty-barrel whale was worth more than a half year's wages (on land) for each oarsman, this was a very good year indeed. Providing an indication as to who was who among Nantucket's second and third generation of whalers is the following list of boat captains and the number of whales taken in that banner year:

> *John Swain, 4; Andrew Gardner, 4; Jonathan Coffin, 4; Paul Paddack [a variation of Paddock], 4; Jason Johnston, 5; Clothier Pierce, 3; Sylvanus Hussey, 2; Nathan Coffin, 4; Peter Gardner, 4; William Gardner, 2; Abishai Folger, 6; Nathan Folger, 4; John Bunker, 1; Shubael Folger, 5; Shubael Coffin, 3; Nathaniel Allen, 3; Edward Heath, 4; George Hussey, 3; Benjamin Gardner, 3; George Coffin, 1; Richard Coffin, 1; Nathaniel Paddack, 2; Joseph Gardner, 1; Matthew Jenkins, 3; Bartlett Coffin, 4; Daniel Gould, 1; Ebenezer Gardner, 4; ——Staples, 1.*

According to Macy, this shore whaling "continued until about the year 1760, when the whales became scarce, and it was by degrees discontinued."

Early in the eighteenth century, the Nantucketers had their first encounter with what was to become their post-shore whaling destiny—not the relatively mild-mannered right whale, but the aggressive, tooth-jawed sperm whale—when one was found washed up dead on the southwestern part of the island. According to Macy, the carcass "caused considerable excitement," and after a squabble over whose whale it was (see Chapter 9), the islanders became convinced that the "sperm procured from the head" was a nostrum that could cure all ills, and according to Macy it was soon "worth its weight in silver" on the island.

Then in 1712, after being blown offshore by a northerly gale, a Hussey and his whaleboat crew found themselves in the midst of a school of whales with an altogether different spout from what they were used to. Instead of a right whale's forked plume, these whales puffed out a single, forward-arching spout. The Nantucketers soon realized that this was a school of sperm whales, and even though the weather was very rough, they quickly fastened to a whale. According to legend, the blood of the freshly killed whale stilled the waters in an almost biblical fashion, and Hussey was able to bring back his prize to Nantucket.

In the words of Obed Macy, this brought "a new life" to whaling on Nantucket, and it was not long before sailing vessels in the range of thirty tons were fitted out to go whaling in what was referred to as "the Deep." These local cruises lasted in the neighborhood of six weeks. After killing a whale and filling up a few hogsheads with the slabs of its blubber, the sloop returned to Nantucket where the owner took possession of the blubber and sent the ship out again in search of more whales. Nantucket shipowners were not about to absorb the additional cost of these newer and larger whaling vessels. In one deft stroke they cut the lay of the crew in half (relative to what it was in shore whaling), providing the shipowner with a much larger stake in the voyage. Whether or not an ironical reference to the uprising of the previous century was intended, these offshore whalers came to be known as "half-share men," a term that was in common usage as late as the 1760s.

Initially each owner had his own tryworks, commonly located near his house. By the early eighteenth century, however, the town had begun to shift to its present-day location on the harbor, enabling the fishery to evolve from a cottage industry to a more centrally located enterprise, with a group of tryhouses being constructed on the beach to the south of the harbor landing. Acting as a buffer between the docks and these smelly and smoky structures was a group of small warehouses built for the storage of whaling equipment. At this time there were no solid-fill piers along the harbor, only temporary "landing places" that were often destroyed during winter storms. At the close of the season, even the larger sloops and schooners were pulled up on shore, which was thought to be safer than leaving them tied up to the relatively rickety docks.

The offshore whale fishery at Nantucket grew steadily throughout the first half of the eighteenth century. In 1715 there were six sloops based on the island in the thirty- to forty-ton range that brought in a total of 600 barrels of oil. In 1730 there were twenty-five vessels, some of which were in the fifty-ton range, bringing in a total of 3,700 barrels of oil; by 1748 there were sixty sloops and schooners operating out of Nantucket in the fifty- to seventy-five-ton range that brought in 11,250 barrels. These large vessels were commonly sent to what was known as the "southward" along the edges of the Gulf Stream, where they fished until the end of June before refitting for another cruise to the Grand Banks.

Although the scope of the enterprise had expanded, this was still very much a local business, with the youth of Nantucket comprising the majority of the crew members. Island Indians also remained a part of the workforce, with each vessel usually containing four to eight Indians among its crew of thirteen. If an anecdote of Obed Macy's is to be believed, a fairly high level of trust still existed between the two cultures, with at least some Indian crew members allowed access to English firearms. According to Macy, Captain John Coffin was resting in his cabin when he was startled by a sharp report. Once on deck he discovered that an Indian crew member had taken it upon himself to load the captain's gun and fire it at a nearby whale, killing it instantly. Thanks to the Indian's ingenuity and quick reflexes, Coffin and crew made forty barrels of oil from the whale, the only success they met with during the entire cruise.

No matter how good or bad things were between Nantucket's English and Indian whalemen throughout the eighteenth century, when it came to the conduct of their daily lives they were both, figuratively and literally, in the same boat. Zaccheus Macy tells the story of a whaleboat caught in a vicious winter storm during the days of along-shore whaling. As the crew, composed of two white men and four Native Americans, rowed into the teeth of the gale, an old Indian at the head of the boat encouraged them in his native language: "Momadichchator auqua farfhkee farnkee pinchee eyoo fememoochkee chaquanks wihchee pinchee eyoo," which means, "Pull ahead with courage; do not be disheartened; we shall not be lost now; there are too many Englishmen to be lost now." According to Macy, "His speaking in this manner gave the crew new courage. They soon perceived that they made headway; and after rowing, they all got safe on shore." Clearly, English and Indian Nantucketers shared something more than a common job description.

As we have seen, long after the Plague of 1763, Nantucket whalemen continued to use Indian phrases, demonstrating that Native American churches were not the only avenue of cultural cross-pollination on Nantucket. At the earliest possible age, young colonial Nantucketers were lisping Wampanoag phrases that would have baffled most other New Englanders. According to one observer in the late eighteenth century, "The boys, as soon as they can talk, will make use of the common [whaling] phrases, [such] as 'townor,' which is an Indian word, and signifies that they have seen the whale twice."

The legendary personality of the Quaker whaleman—laconic, austere, spiritual, and fearless—probably owed as much to the influence of the island's Native Americans as it did to the combination of whaling and Quakerism. Although an islander would have been the last to admit it, the similarity between the Nantucket whaleman and the American Indian was obvious to at least one New Yorker writing in 1829: "The whalers of Nantucket may be called the free Indians of the Ocean, for their life partakes of all that enthusiasm and suffering which the latter experience in the wild woods of the west." Just as the frontiersman of the nineteenth century would assimilate many of the values and customs of the western Indians, so was the Nantucket whaleman of the eighteenth century inevitably influenced by his Native American coworkers.

If the story of Ichabod Paddock ultimately amounts to little more than a convenient and, from the English perspective, self-serving fiction revolving around a mythic white man, the tale also contains at least one undeniable truth: the whaleman did not exist in some deep-sea vacuum. After the voyage was over, there was always his native island. And it was here, where the English had been molded by more than a half-century of contact with Native Nantucketers, that a relatively new cultural force had begun to assert itself. Whereas the beginning of whaling is very much a man's story, the beginning of Quakerism belongs to a woman.

CHAPTER 8

Mary Starbuck, High Priestess
of the Company Store

W
E HAVE SEEN the almost biblical fervor with which
the Nantucketers viewed their whaling destiny: the
first sighting of their blubbery promised land from
a seaside hill, the mystical stilling of the waters with a sperm
whale's blood. But if what the Nantucketers called the "whaling
business" was tantamount to a religious quest, the island's new
religion, Quakerism, was the spiritual equivalent of a business.
Stripped of all pomp and circumstance, Quakerism offered a
low-budget pathway to spiritual fulfillment that only enhanced
the islanders' ability to make a profit on the high seas. For the
Quaker Nantucketer, as it was for the Puritan New Englander,
being righteous need not interfere with being financially successful; on the contrary, one's worldly station was looked to as
an indication of what would one day be one's spiritual destiny.

By the beginning of the eighteenth century, Quakerism in
the American colonies had come a long way since the days of
Thomas Macy's troubles in Salisbury. As Penn's Philadelphia
blossomed into a major port and Friends in nearby Newport
and Cape Cod gained increasing status and respectability, the
religion moved from the radical fringe to the comfortable margin of the colonial establishment. Throughout this process, what
had once seemed so doctrinally outrageous began to look more
and more like Puritanism. Although the Quaker depended on
his own experience of God's presence—the "Inner Light"—for

guidance rather than relying on a Puritan minister's interpretation of Scripture, the fact of the matter was that Quakerism encouraged a sense of community that was as carefully controlled and regimented as that of any seventeenth-century New England society. If there was a difference, it was the way in which Quakerism, in the words of one religious scholar, "promoted an attitude remarkably conducive to success in our competitive business system."

On Nantucket, it is a little bit like the chicken and the egg—which came first, the islanders' determination to make a buck, or Quakerism's nurturing influence on this resolve? The answer lies not so much in the generalizations of social history as in the personality of a single individual. For it was in Mary Starbuck, Tristram Coffin's youngest daughter, that the interplay of worldly success and spiritual destiny created the truly prototypical Nantucketer.

⤸

From the beginning, all eyes were on Mary Coffin and Nathaniel Starbuck. In 1662 they were the first English couple married on Nantucket. A year later, at the age of only eighteen, Mary gave birth to the community's first child. With gifts and inheritances from their parents, Mary and Nathaniel quickly emerged as the most influential couple of their generation, with control over a total of two and a half shares in the proprietary.

From the start, it was Mary Coffin Starbuck who directed the rise of the Starbuck family to the forefront of the community. Although her husband became a rock-solid member of the community, he never learned to read and write (signing documents with "his mark") and, early on at least, he seems to have fallen into some less than upright ways. On September 26, 1673, he was ordered to pay the court four pounds and "also bound to his good behavior for six months" for an unknown offense.

During the turbulence of the Half-Share Revolt, it was Mary who apparently determined the family's loyalties, with the Starbucks throwing their support to Mary's father, Tristram Coffin, rather than to Nathaniel's father Edward, who was one of the few full-share men to back the Gardner group.

If it was Mary who called the shots in the Starbuck family, she made sure to go through the motions of making it seem like a joint decision. As her stature in the community grew to the point that, according to one source, she was "esteemed as a judge among them, for little of moment was done without her," she always included the name of her husband in whatever opinions she might express. Tradition has it that whenever she took part in debates during town meetings (which she attended regularly), she was careful to preface her remarks with the claim, "My husband and I, having considered the subject, think. . . ."

While raising a family of ten children, Mary kept the books for the family store—a primitive frontier trading post that evolved into a highly complex business as the island's economy turned to whaling in the eighteenth century. In the possession of the Nantucket Historical Association is one of Mary's ledgers. Eight and a half by twelve and a half inches, with a sheepskin cover, cracked and warped with age, its leather clasps long since broken, this 147-page volume begins with the inscription: "Mary Starbucks Account Book with the Indians began in 1662—Nathaniel Junior continued it."

Although the entries begin in 1683, the earlier date probably indicates when the Starbucks first went into business. The account book, at times next to impossible to decipher, provides a fascinating glimpse into the economic development and daily life of early Nantucket. In the beginning, the Indians mainly followed traditional pursuits such as fishing and bird-hunting, with the Starbucks providing them with flints, powder, shot, fish hooks, and sinkers in exchange for the delivery of feathers and fish. The entries in the account book make it clear, however, that the Indians became increasingly involved in a wide variety of activities within the English economy—from threshing corn, hewing posts, carting dung, and plowing fields, to mowing hay and washing sheep. And as the whale fishery began to dominate island life, Starbuck provided candles, molasses, kettles, shoes, boards, jackknives, stockings, buttons, and calico in exchange for "oil and bone" from whaling either "alongshore" or "in the Deep."

Inevitably, the advancement of credit to island Indians brought with it the potential for them to fall into debt with what was Nantucket's equivalent of the company store. Whether or not Mary and Nathaniel were guilty of unjustly enriching themselves at the Native Americans' expense, this was the pathway that would lead many an Indian into a lifetime of servitude. Indeed, while a large number of white Nantucketers would owe their salvation to Mary Starbuck's efforts, many Native Americans would owe their souls, if not to the Starbuck company store, to another one just like it.

Whereas Mary had clearly stepped into her father's shoes when it came to business and civic life, she seems to have followed her father-in-law's path when it came to her radical religious leanings. Tradition has it that Peter Folger baptized her in the waters of tiny Waqutaquaib Pond (one of the boundary markers in the original Indian deed), and throughout her life she demonstrated an impatience with traditional religious practices. Although there was no organized church on Nantucket, there were often one or more itinerant clergymen attempting to establish ministries on the island. According to the Quaker Thomas Story, who came to Nantucket in 1704, it was Mary Starbuck—"in great reputation throughout the island for her knowledge in matters of religion, and an oracle among them on that account"—who always convinced her fellow Nantucketers to deny the temptations of hiring a permanent minister.

If this was indeed the case, why then, we must ask, did she wait until she was fifty-eight years old to embrace the anti-clerical cause of Quakerism? Part of the problem may have had to do with a person who is already familiar to us—Stephen Hussey. As one of two practicing Quakers on the island (Richard Swain's son John was the other one), Hussey seems to have given the religion a bad name on Nantucket. Ever since the days of the Half-Share Revolt, he had developed a reputation for mean-spirited combativeness. Even when fellow Quakers traveled to the island, Hussey could not resist the opportunity for an argument.

In 1698, Hussey's willingness to make a public spectacle of himself caused the visiting Quaker Thomas Chalkley to mistake him for the chief magistrate of the island. Hussey, it appears, had been nursing a grudge against Chalkley's "Friends in Barbados" who had made some reference to the spiritual significance of the body of Christ. An exceedingly literal-minded fellow, Hussey asked, "Is it not a contradiction in nature, that flesh and blood should be spiritual?" When Chalkley pointed out that Christ himself had spoken figuratively when he said, "Except ye eat my flesh and drink my blood ye have no life in you," Hussey snorted, "I don't think they were to gnaw it from his arms and shoulders." Undoubtedly with an ironic smile, Chalkley suggested that Hussey had just answered his own question.

With a man such as Hussey as the religion's leading advocate on the island, Quakerism undoubtedly had at least one strike against it on Nantucket. And yet, despite such disadvantages, Chalkley's message apparently appealed to a surprising number of Nantucketers, with an estimated 200 people gathering for one of his meetings. Chalkley reported, "Some of the people said that it was never known that so many people were together on the island at once."

Three years later, in 1701, the breakthrough came with the arrival of the English Quaker John Richardson, who after spending a sleepless night on nearby Muskeget Island arrived on Nantucket to find a crowd of people assembled on the hillside overlooking the harbor. As he climbed what he called "an Ascent," he realized that the islanders were in "great fear," thinking that his ship was a French privateer. Holding out his arms as a sign of peace, he reassured them that he was a man of God and asked the way to the home of Nathaniel Starbuck, "who we understood was in some degree convinced of the Truth." Richardson soon realized, however, that it was Mary Starbuck who was the true spiritual leader of the community: "At the first sight of her it sprang in my heart, to this woman is the everlasting love of God."

Already on island was a "nonconformist minister" who was about to conduct a meeting; Mary invited Richardson to attend it with her but he declined, proposing instead that he have his own meeting later in the day, for which Mary volunteered the use of her own house. Richardson described the scene: "the large and bright rubbed room was set with suitable seats or chairs, the glass windows taken out of the frames, and many chairs placed without very conveniently, so that I did not see anything a wanting . . . but something to stand on." When he reached for a chair to use as a speaking platform, Mary—who, no matter how spiritual she might have been, appreciated the value of her worldly possessions—made it clear that "I was not free to set my feet upon the fine cane chair, lest I should break it."

The lack of a platform did not seem to detract from Richardson's performance. Speaking of the need to "be born again" if one was to be "raised into a spiritual and new life," he directed most of his attention not to the overflowing crowd but to the "great woman" seated before him. The depth and sincerity of her spiritual life are evident in Richardson's description of her reaction:

[She] fought and strove against the testimony, sometimes looking up in my face with a pale, and then with a more ruddy complexion, but the strength of the truth increased, and the Lord's mighty power began to shake the people within and without doors; but she who was looked upon as a Deborah by these people was loth to lose her outside religion, or the appearance thereof; when she could no longer contain, she submitted to the power of truth and the doctrines thereof and lifted up her voice and wept: Oh! then the universal cry and brokenness of heart and tears was wonderful!

After an hour of speaking, Richardson, who had not slept in more than a day, began to grow faint and requested that the meeting be ended. But the crowd was too overcome to disperse. Finally, Mary Starbuck gained enough composure to address the multitude. "[She] stood up, and held out her hand, and spoke tremblingly and said, 'All that ever we have been building, and all that ever we have done is all pulled down this day, and this is the overwhelming truth. . . .'" Added Richardson, "I observed that she, and as many as could well be seen, were wet with tears from their faces to the foreskirts of their garments, and the floor was as though there had been a shower of rain upon it."

Contrary to what some have maintained, Mary Starbuck's conversion did not mark the instantaneous adoption of Quakerism on the island. When another Friend, Thomas Story, came to Nantucket three years later, in 1704, he found an island still "inhabited by a mixed people of various notions" with no organized meeting. One person standing in the way of the Quaker cause was Captain John Gardner, now "an ancient man," according to Story, "who had much sway in the affairs of the government of the island." Despite his age, Gardner had lost none of the feistiness that had characterized his conduct in the Half-Share

Revolt. When Story came to visit him in his own house, Gardner proved to be in no mood to be proselytized, claiming that thirty to forty years earlier in his hometown of Salem, a Quaker had asserted that Jesus Christ never rose from the dead. Although Story insisted that this was not a tenet of Quakerism, Gardner persisted in his vehement denunciations of the faith to the point that "his wife (an ancient person) was much grieved at the ill-nature and behavior of her husband toward us . . . and she wept much whilst we talked together."

The Gardners were not the only couple who disagreed with each other in matters of religion. Stephen Hussey's wife Martha, whom Story describes as "a very rigid and ignorant Presbyterian," proved as irascible as her Quaker spouse. In this instance, however, Story's logic appears to have won out: "At length, finding herself hedged round, and her way blocked up on every hand, she burst into a very great degree of weeping, and endeavoring to hide it, went away a while. . . . [Eventually] she became very gentle, loving and sweet spirited, and would have had us stay longer."

Story quickly recognized, however, that it was not the Mrs. Husseys and John Gardners who held back the growth of Quakerism on the island. Rather, the problem was with Nantucket's two preexisting Quakers, the obnoxious Stephen Hussey and the freewheeling John Swain. At one point during his visit, Story journeyed to the outlying village of Polpis where the Swains had begun to establish a family enclave as early as the 1680s. Story found John Swain in the midst of "raising a timber house," with "a great company of Indians and other people together." Since a "still house" is mentioned in Swain's will, it is probably safe to assume that the promise of free liquor had helped to swell the numbers of the house-raising party. In any event, the grave and solemn Story seems to have been very negatively impressed by the scene, which included a wrestling match between an Indian boy and a non-Quaker minister.

Although not as belligerent as Hussey, Swain (whom Obed Macy described as "of but few words") was clearly out of the mainstream of island life. In one legendary episode, he responded to the news that a French privateer had just landed on the island (see Chapter 5) by hurriedly collecting his money into a sack and burying it somewhere in the woods of Polpis. Swain did such a good job of hiding his stash that he and several subsequent generations of Swains were unable to find the money. For centuries to come, the term "Polpisy" was used by Nantucketers to describe anyone who was countrified or outlandish, and according to Henry Forman, the term "must have had some echo of Swains in it."

In any event, Story had severe reservations about Nantucket's two practicing Quakers, claiming that they "had not been faithful, nor of good report, but a stumbling-block in the way of the weak; for they could not agree between themselves; and one of them [Hussey] was at odds with many of his neighbors. . . ." With the best interests of his faith in mind, Story decided to perform an end-run and appeal directly to Mary Starbuck, who had not yet committed herself in a formal sense to Quakerism. If he could convince her to translate her private beliefs into a more public sphere by organizing a weekly meeting, he knew that the future of Quakerism would be secure on the island.

According to Story, she received his proposal "with Christian gravity, and it affected her much, and became her concern. . . . I proposed it likewise to her children (her husband being freely passive only in such things, and naturally good tempered), who were all discreet young men and women, most of them married, and hopeful; being all convinced of truth, they were ready to embrace the proposal." And so, with her son Nathaniel as her right-hand man, Mary Starbuck launched the English settlement's first attempt at organized religion. Only a few months later, when Thomas Chalkley visited the island for a second time, it was clear that a startling change had come over the island: "There are large meetings, people there being mostly Friends, and a sober growing people in the best things."

Quakerism on Nantucket was initially, at least, very much a family affair. When, in 1708, the Nantucket Friends requested official recognition from the New England Yearly Meeting, seven of the nine who signed the document were Starbucks by either birth or marriage. One of the non-Starbucks was Stephen Hussey; John Swain appears to have not joined the meeting. Soon, however, the litigious Hussey was on the way out.

Quakers believed in the Inner Light, but they also believed that this personal sense of divinity never contradicted Scripture or common sense. This meant that Quakers were expected to conform to rules of behavior that were determined during yearly meetings. If you began to stray from the path of a perfect Christian, you were contacted privately by a member of the meeting; if you continued in your "disorderly walking," even after an official committee was appointed to "labor" with you on the point, you were presented with two alternatives: disownment or a public and very formal repentance.

Stephen Hussey was in the midst of a feud with the town concerning the number of sheep he was allowed to graze on the commons. By 1713, Nathaniel Starbuck, Jr., the clerk of the meeting, was appointed to head a committee whose mission was "to convince him of the evil of so continuing his lawsuit." Finally, in 1717, when Hussey had three of the town's selectmen arrested, the Friends, "being dissatisfied with his actions," disowned him at the age of eighty-seven. A year later, Hussey— who hoped his son would also prove to be a "thorn in the proprietors' side"—was dead, willing his extensive library of law books to future Hussey litigants.

By now the Quaker meeting had moved out of the Starbucks' house to a new building that had already been expanded to fifty by thirty-five feet in 1716. Although Quakers never attempted to impose their Discipline on the rest of the island's population, a somewhat incestuous relationship inevitably developed between town and Quaker government, in part because Mary's son Nathaniel served as clerk in both bodies. In fact, when Starbuck donated an acre of his own land for the first Quaker meeting house and cemetery near Hummock Pond, he felt no qualms in paying himself with an acre of land from the island proprietary!

This overlapping of civic and religious influence, when combined with Nathaniel Starbucks ever-increasing wealth (he has been called Nantucket's first millionaire), meant that Quakerism soon became the religion of power and influence on Nantucket. When in 1712 John Macy, who had business ties with Nathaniel, joined the Society, as did his two brothers, an alliance was forged between the two families that would prove to be both longstanding and exceedingly profitable.

By the 1730s, the meeting had grown to the point that a larger building was required. A new site was chosen in the vicinity of the present-day Quaker burial ground on Main Street and Quaker Road (formerly Grave Street), but it was not until 1760 that people were interred (without headstones) in this "new" burial ground. By 1747, special meetings attracted more than 2,000 people, and in 1761 the meeting house was nearly doubled in size.

The tremendous growth of the Society could be attributed to a variety of causes. Certainly there were many members whose religious convictions were deep and enduring; however, in 1765, it was obvious to Samuel Fothergill that there were other causes as well: "as the rightest part of the inhabitants embraced the principles of the truth from convincement, the others thought the expense of maintaining a priest would be too heavy for them, and have turned Quakers to save money; though I hope, even amongst them, the power of the begetting word is in a degree at work, to give a surer title to the family of Christ."

But Quakerism was more than a cheap alternative to Congregationalism; its emphasis on a staid, highly controlled lifestyle provided what the historian Edward Byers has called the "necessary social cement" to hold this highly diversified group of individualists together. With the introduction of whaling—and with it, an increased exposure to the notoriously wild and profligate lifestyle of the sailor—Nantucket needed all the social cement it could get.

In the terms set forth in the previous chapter, Quakerism was the antidote to the legendary licentiousness of Ichabod Paddock, or more precisely, it was the silver harpoon with which generations of Nantucket wives would lay to rest the moral hazards—as symbolized by Crook-Jaw and the green-eyed mermaid—of whaling. Their husbands might be gone for a year or more harpooning whales and exploring exotic ports, but when they returned to Nantucket it was back to the business of Christian and familial devotion.

Unlike in any other port in America, Nantucket's Quaker culture kept its seamen in line, at least once they were in sight of the waterfront. According to Crèvecoeur:

> *I observe here, at the return of their fleets, no material irregularities, no tumultuous drinking assemblies; whereas in our continental towns, the thoughtless seaman indulges himself in the coarsest pleasures. . . . On the contrary, all was peace here, and a general decency prevailed throughout. . . . The motives that lead them to the sea are very different from those of most other sea-faring men; it is neither idleness nor profligacy that sends them to that element; it is a settled plan of life.*

At the center of this settled plan of life was the Quaker meeting, emitting its magnetic pull throughout the island and beyond. William Root Bliss tells of a whaleship approaching the island one Sunday morning in a thick fog. After the ship anchored outside the bar, the fog lifted just at meeting time. The captain gazed through his spyglass as a crowd of islanders made its way to the huge meeting house. According to the captain, "I could not keep from shouting at the inspiring sight."

As the leader of the family that brought Quakerism and wealth to the island, Mary established an entirely different approach from the one introduced by Ichabod Paddock a decade earlier. The surviving prose of Mary Starbuck amounts to a single letter written in 1715 to an off-island granddaughter who had lost her house to fire. Although her affection for her granddaughter is obvious, the letter is very business-like as Mary enumerates what it is she is sending to the mainland.

These few lines may certify [to] thee that thou are often in my remembrance with thy dear husband and children, with breathings to the Lord for you that his presence may be with you, that there in you may find rest in all your visitations and trials as also that here is a trunk, filled with goods, which is intended to be put on board Ebenezer Stuart's vessel which carries several small tokens from thy Friends, which thou might particularly see by those little invoices here enclosed and by some other marks that are upon the things. . . . [Included were cloth from Aunt Dorcas, blankets from Aunt Dinah, a barrel of mutton from Grandfather Nathaniel, several bushels of corn from Cousin James Coffin and Justice Worth, some wool from Sister James, and seventeen pounds collected from the Quaker Women's Meeting.] More meat and corn will be sent which will be in greater quantities, which thy Uncle Jethro Starbuck will give thee an account of or to thy husband. I should have been glad if he had come over with Stuart, but I hope we shall see him this summer, if not both of you. So with my kind love to thee and to thy husband, children, and to all Friends committing you to the protection of the almighty who is the wise disposer of all things and remains thy affectionate

Grandmother, Mary Starbuck

Thy Grandfather's love to you all, and Uncle Barnabas. Susanna is well and her love [to] you all.

Here is an outlook in which God, family, and the things of this world are all part of a vast and yet highly personal support system. More than Ichabod's restless and daring individualism, here is "the Way" that would lead Nantucket to the top of the whale fishery in the years to come.

CHAPTER 9

Richard Macy, the Master Builder

O N OCTOBER 14, 1691, the Macy family suffered a devastating loss when John, the only surviving son of the
first-purchaser Thomas, died at the age of thirty-six,
leaving behind eight children. Perhaps it was the youngest child
Richard (only two years old at the time) who would be the most
deeply affected by his father's death. As if to compensate for a
childhood of dislocation and loss, Richard would dedicate his
life to building things, providing the lumber, know-how, and
vision that would help transform a rural fishing outpost into the
foremost whaling port in the world.

If Richard Macy is the English Nantucketers' Maushop, it
is only appropriate that most of what we know about him comes
from his grandson, Obed, who was seventeen when Richard
died at the ripe old age of ninety. In his own old age, Obed wrote
"A Short Memorial of Richard Macy," an unpublished account
clearly based on the stories told to him in his youth. When one
considers the alternatives (jingoistic pride, tearful sentimental-
ity), it is a highly refreshing way to glorify a man and his times:
from the point of view of a wide-eyed and awestruck child.

~

As a boy, Richard Macy was apprenticed to Nathan Pease, a
house carpenter, who "chose to keep him constantly at work
rather than permit him to go to school." Throughout Richard's

long apprenticeship, Pease made only one attempt at educating his charge. According to Obed: "A little before he was twenty-one years of age, Richard was called into the shop by his master. His master took a piece of board and chalk and set a sum in addition and did it, and went on to subtraction in the same manner, and charged Richard to look and see how they were done. So he continued from rule to rule, then said, 'There, boy, that's the way to cipher, now go to work.'" Determined to make up for his lack of early formal education, Richard sent himself to school after he "became of age" so that he could learn to "write a legible hand, to read, and keep accounts."

In the collection of the Nantucket Historical Association are the fruits of Macy's belated education: a tiny, three-inch by six-inch daybook that he apparently took wherever he went. The first entry in the book is dated 1712 (two years after he turned twenty-one), and in its margins there is evidence that he was still painstakingly practicing his letters. Macy would use the book until he turned fifty-eight years old in 1747, keeping his accounts in exactly the same way that Mary and Nathaniel Starbuck did in their much larger ledger—debits on the left-hand page, credits on the right. If ever there was a man who came to recognize the value of an education, it was Richard Macy, and, in fact, among his few existing papers is the fragment of a receipt dated September 6, 1729, acknowledging payment to a schoolmistress for instructing his children.

Although a carpenter by trade, Macy, as was typical throughout the island, did a little bit of everything, including whaling and farming. But what distinguished John Macy's youngest born from anyone else on Nantucket was his physical prowess. According to his grandson: "When quite young he showed marks of uncommon strength, and as he advanced in years, his strength increased so that at mature age he was considered the strongest man in the county." It was not long before his feats of strength became legendary. In Obed's words, "he never found how strong he was." Once a horse broke free from its owner and, with cart in tow, came charging toward Macy. Rather than leaping out of the way, he simply grabbed the back of the cart and dug his heels into the sand. After pulling Macy along like a human plow, the horse gradually staggered to a halt. From then on it was said on Nantucket that Richard Macy was stronger than a horse.

One day Macy and some other men were loading sacks of wheat into a cart. Suddenly Macy got down on all fours and told his companions to start piling the sacks onto his back. It was not until the thirteenth sack that he told them to stop. With two and a half bushels of wheat in each sack, it was estimated that there were at least 2,000 pounds on Macy's back.

His fame soon spread to Martha's Vineyard. At one point on the rival island, a company of men in Holmes Hole (now Vineyard Haven) were attempting to set on end a cannon of 1,800 pounds. As the workmen struggled with the huge gun, one of them remarked that Richard Macy of Nantucket happened to be in Edgartown and could probably lift the cannon single-handedly. With a wager undoubtedly resting on the claim, Macy was sent for, and soon a crowd began gathering to see if this Nantucketer were for real. Vineyarders being Vineyarders and anxious for an opportunity to see their rival island taken down a peg, there were plenty of catcalls and jeers as Macy looked the cannon over. Casting a cold eye on the crowd, he said, "You shall soon know whether I can lift it."

As already indicated, Macy was no dummy. Demonstrating a technical understanding that would serve him well all his life, he had the men sling ropes around the cannon, then had jackets placed on his shoulders to pad the ropes. He then requested that boards be put on either side of the cannon to give him a firm footing in the sand. Straddling the massive piece of metal, he lifted his hunched body in the sling until the cannon had cleared the ground. With the gun suspended from his shoulders, he asked the assembled multitude "if they were satisfied that he had lifted it." The crowd shouted in the affirmative. Then, after lowering the cannon to the ground, Macy, "with a flourish round," asked where those were who had expressed their initial skepticism. "But," according to Obed, "they had slunk away and left the company."

In his early years, Macy was not above using his remarkable strength to intimidate people into submission. When the first sperm whale ever seen on Nantucket washed up ashore dead at the Smooth Hummocks on the southwestern part of the island, he was the first white man on the scene. With a sledge and the help of his Indian servant Gregory, he extracted the whale's teeth and quickly buried them, "believing they were of great value." As word of the sperm whale spread throughout the island, a group of English and Indian Nantucketers quickly began to gather, several of them claiming to have rights to it. Then the "King's Officer" arrived and claimed sole possession of the whale for the Crown. According to Obed, "No doubt there was considerable jangling." Everyone in the crowd could agree on one thing, however: Richard Macy must hand over the teeth, with the constable threatening to whip him if he did not do as commanded. But Macy would have none of it. According to his grandson, Richard "made sport and told them he would take the whole company one by one and handle them as a woman would her child. This quelled the dispute, and they joined in saving what they would, the teeth excepted."

Professionally, Macy was not only a carpenter but also a general contractor, and his grandson describes his method of doing business:

His practice was to bargain, to build a house, and finish it in every part, and find the materials. The boards and bricks he bought. The stones he collected on the common land, if they were rocks he would split them. The lime he made by burning shells. The timber he cut here on island. The latter part of his building, when timber was not so easily procured of the right dimensions, he went off-island and felled the trees and hewed the timber to the proper dimensions. The principal part of the frames were of large oak timber, some of which may be seen at the present day. The iron work, the nails excepted, he generally wrought with his own hands. Thus being prepared, he built the house mostly himself.

If this is to be trusted, it seems that some large oak trees still existed on Nantucket well into the first half of the eighteenth century. By this time, the type of dwelling house had evolved from the very simple and symmetrical "English" style (with only two rooms on either floor) to the lean-to, with rooms added in the back first floor as the roof extended into a long "catslide" in the rear. Initially it was common practice to orient these houses to the south, with the long catslide offering protection against the cold northerly winds of winter. This rather humble and asymmetrical form, which evokes the look of someone hunched against the weather, appealed to the austere sensibilities of the Quakers. Long after the lean-to had gone out of fashion on the mainland, Nantucketers clung tenaciously to the style. As late as the 1790s, Richard Macy's nephew, yet another Richard Macy, refused to enter his son Job's new home because it had two stories in the front and rear and no catslide. Such symmetry was viewed as an affront to the lopsided tradition fostered by carpenters such as the first Richard Macy, as well as Elihu Coleman, whose lean-to home (built in 1722) still exists on what is now an impassable section of Hawthorne Lane to the south of Madaket Road.

The year after Coleman built his home in the "old" section of town, Macy built what would become the most important

structure (from a developmental point of view) on Nantucket
in the eighteenth century. In 1723 he began construction of
Straight Wharf, so called because it extended "straight" out into
the harbor from Main Street. Pegging together huge logs that
were then weighted down with rocks and sunk deep into the
mud, Macy piled layer upon layer of logs and rocks until this
sandwiched structure was well above the waterline. He then
drove piles around its edges, topped it off with a layer of sand,
and Straight Wharf was completed.

Six years before Macy built his wharf, the town had already
begun to reorient itself to the newer, larger harbor, with the
Fishlot Division of 1717—a distribution of land that may have
been spurred by the filling in of Cappamet Harbor. The Fishlots
extended the length of modern-day Fair Street, which acted as
an access road to lots on either side. During the same year that
Straight Wharf was built, another division of much smaller lots
known as the Warehouse lots was made in the vicinity of the
wharf.

The town was now positioned to enter into a whole new level of
commercial activity as Macy's wharf became the place where not
only whaling vessels off-loaded their oil but also trading vessels—
from "apple merchants" to "wood coasters"—sold their wares.
For the first time, Nantucket had what could be properly termed
a waterfront, and with it came the necessity of policing what
inevitably became the more lawless side of town. The same year
the wharf was built the town established a "constable's watch
in the night season, for suppressing disorders" caused by "Indians, Negroes, and other suspected persons," and "if they shall be
found upon the wharf and about town after nine of the clock at
night, they shall be taken up and carried before a Justice."

But if Richard Macy's wharf quickly became a focal point of
vice, the evil reputation was not enough to prevent the wholesale
movement of the town in its direction. Since wood was such a

valuable commodity on the island, all the original homes in "old" Sherburne (approximately fifty in number) were either moved in their entirety or cannibalized for their lumber and reconstituted as part of the new town, leaving Elihu Coleman, who had once lived on the eastern edge of town, far to the west of new downtown Nantucket. This giant shellgame was going on throughout the island. To the east, fishing villages in Sesachacha and Peedee would gradually and irresistibly lose most of their houses to Siasconset as it proved the better place for codfishing toward the end of the century.

Meanwhile back at Wesco, all this movement meant that it was an excellent time to be a carpenter. Besides building houses, Richard Macy also had the income he derived from his wharf, of which he would maintain a substantial interest for the rest of his life. But his innovative building did not stop here. As it became more and more obvious that there were not the waterways required to power a sufficient number of grist and fulling mills and that the one thing there was not a shortage of on Nantucket was wind (statistically, it is one of the windiest places on the East Coast), Macy recognized that what the island needed was a windmill. Unfortunately, he had never even seen one. Given the complexity of the undertaking and his lack of experience with the technology, Richard was on the verge of sending for a millwright when he had an extraordinary experience. According to his grandson, "His mind became so absorbed in the subject that he dreamed how to construct the building in every part. He placed confidence in the dream and conducted the workmen accordingly. It proved a good strong mill."

Part Hercules, part intuitive genius, Macy remained "a hard laboring man from his youth to old age." As his daybook shows, besides houses, wharves, and windmills, he made calashes, coffins, chests, and oaken bedsteads that he banged together with a sledge. He also built whaleboats, an art that he would pass on to his eldest son Zaccheus. Just how closely the Macy family stuck together (Richard and his first wife Deborah had twelve children, seven of whom lived to maturity) is suggested by a court case involving Zaccheus and an Indian by the name of Panjame. According to Zaccheus's testimony, he had lost a saw his father had given him in 1731 when he was only eighteen years old; now, nine years later, he had discovered that Panjame was in possession of the saw, which had "RM" marked on it, and accused the Indian of stealing it. Zaccheus's father Richard appeared in court and "made the same attestation," as did Jabez Bunker, who claimed to have seen the saw "at Panjame's house." Although Panjame denied the accusation, he was found guilty, and, as was typical for the time, was sentenced to pay triple damages and court costs.

Throughout his long life, Richard Macy dealt regularly with the Indians much in the same way that Mary and Nathaniel Starbuck did, but on a smaller scale. With cash difficult to come by not only on Nantucket but throughout colonial America, what has become known as "bookkeeping barter" was the rule. English and Indians alike kept account books in which they recorded their dealings with various individuals. Although Nantucket Court records are filled with cases involving debt disputes among the English and Indians, Richard Macy appears to have taken matters into his own hands when he ran into trouble collecting what was owed to him. Certainly, his impressive physical presence must have facilitated credit negotiations. In 1717 he recorded in his daybook two nearly identical "agreements" between himself and the Indian "young Ephram," one of which reads: "Ephram having taken money 40 shillings he doth engage to bring the money in two months or to bind his 2 young sons for fishing upon whaleboat till they are of the ages of 21 years. . . ." A tentative circular scratch is recorded as Ephram's "mark," while Ruth Pease signed on as a witness. Whether or not Ephram was ultimately forced to sell his "2 young sons" into bondage, four years later in 1721 Macy was still extending credit to "Ephram Indian," as well as selling him a hat for 18 shillings, all of which Ephram paid off in full through mowing hay, tending corn, and paying Macy over a pound in cash.

Macy's daybook is not all about debits and credits. On page twenty-three, the Quaker carpenter recorded the following homily under the title "Certain good":

> *A good man walks in straight*
> *parths and is not easily led*
> *aside into crucked parths*
> *that leads to theare*
> *destruction but ceaps his*
> *mind stidfast apon the Lord.*

And yet this little passage may have had to do with credit after all. Perhaps Richard read this passage to those who owed him money so as to remind them of the unpleasant consequences of following "crucked parths."

With interests in Straight Wharf and a mill, not to mention whaling, farming, and sheep-raising, as well as his carpentry business, Richard Macy was positioned to take advantage of Nantucket's economic growth in the years preceding the Revolution. Throughout this period, he and his brothers and sisters would remain very close, never straying from the tight circle of old Nantucket families that had come to their aid soon after John Macy's death. This meant that the Macys' growing influence and wealth remained concentrated within a small group of kin. In the words of Lydia Hinchman, "The Macy family was a close corporation for many years. Up to 1800 very few surnames appear [in the marriage records], excepting such as may be classed among orthodox Nantucket names." Hinchman's use of the word "orthodox" is appropriate, for it was within the adopted family of the Friends Meeting that the Macys put together the pieces of a family unit that had been so cruelly disbanded by the death of father John Macy in 1691.

Richard was a member of the Society of Friends, but his sense of the Inner Light sometimes led him in unusual directions. When his wife Deborah died, Macy—at the age of eighty—decided to marry a woman by the name of Alice Paddock and went to his son Caleb's house to inform him of his decision. When Caleb objected to the plan on account of his father's old age, Richard told his son that he misunderstood the reason for his visit. He had not come for advice or support, he had come simply to tell him that he was going to marry Alice Paddock. Perhaps contributing to Caleb's objections was the fact that Richard had signed a prenuptial agreement with his new fiancée in which he guaranteed her 13 pounds, 6 shillings, and 8 pence "annually upon his decease."

Three years later at the age of eighty-three, he apparently made some remarks that his fellow Friends viewed as inappropriate. As was required by the Discipline, he made a public and formal apology, which read: "Through inadvertency and old age at our last monthly meeting, I spoke to recommend that which was contrary to the good order of Friends which hast since been a grief to my mind as well as brought a burthen to my honest Friends on that account, for which I am sorry and desire Friends to pass it by."

Then, two years later in 1774, Richard and his wife became very ill, requiring that they move in with Macy's daughter Judith and her husband Jonathan Bunker. For twenty weeks, both of them were so sick that they required around-the-clock attention. This prompted Richard to enter into an agreement with his son-in-law in which he acknowledged that "through weakness of body and infirmity of old age" he was "now incapable of managing my estate." Except for his "little new dwelling house and half share of old wharf which I reserve the income thereof to myself," he handed over the management of and income derived from his now considerable estate to Jonathan Bunker, under the provision that he agree to take care of Richard and his wife.

Although Macy was no longer the strong, quick-witted man of action he had once been, he was still an inspiration to not only the young Obed, who seems to have been a rapt listener to many of his grandfather's stories, but also another grandchild, Elihu Bunker, who wrote to him in the final year of Richard's life. Elihu, the father of two children and living in New York, had recently lost his wife and wrote: "I . . . should be glad at all times to hear that you was [*sic*] so far favored as your great age and infirm year can afford, but you have lived to see that no age is exempted from that stroke of Death which is great and awful."

At the age of ninety years and twenty-two days, Richard Macy, once known as the "strongest man in the county," died, according to Obed, "in peace with all mankind and in full belief of the Christian religion as professed by the Society of which he was a member." The youngest son of a father he had scarcely known, he left a lasting impression not only on his island community but also on the memories of his grandchildren.

CHAPTER 10

Of God, Indians, and Getting By: The Hireling, Timothy White

D ESPITE ITS QUAKER reputation, Nantucket was not, religiously speaking, a one-horse town in the eighteenth century. About fifteen years after the Friends built their meeting house, the Congregationalists built their own place of worship on a slight rise of ground just to the north of No-Bottom Pond. However, just because they had a meeting house did not mean they were about to pay for a minister.

Traditions died hard on old Nantucket, particularly if they had to do with religion and money. Nantucket's Congregationalists were not alone in their determination to avoid the temptations of a "hireling priest." In 1720 the Boston divine Samuel Danforth mentioned the southeastern communities of "Freetown, Tiverton, Dartmouth and Nantucket" as "frontiers, bordering upon or near to the place where Satan hath his throne," that were in desperate need of the civilizing influence of a Harvard-educated minister. Two years later, the Boston Congregationalists put their money where their rhetoric was and sent one Nathan Prince to the island. He would last only a year. In a letter to his brother, Prince describes what he is up against. Although Congregationalists outnumber most of the nonconformist sects on the island (including Baptists and Philadelphians), they are still running a very distant second to the Quakers:

'Tis strange how they have increased. Twenty years ago there was scarce one and now there are several hundreds, all proceeded from a woman (one Starbuck) turning Quaker; who being a person of note for wisdom in this place became a preacher and soon converted so many as that they formed themselves into a society and built a meeting house and became the prevailing profession of the island.

Five years after her death, the island was still possessed by the charismatic ghost of Mary Starbuck.

Enter a twenty-five-year-old minister by the name of Timothy White.

In the beginning, this Harvard graduate from Haverhill (deep in the heart of the Merrimack Valley) seems to have been blissfully oblivious to the extent of the challenges he had assumed. For one thing, he had some money in his pocket, provided to him by the Congregationalists in Boston. For another, he was in love.

In a letter to his sister Abigail, written during his first year on Nantucket in 1725, he explains that he has been "stiffly engaged in courting," and as a consequence has been "very forgetful of those lesser things," such as writing letters. This is no solemn and bloodless Puritan but a young man who seems to relish the rumors concerning his romantic attachments: "Whether the reason is, because my company is so very delightsome & charming, or what it is, I can't tell, but it has been my portion to be honor'd with such suspicions wherever I have yet lived for any time. But if this be not true, I could wish it were, for I am no enemy to proceedings of this nature."

Three years later he would marry the seventeen-year-old Susanna Gardner; two years later they were building a house on land given to them by Susanna's father at the corner of North Liberty and Cliff Road. Behind them was a swamp that abutted the Jethro Coffin House where Timothy and Susanna kept a garden. By that point they had already lost two children in infancy; in 1731 they would finally have a daughter, Susanna, and then, two years later, a son, Timothy. The Whites would ultimately have a total of thirteen children, of whom only six would survive to maturity.

Even though White had married into one of the more influential Congregational families on the island, it soon became clear that his connections were to no avail when it came to securing a fixed position in the community. Whereas Starbucks and Macys occupied the positions of power among the Quakers, Coffins, Gardners, and Bunkers were the island's most prominent Congregationalists. Over the years White would add close to 200 members to the church and seems to have been a popular minister. Even so, the congregation remained steadfast in its refusal to provide White with a steady income.

In order to support himself and his growing family, White, as so many people have done on this island, was forced to do a little bit of everything. In 1728 he began to preach to the Indians on a monthly basis, his efforts financed, once again, by off-island religious authorities. For the next thirteen years he preached to gatherings of between twelve and eighty Indians at meeting houses in Miacomet, Siasconset, Squam, and Okorwaw, carrying with him a small three-and-a-half by six-inch notebook in which are scribbled the notes to hundreds of sermons.

He seems to have been a forceful preacher, who was not afraid to speak his mind. In one existing sermon, he scolds his listeners for their behavior during a recent "disturbance":

> *Is it agreeable to the good government of the family for either the heads or members of it to be from home (especially at the tavern) till eleven or twelve o'clock at night, or one or two in the morning? Is it not offensive to disturb people in their*

houses in the evening by needless noises, and in the proper
hours for rest, beating the drum or firing guns? And how
can that be justified which obliges the careful owner to watch
till after midnight to prevent his house or substance being
destroyed by fire?

Although this sermon (on a separate sheet of paper) is not dated, making it impossible to determine when as well as where it was delivered, the text suggests that the Congregationalists may have been a little less sedate than their Quaker counterparts.

But even preaching before the English and the Indians was not enough for White to make ends meet. So he established a school. In his memorandum book he kept a strict account of not only attendance but payment by his pupils' parents. The tuition was in the neighborhood of ten shillings per quarter, and it was not unusual for him to have as many as thirty-four pupils, mostly Coffins, Gardners, Bunkers, Chases, Brocks, Chadwicks, and an occasional Folger. More often than not he was paid in hay, wool, wheat, wood, molasses, cheese, and tallow instead of money.

Although now burdened with more than his share of the cares of this world, White, who carried a monogrammed ivory-headed cane, does not seem to have entirely lost his sense of fun and good humor. Among his papers are several fragments of doggerel verse describing the challenges of being a schoolmaster:

Scholars being come each from his home, we set all
*   things in order.*
One takes his book with scowling look, to writing
*   goes another.*
To warm the rooms run Nat or Tom and fetch a
*   coal of fire.*
Some take the wood such as is good. Put that stick
*   here, this there.*

*Come hither, Jo, your mouth clap to and make the
    fire blaze.
At which the boys without much noise, with smil-
    ing faces gaze.
Come, Ben, and read your letters, heed and keep
    your line with care.
A school so green I've never seen, I solemnly declare.*

With money tight, the students provided their own books:

*Bibles for spellers, testaments as well as psalters and
    primers, too,
Spelling books some, old psalm books one, Pilgrim's
    Progress also,
Tattered and torn letters, old and worn, but few
    without his mark;
From where they're bro't puzzles my tho't, unless
    from Noah's Ark.*

Soon the strain of being not only a minister to the English
and Indians but also a schoolmaster began to catch up with
Timothy White. Although the Nantucketers' refusal to support
him financially seems to have been a matter of principle, it was
difficult for White not to take it personally. In a letter written
in 1731 to Benjamin Colman in Boston he expresses his "great
discouragement" and complains of "a numerous company of
heretics who are continually plotting against, and will spare no
pains to overthrow, the truth." Colman in turn spoke to the governor of Massachusetts, Jonathan Belcher, who on October 3,
1732, took the extraordinary step of writing directly to George
Bunker, a leading member of the Nantucket congregation. The
letter provides a fascinating portrait of Timothy White and his
dilemma:

I understand he has been now about seven years in Nantucket and preached (twice every Lord's Day) to a congregation of between 200 and 300 souls, among which you are one of the principal, and I find his chief support hitherto has been from private funds, arising out of collections and subscriptions in and about this town [Boston], . . . and although there are about 60 men that attend on his preaching, yet he has been obliged to support himself for more than two years past wholly by his school; and the funds from which he formerly received considerable being now exhausted, he is at present under great discouragement, not seeing how he shall subsist himself and family, but thinks he must be obliged to come away. Upon the representation of these things I sent for him and told him he must by no means think of leaving you. He bears an extraordinary character among the ministers here for a gentleman of good learning and religion, and of great modesty and humility. I, therefore, think that the whole Island, and particularly those that attend him at public worship, have a great blessing in him, and I hope you will think so, and show him your respect and affection by being willing to make him able to live and to do his work among you. . . . Pray, consider seriously of all I have said, and how easy and light a thing it is to maintain a Gospel minister if it pleases God to incline your hearts.

But the hearts of the Nantucket Congregationalists were not so inclined. For many islanders, the Congregational "Establishment" emanating from Boston represented everything their forefathers had come to Nantucket to escape. Even if their personal religious beliefs were essentially Congregational, they were not about to knuckle under to an off-island authority—particularly if they were going to have to pay for the privilege. But there was another factor in the way of establishing a Congregational ministry on Nantucket, and it had to do with the Indians.

Congregationalism was not only the Boston way, it was also the Indian way on Nantucket, and English Nantucketers were in no hurry to emulate this "heathen" mode of worship, which predated their own appearance on the island. By the 1730s, the Indians' situation on the island had degenerated dramatically. The population had plummeted from 1,500 in 1675 to less than half that number as disease and alcoholism took their toll, a process that many of the English helped to accelerate. Obed Macy describes the vicious circle in which so many island Indians found themselves: "Some of the English were so wicked as to . . . trade with them for their baskets, fish, corn, and vegetables and pay them in spirituous liquors and frequently get them in debt and cause them to go a whaling to pay their 'masters' as they called them. This kept them in a low degraded state."

For the Indians, the last bastion of their cultural identity was the meeting house. These primarily Congregational assemblies provided what one historian has called "a buffer" against the cumulative effects of disease, alcoholism, and debt servitude and were vital to the Indians' survival as a viable community. English Nantucketers, who had never operated under the watchful eye of a hireling minister, had little sympathy for the Indians' century-old tradition of Congregational worship. For the English, making money was the true religion, and all other spiritual and cultural needs (especially those of the Indians) took a very distant backseat. Just how destructive the Nantucket whale fishery and its system of debt servitude were to the Indian community is made plain in petition after petition sent to the Massachusetts General Court throughout the first half of the eighteenth century. According to the Indians' own testimony, when out at sea they are forced to spend "the Sabbath day rowing after whales or killing whales all day long . . . and when we are on land then we have no time to go to the meeting and then we are called to go away again to sea whaling." The Indian boys who have been brought up by their English masters "take no notice of the Sabbath day"; instead of going to the meeting house, they "go away to see their friends." With their traditional ways being irrevocably eroded by the whaling interests of the English, the Indians ask how they can be expected to continue on "when our masters lead us to darkness and not in light?" It would prove to be a rhetorical question.

As Obed Macy so insightfully observed, "all the Indians lacked was encouragement and proper management." And to a certain extent, Timothy White, who was being paid by the off-island spiritual leaders to inspect the Indians' religious meetings and schools, attempted to provide this "proper management." He made conscientious efforts to insure that the four Indian ministers received their duly allotted stipends from Boston. In one letter he expresses genuine concern about the effects of recent cutbacks on the Indian schools: "I am under great discouragements about the Indian schools, and I find the Indians themselves under the like—for as the books fail, so the schools (at best) are so unsteady that they complain of their children's loafing in the vacant times what they gain when at school."

But if White clearly cared about the island's native people, his ties to the English community meant that he would never become an outspoken advocate of the Indian cause. To illustrate the impossible tightrope act White was forced to perform in his dual role as minister to both the English and Indians, let us look to the example of Cromwell Coffin. White's memorandum book records the baptisms of several of Coffin's children; he was apparently an upstanding member of the church and community. The Nantucket Court Records are also filled with Cromwell Coffin's name, but in these instances it is in connection with an Indian by the name of Abraham Monkey. In October of 1731 Monkey was convicted of stealing "leather and some tools" from Thomas Clark and "two shirts and a pair of stockings" from William

Smith. Unable to pay triple damages and court costs (while also suffering a whipping of "15 stripes"), Monkey was sentenced to serve on a whaler until he had paid off the debt. Then in February of the following year, he once again ran into trouble for stealing "a great coat, a gun lock, some shot, and a shirt" from Tabor Morton. It was then that Cromwell Coffin entered his life, offering to pay "for him and let him at liberty" if Monkey agreed to add three years to his debt servitude on Nantucket whalers. In October, Coffin and Monkey were back in court:

> *Abraham Monkey being brought into court by his master Cromwell Coffin and it appearing to this court that his master hath paid for him twenty pounds for sundry thefts committed by the said Abraham, it is therefore ordered by the court that the said Abraham shall serve the said Cromwell Coffin or his assigns three years and six months after his former time is expired.*

Suffice it to say that the future of Cromwell Coffin's investment was assured.

If Timothy White was to attend to the spiritual needs of the island's Indians (without losing all hope of English financial support), he would have to do it in such a way that did not alienate the likes of Cromwell Coffin, whose business interests were so intimately involved in Indian debt servitude. This meant that while White might give the Indians (in Macy's words) "encouragement," he was not about to question what constituted their "proper management" by the English. As a consequence, he never seems to have rocked the boat when it came to Native American–English relations on Nantucket, and at least some of the Indians' own religious leaders were less than pleased with him. In 1733, five years after he had begun preaching to the

Indians, White was issued a certificate from Boston addressed "to the ministers of the several Indian Congregations of the island of Nantucket," reminding them that the Commissioners had appointed "Rev. Mr. Timothy White to preach lectures to you, to oversee, counsel & advise you from time to time as occasion shall require, and to inspect the schools and churches and to catechize the children & such as are proper for it, & you & all concerned are to pay a proper regard to him accordingly."

Rather than become a whistle-blower, White chose to become a player in the Nantucket economy, using his knowledge of the Native American community to help English "masters" get the most out of their Indians. In 1747, Bellamy Bosworth of Chilmark, Martha's Vineyard, wrote to White, requesting him to settle his account with a Nantucket shipowner concerning his "two Indians' voyages" and then added, "I also desire you to write to me what you think to do with my Indians: and when you want them I hope you will send orders for them, or order who you please to come for them. I can fit them out in part, the rest you must supply them with." If White was sympathetic to the Native Americans' plight, it did not keep him from making a much needed dollar in the business of Indian debt servitude.

During White's tenure on the island, the Indians' frustrations apparently reached the breaking point. The whale fishery was not the only threat to their way of life. They were also running out of land. Numerous complaints were filed with the General Court describing how the English had obtained land deeds from Indians who did not have the proper authority. The English also abused their grazing rights on what little land the Indians still possessed, making it difficult for them to grow their crops. Unable to get any satisfaction from the court system, the Indians may have hatched a plan to retake the island by force. In the *Boston News-Letter* of October 5, 1738, is a report that an

Indian friendly to the English had disclosed a plot to attack the English settlement. According to Obed Macy:

> *Intimation was . . . given to the whites, that the Indians had entered into a conspiracy to rise upon them, on a certain night, and to massacre men, women, and children. At the appointed time, agreeably with the information, the high sheriff, with fifty well armed men, issued out of the town to reconnoiter the settlements of the natives, and ascertain whether they were making any hostile movements. They found all quiet; it was harvest time, and the Indians were merrily husking their corn.*

The *Boston News-Letter* report makes it clear that the fears of the English remained high, however, especially since their whalers contained such a large percentage of Indian crew members. Timothy White was certainly no Peter Folger, ready to leap into the fray when Indian-English relations reached a flash point. As much a part of the problem as he was a potential solution to it, White could do little more than watch the sad and slow decline of a people whose spiritual life had become a casualty of the English community's remorseless pursuit of worldly success.

As the years dragged on and his family increased—while funds from Boston and his Nantucket congregation, if anything, decreased—White inevitably looked to other sources of income. The whale fishery was not, by any means, the only way people made money on Nantucket. By this time, the island had become the focal point of a vast "coasting trade" along the eastern seaboard, while also establishing a direct and profitable link with London. Crèvecoeur described the extent of the island's commercial ties in the 1770s:

> *[T]hey are well acquainted with the cheapest method of procuring lumber from Kennebec River, Penobscot, etc.; pitch*

and tar from North Carolina; flour and biscuit from Phila-
delphia; beef and pork from Connecticut. They know how to
exchange their cod-fish and West Indian produce for those
articles which they are continually either bringing to their
island or sending off to other places where they are wanted.

White started out slowly, initially acting as an agent for
goods provided by family and friends in Haverhill. In 1733 he
received five barrels of cider from a Mr. Brown, which after selling to a Gardner and three Coffins, gave him "neat proceeds"
of close to five pounds, with which he purchased wool and fish
that he then shipped back to Brown. He also sold books, such as
almanacs and bibles, to the parents of his pupils. Then, in 1745,
he made the plunge, purchasing an eighth interest in the "good
sloop *Susanna* [also the name of his wife], burthen about fifty-six
tons, now out on a whaling voyage." In a letter written during
the following year, he describes the vessel as "an excellent sea-
boat . . . but dull upon a wind," while outlining plans to outfit
her for the London trade.

As White's mercantile interests expanded, he became increasingly disaffected with his ministerial efforts on Nantucket. By 1749,
he seems to have determined that he must soon leave. The powers-
that-be back in Boston did their best to convince him to carry on:

We are sensible, indeed, your services among them have been
attended with many peculiar difficulties; and that you have
been but poorly requited by man for your laborious endeavors
to serve the Kingdom and interest of our Lord Jesus Christ
in the place where you are. But remember, Dear Brother, we
serve a good Master, who will one day richly reward the little
he enables us to do in his service.

And as you have been long acquainted with that people,
and, we hope, have a great interest in the affections of many

*of them, we can't but fear your leaving them in their present
state will greatly disserve the cause of Christ in his holy religion, which we trust are exceeding dear to you.*

The following year, Timothy White left Nantucket. After
serving a brief stint in Narragansett, where once again he failed
to secure an established ministry, he was back in his hometown
of Haverhill. He still owned part of the *Susanna* but complained
that "being about 150 miles from Nantucket I can but seldom
get any intelligence from thence of the managements of my
partners." Increasingly he looked to exploit the benefits of living on the Merrimack River, "where we abound with the best of
Plank & Ship timber" as well as staves, clapboards, and shingles
that he might trade in London for woolens, linens, gloves, soft
pewter, nails, cutlery, and other items.

On September 13, 1755, he wrote the letter with which he
broke his final tie with the ungrateful congregation back on
Nantucket. Writing to the commissioners in Boston, he recounts
how in 1732 Reverend Colman sent him a set of "Baxter's
Works" for both himself and the trustees of his congregation.
Now that he has left the island, and there being "neither minister nor trustee" on Nantucket, he wants to know if he is justified
in keeping the books, explaining: "Inasmuch as I supplied that
pulpit for more than eighteen years after they were put in my
hands, & during this term of years lived chiefly upon my own
means, I am justified in accounting them my own." Certainly,
the Boston Congregationalists would have found it difficult to
disagree.

In 1763, thirteen years after White's departure from Nantucket, a "yellow fever" killed 222 out of 358 island Indians, thus
reducing at a stroke the vitality of the strongest rival of Nantucket's white Congregational community. Four years later, in

1767 (two years after the death of Timothy White in Haverhill), the Nantucketers at last decided to foot the bill for an established minister. With the Indians wiped out (and with them, their churches), English Congregationalists were finally willing to put their own religious house in order.

CHAPTER 11

Peleg Folger, the Poet Whaleman

IN *MOBY-DICK* Ishmael claims that "a whaleship was my Yale College and my Harvard." Nantucket's real-life counterpart to Ishmael was Peleg (pronounced "PILL-ick") Folger who, after growing up as a farmer on Nantucket, went to sea at seventeen. It was then, in the year 1751, that the primarily self-taught Peleg began keeping a log. On the very first page of his journal it becomes obvious that this is an exceptional document from an exceptional individual:

> *Many people who keep journals at sea, fill them up with some trifles or others; for my part, I propose in the following sheets, not to keep an over strict history of every trifling occurrence that happened; only now and then of some particular affair; and to fill up the rest with subjects wither mathematical, theological, historical, philosophical, or poetical, or anything else that best suits mine inclinations. . . .*

As Peleg makes abundantly clear, there is more to his log than just whales. When he is not quoting Latin or British poetry, he is moralizing on man's mortality ("Death summons all men to the silent grave" is a favorite phrase). And yet, while reading this slender volume of ancient papers that have been stitched together with string, we never lose the sense of being in the midst of a whaling voyage. Sometimes the action is almost frighteningly understated:

> *July 30. We struck a large spermaceti and got in three irons*
> *and one tow-iron put in by John Way, one of our mates. As*
> *soon as the tow-iron went into the whale she gave a flank*
> *and went down and coming up again she bolted her head out*
> *of the water almost if not quite as far as her fins. And then*
> *pitched the whole weight of her head on the boat—stove the*
> *boat and ruined her and killed the midshipman (an Indian*
> *named Sam Lamson) outright. A sad and awful Providence.*

Even amid the boredom and discomfort that was also a part of the whaling life, Folger is able to devise wonderful similes and metaphors. As his ship wallows in a jumbled sea, he writes, "It feels tiresome and tedious to lay by. So much rowling and tumbling very uneasily like the conscience of a wicked man. How many are the tedious cares and anxieties of human life. But I carry my discontent about with me for I cannot run away from myself." Almost exactly 100 years before the publication of *Moby-Dick*, Peleg Folger was already extracting philosophical and poetic truths from the blubbery business of whaling.

As is true with any great literary work, Peleg's log tells us as much, if not more, about the times in which he was writing as it does about Folger himself. In fact, his log is probably one of the best sources we have for information concerning eighteenth-century whaling. At this time, sloops between forty and fifty feet were standard; two whaleboats were used, and the crew typically consisted of thirteen men, leaving only one man to tend the ship when both whaleboats (six men each) were in use. The first voyages that Peleg describes, made in the spring and early summer of 1751 and '52, were to the south, where sperm whales frequented the edges of the Gulf Stream between the Carolinas and Bermuda. In these voyages there is no mention of trying out the oil; instead, the blubber was stored in hogsheads and then returned to Nantucket for processing. Due to the perishable nature of the blubber, these voyages never lasted much longer than six weeks, and after unloading the blubber, the sloop would head out once again. For example, in 1751 Peleg's sloop the *Grampus* made three different voyages: April 10th–May 15th; May 18th–June 18th; and June 23rd–July 20th.

Although this voyaging pattern meant that Nantucket whalers were never too far from home, it also required that they spend an inordinate amount of time amid some of the most dangerous shoals in the world, with which they became intimately acquainted. Simply by taking a "sounding," which would indicate not only the depth of the water but also the nature of the bottom, a Nantucketer could determine his position with an amazing exactitude. For example, Folger notes in his journal,

> *Last night at 8 o'clock we had 34 fathoms depth of water; fine black and white sand, so we kept her NW till 12 o'clock, then sounded and found 23 fathoms; half an hour after found 22 fathoms; so we kept our luff till we found 16 fathoms. To the eastward of the south shoal we found for the most part black and white sand. . . . So now here we are in the southward of Nobadeer and hope to be at our bar before sunset.*

The shortness of the voyages meant that whaling was a much less lonely occupation than it would ultimately become. Throughout the spring and summer, sloops were constantly going in and out of the harbor. In one entry Peleg notes: "We sailed from Nantucket May 6th in company with about 30 sail of whalemen and when we anchored under the east end of Nantucket we appeared like a forest." During these southern cruises, fellow whalers were encountered on a daily basis. In one entry, Folger mentions that they "spoke with five whalemen"; in another, "We have seen almost one half our fleet, nay, more than half for ought I know; as also divers whalemen from Martin's Vineyard, Cape Cod, Rhode Island, and Cushnet." That these encounters were not purely recreational is indicated by Folger's entry for May 16th, in which he launches into a typical rumination:

> *About 12 o'clock we spoke with a Capeman who told us oil bore a very good price in Boston—140 pounds old tenor per tun to be paid in dollars on the spot; and the small pox which hath been in Boston some time still continues very great there. It seems to me as if there is nothing but fear and care and trouble on every side. No man can be born and live and die, without his share. . . . And yet how the fear of death will terrify poor mortals. So I conclude this day's remarks hoping all are well at home, male and female.*

During this era, it was common practice for the crews of two whalers to combine forces or "mate" in their pursuit of whales. On April 27th of the same cruise referred to above, Folger records: "We concluded to keep company with Beriah Fitch and mated with him while we kept company. In the afternoon we struck a large spermaceti and killed her and cut off her body blubber the same day." The following day, the two sloops once again assisted each other in finishing up with the whale's head: "We got her between both vessels and got a parbuckle [a sling-like block-and-tackle system] under her and four tackles and runners to her and hoisted her head about 2 feet above water and through cut a scuttle in her head and a man got in up to his armpits and dipped out almost 6 hogsheads of clear oil out of her case besides 6 more of the noodle."

During this same voyage, Folger's vessel also "mated" with

a sloop captained by Charles Gardner, in whose company they kept throughout a particularly bad spell of weather. Note that Folger refers to the sails of what was most definitely a feminine ship in the masculine:

> *This day a very hard gale of wind at the NE. We first carried a trysail, foresail, and jib. By and by the wind coming on, we hauled down our jib and reefed him through, set him again, but the wind soon tore him sadly so we hauled him down again and unbent him and got him into the cabin and mended him in order for a good time to bend him to again. So stood in under a trysail and foresail till night when the wind blowing harder and a very large swell rising, we were obliged to haul him down and stow him snug.*

Two days later, the wind shifted and moderated to the point that they were able to haul up a reefed mainsail, foresail, and jib, and with all three sails "perfectly" set, the *Grampus* ran before the breeze "like a blaze all night," headed for home in the company of Gardner.

In 1752, after a series of spring voyages to the south, Peleg signed on with "the good sloop *Seaflower*, Captain Christopher Coffin, Commander," for what Folger describes as a voyage "to Newfoundland to kill some humpbacks." This much longer voyage (they would not return until the end of August) was made possible through the development of a relatively new technology. By the late 1720s, Nantucket offshore whaling vessels began carrying their own portable tryworks, which they would set up and operate on a nearby shore. This worked well in and around Newfoundland, where the many islands provided the whalers with relatively easy access to shore.

However, since the whalemen invariably left a putrefying whale's corpse behind them, it was not long before they had begun to wear out their welcome with the Newfoundlanders. (Folger refers to one of their stopping points as the "Stinking Islands.") In "Misketo Cove" the crew of the ironically named *Seaflower* had a run-in with an angry group of locals:

> *There the Irishmen cursed us at a high rate for they hate the whalemen in this harbor. Here we lay till June 27th, and in that space of time bore many an oath of the Paddies and bogtrotters, they swearing we should not cut up our whale in the harbor. But, however, we cut up one or two and then on the 27th of June they raised a mob in the evening (one "Pike," an Irishman, who called himself Captain of the harbor, being the Chief Head) and fired upon us, and the shot struck all round us, but through mercy hurt no man. So we towed our vessels out of the harbor, being 6 or 7 sail of us, and lay off in the Bay that night.*

Throughout this voyage, the *Seaflower* went from island to island in the company of three other Nantucket sloops, ultimately trying out "something better than 100 barrels of humpback oil."

The 1750s were a pivotal time in the whale fishery; by this point many vessels were being outfitted with on-board brick tryworks that enabled them to process the blubber at sea. This broadened their range to the extent that they could now voyage far beyond Newfoundland into the arctic waters of the Davis Strait. For the whalemen, this new technology was a very mixed blessing. Cutting into the whale and trying the oil in the midst of the ocean (as opposed to the island harbors around Newfoundland) was not only dirty and exhausting but could also be extremely dangerous on a vessel of only fifty feet in length when the sea kicked up. During a voyage to the Davis Strait in 1754, Peleg Folger describes a typical experience: "Still cutting our whale. A chopling sea agoing and but little wind. Our sloop girded most violently and we parted our runners twice and split one of our runner blocks and hurt one of our hands (splitting his fingers, one of them most sadly) and made most racking work. About 6 PM we unhooked our tackles and runners, not daring to cut any longer for fear of our lives and limbs."

With the advent of the on-board tryworks, the average length of a whaling voyage during the next ten years would jump from six weeks to four and a half months, dramatically increasing the level of boredom and loneliness. Although these longer voyages still offered the excitement of the hunt, whaling was no longer the varied and extremely social occupation it had once been. Instead of fishermen and sailors, whalemen were increasingly becoming ship-bound factory workers.

As the technology of whaling began to change, so did the composition of the crews. By this time the number of Indians in the fishery had dropped significantly, from more than fifty percent of the workforce in the 1730s to less than fifteen percent in the 1760s. To fill this void, Nantucket whaling merchants actively recruited sailors from coastal towns throughout New England and New York. Since the vast majority of these recruits were white, the Nantucket fishery became much less racially diverse than it had once been (and would ultimately become in the years after the Revolution).

That whaling was indeed entering into a new era is evident in Folger's log, particularly his account of an almost five-month voyage to the Davis Strait on the sloop *Greyhound*, Richard Pinkham, Captain. While the irrepressible Folger cannot help but bring an eye for delightful detail to his material, his log describes a voyage with an altogether different pace from the six-week jaunts to the Gulf Stream or the colorful island-hopping of his cruise to Newfoundland. Although the extreme northern latitude meant that, in Peleg's words, "the daylight goeth not out of the sky during the whole 24 hours," persistent fogs and icebergs kept the crew "uneasy." A typical log entry: "Very thick and foggy weather. We saw some large cakes of ice and passed one about midnight but did not see it. Only heard it roar. There is need of a good watch upon these countries."

The months spent hunting spermaceti and right whales in the Arctic Circle did have, however, their pleasures. Despite the miserable weather outside, a good deal of camaraderie seems to have existed below-decks. At one point during the Davis Strait cruise, Folger states: "The weather is freezing cold. Days long. Nights short. Sea rowling and tumbling. The deck tedious. Our cabins our delight. The fire pleasant. Our allowance to every man aboard—his belly full and more too if he wants. Alas! if it was not for hopes the heart would fail." Indeed, Peleg and his fellow shipmates seem to have been very well provided for throughout their cruise. Only a few days out from Nantucket, the *Greyhound* "spoke" with a trading schooner from Montserrat that provided them with "two bottles of rum and some limes and some sugar oranges." Once in the northern latitudes, Peleg describes how the crew spent the morning "pouring some hot chocolate down our bellies" before being interrupted by the appearance of a whale. He also mentions meals of corned fish, pancakes, homecakes, "doboys," plum pudding, and haglet pie.

It is clear from Peleg's log that these early Nantucket whalemen shared something more than good food and a common home port; they also shared a good deal of justifiable pride in their expertise. Among whalers, they were not only the new kids on the block, they were also the ones with the "Right Stuff" who succeeded where others failed. While most whalers in New England and Europe pursued the cow-like right whale, the Nantucketers were the first to specialize in the more bull-like sperm whale whose oil represented the "high end" of the market. At one point Peleg describes the sheepish response of a whaler from Glasgow soon after the Nantucketers killed a "large spermaceti": "The Scotchman stood away till he had gotten out of sight, having no luck amongst the whales."

It was not just his expertise that set the Nantucketer apart. His religious beliefs also made him a different order of whaleman. And in 1758 Quakerism gave the Nantucketers a very tangible advantage over all others in the colonial fishery. During this period of the Seven Years War, a large number of men throughout the colonies were called upon to serve their mother country. However, since most Nantucketers were Quaker pacifists, the British authorities saw fit to award them an exemption, giving them the right to continue whaling even though an embargo had been placed on all other colonial fishing in the Grand Banks. Having this select status granted to an island that already enjoyed its share of advantages when it came to the whale fishery must have irked more than a few New Englanders, laying the seeds for a regional bitterness toward Nantucket that, as we shall see in the next chapter, would only grow in the years to come.

So, while their fellow whalemen were pressed to fight the French, the Quakers of Nantucket continued to fight the sperm whale, a form of bloodshed for which these pacifists proved amazingly well-adapted. When in pursuit of their prey, the Nantucketers showed no mercy, using their ever-growing knowledge of the whales' habits to their advantage. One common trick was to single out a mother and her calf; since the whalemen knew the mother would never abandon her child, they would first kill the calf and then have a relatively easy time of fastening to the mother. However, at one point this strategy backfired on Peleg and crew. After killing the calf, they harpooned the mother:

> *In her flurry she came at our boat and furiously ran over us and overset us and made a miserable wreck of our boat in a moment. A wonder it was we all had our lives spared, tho' the whale had divers warps over her and divers of us all were*

*sadly puzzled under the water. Yet we were all taken up well
and not one hurt. Praise the Lord for his mercies & for his
wonderful works to the children of men.*

The final sentence of this passage goes to the heart of the fascinating paradox of the Nantucket whalemen. Although some of
the deadliest, most conniving hunters the earth has ever known,
they were Quakers, a sect that stood against war and conflict
and anything that might excite undue emotions.

Certainly it is unfair to apply our generation's sensitivity
to the plight of the whale to the Nantucket whalemen, whose
Bible granted them dominion over the fishes of the sea. As Peleg
expressed it in poetry:

> *Thou didst, O Lord, create the mighty whale,*
> *That wondrous monster of a mighty length;*
> *Vast is his head and body, vast his tail,*
> *Beyond conception his unmeasured strength.*
>
> *But, everlasting God, thou dost ordain*
> *That we, poor feeble mortals should engage*
> *(Ourselves, our wives and children to maintain,)*
> *This dreadful monster with a martial rage.*

Since they were fulfilling God's will, the Nantucket whalemen
were able to kill, according to Obed Macy, "without brutal excitement." But as Folger's log makes clear, whaling could be as brutal
and exciting as any war—a holy war in the case of the Quaker
whalemen. No wonder they were better at it than anyone else.

⟡

Peleg made his last recorded voyage in 1760, when he was twenty-
six years old. The consummate observer, he may have been too

brainy, too bookish to make it as a whaling captain. Apparently his peers viewed him as an unusual sort. Scrawled across a portion of Peleg's log is this: "Old Peleg Folger is a Num Scull for writing in Latin. I fear Peleg Folger will be offended with me for writing in his book but I will intercede with Anna Pitts on his behalf for retaliation for the same. Nathaniel Worth." Despite Worth's efforts, Peleg never married, ultimately becoming a schoolteacher and clerk of the Monthly Meeting. According to Macy, "He was considered as a monitor in all his conduct through life; beloved by all good people, he commanded the respect and obedience of those who looked to him for support and protection, among whom were several fatherless children."

But, as Worth's log entry also suggests, Folger was undoubtedly viewed as something of an eccentric on an island where "book learning" was a relative rarity; hence the reference to him as "old" even though he was less than twenty when Worth made the comment in his log. In the same vein is this slightly irreverent piece of doggerel concerning "Uncle Pillick," passed down to us from the 1750s:

> *Old Uncle Pillick he built him a boat*
> *On the ba-ack side of Nantucket P'int.*
> *He rolled up his trousers and set her afloat*
> *On the ba-ack side of Nantucket P'int.*

In any event, Peleg's ambitions inevitably lay beyond the harpooning of whales. On the occasion of his twenty-fourth birthday he wrote a long poem that includes this stanza:

> *My flying time! How soon 'tis gone*
> *Full three and twenty fruitless years*
> *My work, alas, remains undone*
> *I may strive with prayers and tears.*

Whether or not Folger saw his whaling years as "fruitless," they ingrained in him certain habits that he would maintain for the rest of his life. Just as he had once calculated a never-ending series of navigational problems in his logs, he would write out translation after translation of Latin poetry and prose. He also developed a remarkable expertise in not only mathematics but the natural sciences as well. According to Macy, he "was considered by judges to be far superior to . . . many who had had the advantages of a classical education."

Of special importance to us today is that he maintained his journal-writing habits, recording deaths and noteworthy storms in the same quirky style that characterizes his logs. Indeed, whenever a storm swept across the island and its surrounding waters, Peleg inevitably took pen to paper, anticipating Ralph Waldo Emerson's observation that Nantucketers "remember the quarter deck in their homes":

5th of 3rd mo. 1771. A most terrible gale of wind with abundance of snow. It began to snow soon after 12 and by sunset was a hard storm and lasted till the afternoon of the next day when it moderated. Effects: a vessel cast away on the east end of Nantucket of which the master and mate both died and the people that survive suffered great hardships. A great deal of shipwreck between here and New York wherein great numbers of people endured a world of misery and distress. 35 or 60 sheep drowned in Copalm [Capaum].

20th of 3rd mo. 1772. A terrible gale of wind with abundance of snow. What effects we know not as yet.

3rd of 4th mo. Monthly meeting day by adjournment: A very hard gale of wind at NE with abundance of rain, sleet and snow. It began yesterday morning and is at this present a hard wind and rain. While I write this I perceive the wind to sound hollow in the chimney and plenty of rain and sleet against my chamber window.

16th of 4th mo. A southerly wind with a great deal of rain. I am at this time in my chamber in pretty good health. Where I shall be tomorrow at this time, alas who can tell.

21st of 3rd mo. 1773. A terrible gale of wind at NE or NNE. While I write this it is as terrible a storm as is commonly known at any time of year. Snow, hail, rain, and sleet.

In comparing Peleg's sea log and island journal, we begin to understand how the Nantucketers managed to bridge the gap that was so often imposed between themselves and their loved ones. As far as they were concerned, Nantucket was not so much a piece of real estate as it was, in the words of the contemporary chronicler Edouard Stackpole, a "Mother Ship," in which all Nantucketers—whether they were on island or hundreds of miles out to sea—experienced the same storms and the same misfortunes.

As a final testimonial to this sense of interconnectedness, and how Quakerism provided the glue that held them all together, let us return to Peleg's log. It is 1754; he is twenty years old and bound for the Davis Strait on board the good sloop *Phebe*; it is an unusually fine day; it is also a Sunday, and inevitably his thoughts turn to Nantucket:

And if the weather is so pleasant at home it is a charming day for the young ladies to go to meeting, and if they do but get any good by it, it will be very well. So remembering all at home both male and female, mother, brothers, sisters, Friends, and acquaintances and all others without exception

and wishing them all well and a happy and prosperous meet-
ing in the Royal Assembly while we are drinking flip and
chasing whales, and wishing them all well till we once more
meet together which I hope will not be long (by the blessing of
God), I conclude the remarks of this 24 hours being in the vast
Atlantic Ocean and how far to eastward of the Grand Bank
of Newfoundland we know not nor greatly care, for we are
all in health and all merry together.

CHAPTER 12

Kezia Coffin's Revolutionary
Rise and Fall

N O FIGURE in Nantucket history has captured the imagination of subsequent generations in quite the same way as Kezia Folger Coffin. Crèvecoeur met her when he came to Nantucket in the 1770s and claimed that on this island of "superior" wives, Kezia (pronounced "Ka-ZYE-ah") stood out above the rest. While her husband was away on whaling voyages, she began trading with "pins and needles and kept a school." It was not long, however, until she had entered the mercantile big time, becoming the sole agent for a leading trading house in London. In a matter of years, she and her husband were among the wealthiest couples on the island. Crèvecoeur raved, "Who is he in this country and who is a citizen of Nantucket or Boston who does not know Aunt Kesiah?" Here was a Mary Starbuck with an attitude—a little less holy and a lot more ambitious—a "she-merchant" who achieved the kind of financial success that the Reverend Timothy White could only dream about.

But if Kezia may have been Nantucket's first famous person, she would ultimately become one of its most infamous persons. When a writer by the name of Joseph C. Hart visited the island in the 1830s, Nantucketers were still talking about Kezia Coffin, and Hart grasped hold of her story as material for a novel. But whereas Crèvecoeur had seen her as a paragon, Hart portrays her in his potboiler *Miriam Coffin* as a pariah—a Lady Macbeth of whaling whose nefarious schemes ultimately end in financial ruin during the dark days of the Revolution.

The novelization of Kezia Coffin's story—lurid cautionary tale that it might be—bears out the supposition that there is no such thing as bad publicity. Even though one of their own had been portrayed in a less than flattering light, Nantucketers loved the book. The local paper praised *Miriam Coffin* for its "thrilling interest" and historical accuracy. The rest of America liked it, too, and *Miriam Coffin* went on to become a run-away bestseller. In fact the continued popularity of the novel throughout the nineteenth century prompted the wife of William Starbuck, a subsequent owner of Kezia's house, to lament having torn down the original structure. So many people had offered to pay her for "just a shingle or little trifle of what used to be Miriam's" that Mrs. Starbuck believed she could have turned the home into a profitable "resort."

So who exactly was Miriam, a.k.a. Kezia, Coffin? Certainly she was not as "perverted" as Hart's novel might lead us to believe, nor was she the ideal helpmate Crèvecoeur claimed her to be. Indeed, the story of Kezia's spectacular rise and fall is in many ways emblematic of the island as a whole during the Revolution, a conflict that served as a horrific wake-up call to a community that had begun to think of itself as the "Nation of Nantucket."

∽

Although Crèvecoeur claimed that Nantucket wives were never "turbulent, of high temper, and difficult to be ruled," Kezia Coffin appears to have been the exception that proves the rule. Whereas tradition tells of Mary Starbuck's routine deference to her much less capable husband during town meetings, Kezia established a tradition of an altogether different sort when, in the words of the Nantucketer George Worth, she reputedly dismissed "a town meeting with all the authority and determination of a Cromwell dispersing an obdurate parliament."

While exemplary wives such as Kezia's sister Judith (mother to Obed Macy) quietly guided and sustained the business interests of their husbands, Kezia was not about to take a backseat to anyone. Her business dealings in London put her in contact with some of the movers and shakers of her time, including none other than her cousin Benjamin Franklin, who in a letter written from London in August of 1765 asked her to remember him "kindly to your husband and daughter, tho' I am unknown to them." Clearly, Kezia was no second fiddle to her spouse (who was fifteen years her senior) when it came to her dealings throughout England and America.

In 1770, she built what was claimed to be "the most regal private mansion" on the island. Located on the west side of Center Street between India and Hussey Streets, it broke with all local traditions of frugality and simplicity, introducing the boldly symmetrical architectural fashion of the mainland to an island still clinging to the lean-to design. And rather than facing it to the south, as was still customary on the island, Kezia took the audacious step of positioning her mansion so that it ostentatiously faced the street.

Although nominally a Quaker, Kezia did not let the religion's strict code of conduct cramp her style. She and her daughter were advised "not to dress so fashionable" by a committee of Friends, and in 1773 she was disowned for purchasing a spinet for her daughter. Providing a revealing glimpse into the dynamics of the Coffin household is the following testimony from Quaker Disciplinary Records: "John Coffin declares he had no hand in bringing the spinet to his house and had forbidden it being used there and was sorry it was even brought into his house." In order to appease the Quakers, of which Kezia's daughter and husband remained members, the spinet was moved to "Esquire Hussey's house," where her daughter continued to play the instrument on the sly.

Kezia broke with another Nantucket tradition when she obtained the services of a Yale-educated lawyer by the name of Phineas Fanning, who was officially sworn in as a "lawful attorney" on Nantucket in March of 1773. This marked the first time in the history of the island that an attorney decided to take up residence on Nantucket. According to one account, Fanning originally came to the island "out of curiosity merely," but after meeting Kezia's only daughter, ultimately married her and settled on the island. However, in 1773, the year Fanning began to practice law on the island, Kezia Coffin's daughter (who was named after her mother) was only fourteen years old. According to another tradition, it was Kezia "Sr." who first convinced Fanning to relocate, inviting him into her household so that she could take advantage of his legal expertise in her various business dealings, specifically using him to draw up a power of attorney that gave her total control over her husband's business interests. In any event, on an island where the courts were avoided at all costs in favor of the time-honored tradition of mediation, Kezia's intimate connection with a lawyer was highly unusual.

But Kezia's flirtation with scandal was not limited to just flashy clothes, palatial homes, and fancy lawyers; she may have also been a drug user. When on Nantucket, Crèvecoeur became well acquainted with Kezia and her circle of friends, which included the physician and sheriff, Dr. Benjamin Tupper, who readily admitted to taking opium. According to Crèvecoeur, "He takes three grains of it every day after breakfast, without the effects of which, he often told me, he was not able to transact any business." Crèvecoeur claimed that this "Asiatic custom . . . prevails here among the women," and certainly, Kezia's many commercial ties would have given her ample opportunity to acquire the drug. Whether or not the more mercurial aspects of her personality can be attributed to an opium addiction, she was a person who thrived on controversy.

If Kezia seems to have been a character straight out of Tom Wolfe's *Bonfire of the Vanities*, Nantucket in the years prior to the Revolution had some undeniable similarities to the "good times" of the 1980s. While the rest of New England suffered through the series of economic disasters that made the Revolution an inevitability, Nantucket experienced thirty years of steady growth, with its most dramatic period of expansion occurring between 1770 and 1775. By this time the Nantucket whale fishery had reached the west coast of Africa and the distant Falkland Islands, annually sending out 150 vessels while employing more than 2,000 seamen.

One of the main reasons Nantucket had succeeded where others had failed was that almost every segment of the community was involved, in one way or another, in the whale fishery. Even if a voyage was unsuccessful, it had at least kept a significant portion of the population employed. And since virtually all Nantucketers felt obliged to invest whatever they had available in the whale fishery (prompting Crèvecoeur to comment, "the greatest part of their property is floating on the sea"), this "mode of conducting the business" had the potential, when things went well, of spreading the wealth throughout the community.

But all was not sweetness and light on Nantucket during this era. Human nature being what it is, the urge to make a profit often got in the way of Christian charity and familial good will; there was also a fair amount of envy directed toward those who began quietly and not-so-quietly to amass fortunes. In 1764 Sylvanus Hussey complained that the island's leading firm of Joseph Rotch (pronounced "Roach") and Sons would "break through all the solemn ties of nature where it grates with interest." During that same year, William Rotch, the eldest son of the company's founder and a devout Quaker, informed a candle manufacturer "that all the friendship that can be expected in trade is to let your friend have a thing at the same price that others would give for it." The message was clear: Even on an island where almost everyone was related in some way or another, nothing got in the way of business.

But if Nantucket whaling merchants had what one historian has called a "combative hierarchy" among themselves, they were even more difficult to deal with if you happened to be a merchant from elsewhere in New England. Since they were involved in virtually all aspects of the fishery—from harpooning the whale to manufacturing candles—Nantucket whaling merchants were in a position to insist upon their own terms, especially since they had a direct trade link with London. One Boston merchant warned a counterpart in Newport, "'tis vain to attempt to tie [the Nantucket men] down to any measures they do not like."

It was a no-holds-barred, dog-eat-dog environment in which someone of Kezia Coffin's temperament apparently thrived. It was also an environment in which it was easy to develop more than a few enemies—both on and off island. Complicating the picture was the inexorable approach of the Revolution, a conflict in which the high-flying island of Nantucket had absolutely no interest. Indeed, it was hardly accidental that two of the three ships in the Boston Tea Party were owned by Rotch and Sons, whose Counting House at the foot of Main Street was built in the midst of this pre-Revolutionary boom in 1772.

Rather than attempt to temper some of the hostility they had engendered over the years, Nantucketers continued to press for every possible advantage, even as the colonies teetered on the edge of rebellion. During the winter of 1775 the island petitioned for and won an exemption from the Restraining Act that dramatically curtailed fishing elsewhere in the region. When the bubble burst that spring with skirmishes in Lexington and Concord, Nantucket was in no position to expect any favors from the Massachusetts Provincial Congress, which ordered a boycott on all trade with the island. Although this was later amended, Nantucketers continued to pay the price for years of willful autonomy from the region.

As far as the rest of America was concerned, Nantucket was an island of British sympathizers. The governor of Connecticut advised all those Nantucketers who were for the rebellion to remove to the mainland and "leave the rest to be supported by their good friends the [British] administration." In Philadelphia a Nantucket coasting vessel was refused a shipment of flour; the reason given: "You are all Tories at Nantucket." In July of 1775, a Cape Codder wrote to the Continental authorities in Watertown concerning "particulars I have heard about Nantucket," specifically mentioning 70 to 100 "Boston people (supposed to be Tories mostly) [who] arrived there last week." According to the informant, "Many of said inhabitants were against their landing, but the sages of the Friends [i.e., William Rotch] overruled, observing they were rich and would be an advantage to the island."

Rather than admitting that his own notoriously hard-nosed business practices may have contributed to some of the ill feeling directed toward the island, William Rotch chose to see it in terms of religious persecution. According to Rotch, Nantucket had been "marked out by this part of the country for destruction" largely because of its pacifist Quaker beliefs. While Rotch used his religion as a smoke screen (even as his brother secretly planned a new, London-oriented whaling operation on the Falkland Islands), Kezia Coffin seems to have been more open about her Tory inclinations. Her daughter began keeping a journal in 1775, and the sixteen-year-old diarist (who refers to her parents as "Dadda" and "my ever-to-be-honored Mama") recorded the events of the mounting crisis from a distinct point of view. When a "little vessel" with 100 Continental soldiers arrived on Nantucket in May of 1775, she was unimpressed with their fanfare: "They marched off the wharf with drums beating, fifes playing and colors flying. . . . God save George the King!" A few days later "these rebellious fellows" confiscated "50 odd whaleboats" that would ultimately see service on Lake Champlain as part of Benedict Arnold's ill-fated attempt to seize Canada.

Despite the arrival of the refugees from Boston, it soon became apparent that the island was not going to be any kind of haven during the war. Both British and American privateers had no qualms about taking Nantucket whalers and coasting vessels, making it virtually impossible to carry on the whale fishery as hundreds of island seamen languished in the British prison hulks in New York and Newport.

With no other means of support and with food in increasingly short supply, many Nantucketers turned to farming. To encourage this new endeavor, the town proprietors laid out large tracts of land in the southeastern part of the island as well as in Squam and Pocomo (pronounced "POCK-ah-ma"). Others took up fishing. Two saltworks were started on Brant Point and Polpis to provide a preservative for the fish, but the foggy Nantucket weather was too humid to allow adequate amounts of salt to be extracted. With firewood becoming next-to-nonexistent on the island, peat was dug as a substitute.

In the early years of the war, partly because several islanders were able to maintain a profitable trade route with the West Indies, things were better on Nantucket than elsewhere in New England, where the depredations of soldiers left several towns in flames. Other, more secretive means of conveying goods to the island were also employed. According to Obed Macy, who grew up during the Revolution, it was not uncommon for islanders to set out for "Connecticut and elsewhere" in small open boats "built of frail materials, and purposely made weak in order that, by degrees of pliability, they might pass more easily through the water." It was common practice to set out in these "fast sailing" boats at night and during a storm so as to reduce the chances of capture.

Needless to say, it was a dangerous business, and one in which Kezia Coffin, with the aid of her lawyer and future son-in-law Phineas Fanning, participated. In her daughter's journal there are repeated references to Fanning's smuggling adventures. On October 9, 1775, he sailed from Shelter Island, New York, to Nantucket in "the quickest passage ever made," leaving under the cover of darkness and reaching Nantucket just after midnight of the next day. According to the younger Kezia, "by stealth they took more in than they were allowed," bringing "60 or 70 weight of butter, as much cheese, one cow (dead), 2 bbls. cider, 3 bushels quinces, several bushels of apples, dried cherries, pears, apples, etc., and one deer skin." In December Fanning was at it again, arriving with a new load of provisions "after going through everything but death." Three days later, Kezia records, "Our house has been like a tavern, people coming after provisions."

With prices at an all-time high, the profit to be made by this dangerous trade was huge, and during the summer of 1776 Kezia had a barn built on property she and her husband owned in Quaise, several miles up the harbor from town; by September of the following year—during which her daughter and Fanning were married—a new country estate was built on this same Quaise location, employing five carpenters. Although some Nantucket historians have claimed that there is no evidence Kezia was ever a smuggler, tradition states that this new residence was built with the expressed purpose of carrying on her illegal trade, complete with a beach-side tunnel leading to an underground storage area.

Indeed, it is difficult to imagine why anyone would even consider building a new and palatial home two years into the Revolution (a time when virtually everyone else on the island was suffering devastating financial reversals), unless the house had a direct relationship to his or her ability to turn a profit. Certainly the location of Kezia's new home was ideally suited for smuggling, removed as it was from town and yet within the shelter of Coatue. At the thinnest section of this barrier beach (which Kezia, Jr., refers to as "Courteau"), between fourth and fifth point, there was a "haul-over place" where, according to Kezia's diary, a boat could "put immediately over" to Quaise. Thus, it was possible to reach the Coffins' Quaise residence without passing near Brant Point.

Although most local historians have been quick to attribute all talk of secret tunnels and subterranean warehouses to the overwrought imaginings of an off-island novelist, it must be remembered that during the year of its publication, Nantucketers insisted that *Miriam Coffin* was "faithfully consistent with matters of fact occurrences." At the close of the nineteenth century, Eliza Mitchell, an ancient Nantucketer who had known the famed Siasconset genealogist and historian Benjamin Franklin Folger, recorded Folger's claim that he had actually seen Coffin's tunnel and "storage place" in the early years of the century. According to Folger, "In the center I could stand nearly straight. All was time-worn and very much decayed, but I saw what I needed to convince me [that Kezia Coffin] was a very capable woman but lacking very much in principle."

This was, apparently, the feeling of a growing number of Nantucketers as conditions on the island went from bad to worse during the Revolution. Continental and British privateers, known as "shaving mills," increasingly used the harbor as a battleground, firing upon each other, looting and burning island ships, and generally terrorizing the local populace.

Then in the fall of 1779 Kezia Coffin along with Dr. Benjamin Tupper, William Rotch, Timothy Folger, and Samuel Starbuck were accused of treason for assisting the British in ransacking the warehouse of a fellow Nantucketer by the name of Thomas Jenkins.

It would not be until the following spring that these five, along with fifteen witnesses, were able to travel to Watertown for the trial. In December, what became known as the "Hard Winter" set in. The cold was so severe that ice extended out into the Sound as far as the eye could see, cutting off all contact with the mainland. Food was so scarce that many were reduced to eating sea gulls. Due to the incredible thickness of the ice, fishing was next to impossible, as was digging peat. The cold had one benefit, however. Since the harbor was frozen solid, it was now possible to drive horse-drawn calashes directly to the Coskata section of the island, a normally inaccessible area where there were still some gnarled juniper and oak trees. As many as fifty to sixty calashes began traveling to Coskata on a daily basis, an eighteen-mile round trip past Kezia's Quaise estate. Undoubtedly the subject of its notorious owner was brought up more than once in the conversations of the wood gatherers.

Although Kezia and the four others accused of treason were ultimately acquitted of the charges that spring, the trial seems to have marked the beginning of Kezia Coffin's decline. In October of 1782, she almost drowned in Hyannis Harbor while attempting to board a sloop bound for Nantucket; in March of the following year, her daughter recorded that "my father alias mother" was accused of stealing a vessel from the Continental forces. With Fanning's power of attorney in hand, Kezia went to New York "to answer to the case." In April of that year, news of peace reached the island, and Kezia, Jr., ruefully noted, "Everything the Rebels can wish allowed them." That November her mother finally returned from New York "unsuccessful in laws."

Later in the month, two merchants from Newport successfully sued for 700 pounds that, according to the diarist, "my Mother had taken up to carry on business for that devilish McCauly Company in New York." The Coffins—like so many loyalists—were bankrupt.

On December 27th, the sheriff and several men arrived at the Coffins' house on Center Street, but Kezia, who had just turned sixty, refused to leave her chair, forcing them to carry her, chair and all, out into the street. Her husband put up no resistance, however, as the sheriff and his men remained in the house "sitting around the front room fire"—much to the anger of Kezia's daughter, who wrote:

> *No family, I am certain was ever treated as ours are and have been. I would not wish to enjoy one six pence of my father's estate if he owes money, but to have things taken hold of and torn away in the manner they are, is more than flesh and blood can or ought to bear. I am fearful that my beloved parents will lie in the street, although I believe it is the wish of many, but grant their wishes may be abortive!*

Just how ugly things had become among the once mighty Nantucket whale merchants is indicated by the venom the diarist directed toward Timothy Folger, a fellow Tory who had also been accused of treason: "O! that Demon of a Timothy Folger, he was the first cause of all our trouble. I pray that I may seek vengeance all the days of my life."

But the backstabbing did not stop there. A year later, in 1784, Kezia sailed for Halifax, Nova Scotia, in hopes of getting restitution from the British government for her losses during the war. A year later she was still in Halifax, penniless and in debtor's prison, without "chair, table, nor other furniture in her cell." Although Timothy Folger and Paul Starbuck were also in

Nova Scotia (see Chapter 13), they did not lift a finger to help their island "cousin." In fact, according to Kezia, Jr., "It was by Folger's and Starbuck's means she was imprisoned, they telling all the lies they could invent to her prejudice."

A woman in a man's world, Kezia was outside the "old boy" network that would sustain the likes of William Rotch and Timothy Folger after the conclusion of the Revolution. Just as much of New England had watched Nantucket's colonial rise with a mixture of envy and contempt and then taken a wicked delight in its catastrophic fall during the Revolution, so had it been "the wish of many" on Nantucket that this uncompromising female get her just deserts. Instead of the questionable legality of her trade practices, Kezia's true crime, as far as the Nantucketers were concerned, was being a woman. In *Miriam Coffin* Hart echoes the island's verdict when he has Miriam's husband issue this final chastisement to his over-reaching spouse: "Get thee gone to thy kitchen, where it is fitting thou should'st preside:— Go—go to thy kitchen, woman, and do thou never meddle with men's affairs more!"

If, as Crèvecoeur pointed out, the whale fishery had given Nantucket wives added responsibilities and "ripened their judgment," there was another part of their job description: never be "turbulent, of high temper, and difficult to be ruled." To act as Kezia had done was to run the risk, in Crèvecoeur's words, of "subverting the principles of their society by altering its ancient rules." Instead of acting as a dutiful spouse in a provincial backwater, Kezia had led her life as a wheeler-dealer at the center of a vast and truly cosmopolitan commercial network. Unfortunately the times, and her gender, were not on her side.

Although Hart's Miriam Coffin returns to her kitchen, the real Kezia seems to have remained unrepentant to the very end. After her sufferings in Nova Scotia, Kezia eventually returned to Nantucket but never gave up hope of receiving some form of redress, instructing her son-in-law, "I want thee to keep this in court as long as I live." Tradition has it that she insisted on wearing black as a public expression of her grief over the outcome of the Revolution. And, contrary to another tradition, she proved surprisingly successful in court, winning several decisions against islanders who had taken control of her property, both in Quaise and in town, after her husband's death.

In March of 1798, she went to court in the afternoon before returning to her rented house on Main Street. About dusk she marched up the front stairs in her usual, purposeful manner and then apparently suffered a stroke and fell backwards down the staircase. After remaining in a coma for several days, she died, almost exactly a decade after her husband. Eight months later, Phineas Fanning would follow her to the grave, leaving his wife five months pregnant.

For the Coffins and Fannings—as was true for many others throughout Nantucket and the rest of colonial America— the War for Independence was as much the end as it was the beginning of a way of life. No matter how hard the Nantucketers eventually worked to re-create their pre-Revolutionary prosperity, it would never be quite the same.

CHAPTER 13

The "Removals": From Jethro Coffin to William Rotch

NANTUCKET ISLAND and its whaling life were not for everyone. Although the island's economy continued to grow throughout the first seventy-five years of the eighteenth century, Nantucket lost as many people as it kept. Of course, this was happening all over New England as individuals and families headed west, south, and even north in search of new opportunities. But there was something different about the way Nantucketers went about the business of "moving on."

Having grown up on a tiny island where most of the inhabitants not only were related by birth but also shared the same profession and religious beliefs, Nantucketers had a common bond that few other communities in America could match. When opportunities presented themselves on the mainland or things got so bad on the island that they decided to leave, Nantucketers tended to relocate in groups. Crèvecoeur compared their migration pattern to bees moving "in regular and connected swarms."

Certainly the Quakers' distinction between themselves and the "world's people" encouraged a certain insularity. But it also had to do with their place of birth, where for more than a century Nantucketers had been nurturing a sense of themselves as a distinct culture, especially when it came to the neighboring Cape and islands. They not only had a unique accent (a Nantucketer said "bah" [for bar] while a Vineyarder said "ba*er*"), they also considered themselves more refined and cosmopolitan, an inevitable result of the national and international scope of the whale fishery. For example, Kezia Coffin Fanning's diary has this entry: "One Allen of the Vineyard dined here. Very polite for the Vineyard." The derogatory term of "Coof," which ultimately came to describe anyone unlucky enough to be born off island, was originally applied to Cape Codders.

Given this sense of themselves as a people apart, it is not surprising that when Nantucketers found themselves in a new location and among a different people, they remained fiercely protective of their traditional way of life, a clannishness that sometimes manifested itself in curious ways. Writing from Philadelphia in 1789, Benjamin Franklin commented on his experience with two Nantucket "cousins": "They are wonderfully shy. But I admire their honest plainness of speech. About a year ago I invited two of them to dine with me. Their answer was, that they would, if they could not do better. I suppose they did better, for I never saw them afterwards. . . ."

Although the Revolution would prompt many Nantucketers to leave their home, the island had already been sending out its swarms for quite some time. Take, for example, Jethro and Mary Coffin, the couple whose marriage in 1686 helped to heal the injuries inflicted by the Half-Share Revolt. After living in the "Oldest House" for more than twenty years, Jethro and Mary sold out and moved to what is now known as Mendon, Massachusetts. In 1708, the year of their "removal," Jethro was forty-five; Mary was thirty-eight; their six surviving children had all been born on Nantucket, where whaling was just beginning to take off. Accompanying them were several other Nantucket families, including that of John Gardner, eldest son of the famous leader of the Revolt. Why were these upstanding members of the community willing to begin it all over again in an undeveloped backwater?

Family connections were partly responsible. Jethro's father

Peter Coffin (eldest son to Tristram) had been awarded the land back in 1672 for delivering a shipload of masts to the British government, and in 1713 he deeded the grant to Jethro. Just as the original settlement of Nantucket had provided Peter with a market for his lumber, market forces seem to have determined the relocation of Jethro to Mendon, where many of the resources that were either unavailable or in short supply on Nantucket existed in abundance. In the many swamps in the area grew the white cedar needed for whaleboats; there were also rivers to power sawmills; iron ore with which to forge whaling equipment; and a direct water route to transport the goods back to the island. In short, Coffin and his cohorts became "peripheral suppliers," providing materials that were custom-made for the fledgling whale fishery.

The Mendonites had more than just a commercial tie to the island. Their social and family life still revolved around their place of origin. Marriages tended to be either among themselves or with Nantucketers. And when in 1726 they lost their leader, Jethro Coffin, in a "Great Sickness," the pull of their original home proved too strong, and the community disbanded, with most of the Coffins and Gardners returning that same year to Nantucket.

This was a pattern that would repeat itself more than once. In 1761, in response to an invitation from the British government, forty-eight families (thirty-five from Nantucket and thirteen from Cape Cod) set sail for Nova Scotia's Cape Sable in Barrington township. As soon as they arrived in Nova Scotia, the Nantucketers took steps to insure the integrity of their community. A "dividing line" was drawn across the settlement, with all Nantucketers to the south and the Cape Codders to the north. Although perfectly proficient at hunting whales, the Nantucketers—from an island where the largest wild animal was the Norway rat—had no experience hunting game, and many of them nearly starved to death during their first winter on Cape Sable, in part because they "knew little of woodcraft," according to a local doctor. The next spring, ten families returned to the island. Although the community reached a high of 376 people in 1767, the settlement began to collapse in the next decade as family after family returned to Nantucket.

About this same time, yet another "swarm" headed out from Nantucket, but in an entirely different direction—south, to New Garden (now Guilford), North Carolina, in today's Greensboro area. Rather than the British government, it appears that the Quakers were the original promoters of this new settlement, with no less than five North Carolinian ministers preaching on the island in the years prior to the first migration. Just how organized this initial removal was is indicated by an entry in Peleg Folger's journal:

> *28th of the 4th mo. 1771. This day embarked in order to settle in New Garden in North Carolina: John Macy and his family, Reuben Bunker, Jr., and his family, Daniel Worth and his family, Libri Coffin and his family, Gayer Starbuck and his family. Passengers in order to view the country: David Macy, William Coffin, Daniel Gardner, William Barnard, Stephen Macy, and Jethro Gardner. Prince Gardner, Master; Reuben Barnard, Mate.*

Crèvecoeur arrived on the island a year or so after this first boatload of emigrants had left (in fact, it may have been an earlier visit to New Garden that first inspired him to travel to Nantucket). According to Crèvecoeur, in 1766 the Nantucketers purchased a large tract of land within forty miles of the "spring heads" of the Deep River in North Carolina where "the richness of the soil, etc., made them cheerfully quit an island on which there was no longer any room for them." It may not have been just a matter of space. With the threat of revolution looming ever larger, many of these Nantucketers undoubtedly recognized that an island was no place to be in the middle of a war.

Unlike the earlier migration to Nova Scotia, this Nantucket outpost flourished, largely because of the preexisting support system of Quakerism. The procedure was this: When a Nantucketer decided to relocate, he or she first obtained official certification for "removal" from the Nantucket Meeting—a document that attested to his or her good financial as well as spiritual standing in the community—for presentation to the meeting in New Garden. From 1771 to 1775 there were forty-one certificates recorded from Nantucket. Nantucketers removing to New Garden were thus assured that no matter how different their lives as inland farmers were going to be, there was at least one constant they could count on.

One analysis of Quaker records from this region in North Carolina found more than 600 people of Nantucket birth or lineage, a breakdown of which shows a remarkably representative cross-section of Nantucket first families: 175 Macys, 104 Coffins, 66 Starbucks, 65 Swains, 55 Gardners, 39 Worths, 36 Husseys, 25 Barnards, 18 Bunkers, and 1 Folger. In 1773, New Garden–transplants William and Phebe Stanton wrote to Phebe's father, Zaccheus Macy on Nantucket. After talking about the scarcity of salt and iron; the low price of molasses, flour, and wood; the productivity of their farm; and the progress of the three children born since their removal, they wrote: "Our children remember their love to their grandfather & grandmother & their relations & folks of Nantucket every day & them that was born here talk of Nantucket as much as them that was born there and frequently talk of going there to see grandfather and grandmother."

After the Revolution, this group of Quaker Nantucketers, becoming increasingly uncomfortable with the ubiquity of slavery in the South, began to emigrate once again, this time to the west into Indiana and Ohio. Even though they were now becoming second- and even third-generation mainlanders, they did not forget their origins, looking back with pride to the island that they still considered to be the "Nation of Nantucket." Economy, Indiana, was first called Nantucket by its original settlers from North Carolina and features a "Tucket Burying Ground" full of Barnards, Coffins, Macys, Swains, and Starbucks. In 1819 a Friends Meeting in Salem, Indiana, was organized in which its members vowed "to cherish the memory and emulate the example of the pioneers of Nantucket who established and maintained a commonwealth when there was no other in New England."

Crèvecoeur recognized that this concept of the island as a "commonwealth" was as much a state of mind as it was a function of the physical place on which the Nantucketers lived. Before the conclusion of the Revolution, he correctly predicted that if they were one day "driven from this spot, . . . they might perhaps be allowed to transport themselves in their own vessels to some other spot or island, which they would soon fertilize by the same means with which they have fertilized this."

Soon after the end of hostilities, with the once great Nantucket whaling fleet in ruins, this prophecy became a reality when a band of eighteen Nantucket families relocated to Hudson, New York, more than 100 miles up the Hudson River. Here, on a bay safely removed from the threat of privateers, they reassembled houses that had been taken apart and shipped in pieces from the island. By 1786 there were four wharves, several warehouses, a ropewalk, sail loft, candle factory, and 150 dwellings (many of them lean-tos with roof walks)—all based on the Nantucket model. In the first twenty years of its existence, this offshoot community grew to the point that it temporarily outranked Nantucket as a whaling port. It is reported that in 1802, fifteen vessels a day cleared from Hudson, with the port becoming so crowded that it was possible to walk across the bay on the decks of waiting vessels. According to one Hudson resident writing in 1928, whose great-grandmother had been born on the island, "The news at Nantucket . . . was always a subject of keen interest" among Hudson residents.

As we have seen, many of Nantucket's most ambitious whaling merchants were avowed Tories. The continued strength of their old loyalties combined with the loss of London as a market (not surprisingly, Britain imposed a hefty duty on American whale oil) led several influential members of the community to propose in 1785 that the island remain an independent or "neutral" state. Needless to say, Massachusetts authorities took a rather dim view of this rather extraordinary proposal. So in 1786 Timothy Folger and Samuel Starbuck led a group of Nantucket loyalists to Dartmouth, Nova Scotia. By that summer, a total of forty families had removed to Dartmouth, initiating a whale fishery that would ultimately employ 150 seamen and a total of twenty-two vessels. How big this fishery might have become will never be known. As early as April of 1786, the British government, which had hopes of capitalizing on Nantucket's misfortunes by establishing a whaling monopoly, decided that the last thing it needed was another colonial whaling port to compete against. Rather than setting up a rival Nantucket outpost, the British wanted to divide and conquer the Nation of Nantucket by luring its whalemen directly to English-owned whalers. So, only a few months into its settlement, the Dartmouth enclave (which would continue on for a number of years despite the lack of support) had the plug pulled out by the British government.

Another leading Nantucketer, William Rotch, attempted to convince the British government that it should help finance his relocation to England, where he, too, proposed to create a transplanted microcosm of Nantucket. However, the London whaling merchants once again applied pressure on their political leaders, insisting that Britain had no need of Rotch. So the savvy Quaker merchant took his Nantucket "genius" to—of all places—Dunkirk, France. Here was the ultimate test case: a foreign culture on the other side of the Atlantic. If the Nantucketers could make it work here, they could make it work anywhere.

With the help of bounties on oil and some other inducements, Rotch was able to get a sizeable fleet of twenty vessels up and running by 1789, although only nine Nantucket families actually relocated to Dunkirk. The settlement was less of a community than a marketing ploy, a way for Rotch to funnel Nantucket oil into the European market. As far as he was concerned, what was then known as the "Southern Whale Fishery" was an international business that no single nation (unless, of course, you were talking about the Nation of Nantucket) could call its own. In a letter to Samuel Rodman he rather smugly confided, "I wish our great [states] men may consider they have not sufficient power to overturn us in this branch. . . ." Although Rotch's overseas ventures seem to have been initially motivated by a genuine desire to help his native island, his conduct of the Dunkirk fishery made it increasingly clear where his true loyalties lay. According to the Rhode Island whaling merchant Moses Brown, Rotch had allowed "the profits of so gilded and flattering prospects . . . overbalance the ties of country, friends, etc."

Galled by Rotch's success in France, the English government finally relented when they were presented with yet another plan to initiate a new Nantucket whaling colony on British soil. In 1790, Lord Charles Greville, nephew of Sir William Hamilton, was empowered by Parliament to begin developing a Welsh harbor known as Milford Haven into a whaling port. To drum up interest, Greville immediately sent an emissary to both Nantucket and Dartmouth. Unlike the London whale fishery, where seamen received wages, the Milford Haven fishery would be based on the American lay system. At one point, Greville explicitly stated his three aims in establishing a whaling port in Milford Haven: "1. To cut up both French and Colonial competition in the Whale Fishery. 2nd. To separate the detached Nantucketers from the Nantucketers remaining in America. The 3rd object is personal to me, vizt.—To give permanency to my establishment by a further addition of original whalers, either by general invitation or by a partial one."

Whether they were in Nova Scotia, Dunkirk, or still based on their native island, the Nantucket whalemen were what Greville was after, but he was only partially successful in achieving his aims. In Dartmouth both Starbuck and Folger agreed to make the switch, but the two merchants seem to have alienated many of their fellow Nova Scotian Nantucketers by negotiating private pensions for themselves (of 150 pounds per year) when they were supposedly negotiating for the colony as a whole. Feeling against Starbuck ran so high that the Nantucket Monthly Meeting (which maintained jurisdiction in Dartmouth) refused to grant him a removal certificate. Writing from Milford Haven in 1794, he complained of his "grievous hurt" in respect to the accusations. Folger's family does not seem to have been thrilled by the move either. Timothy's wife would record in her diary, "I step'd my feet on Welsh land and a grievous day it was to me."

Despite the controversy, Folger and Starbuck were soon sending out whalers from a port that was being designed and built to their specifications. Meanwhile, back in Dunkirk, William Rotch was in the midst of the French Revolution—certainly an ironic fate for the Quaker pacifist who had voyaged across the Atlantic in search of an alternative to his own revolution-ravaged island. In a letter he admitted that "I never expected to be in this midst of a second Revolution," and in 1794 he would finally return to Nantucket when war erupted between France and England. His son Benjamin went to Milford Haven, where he soon became the port's leading whaling merchant.

Although Milford Haven enjoyed its share of prosperity, the War of 1812 had a devastating effect on the whale fishery. Benjamin Rotch would go bankrupt; back in America, even the once booming port of Hudson, New York, would fall into a disastrous decline. On Nantucket, the war provoked yet another wave of migration as islanders left for the Kennebec River area in Maine (a favorite destination for Nantucketers even before the Revolution) and the west, with a raft of Quaker removal certificates being issued to the "Miami Monthly Meeting, State of Ohio." In 1811, Micajah Coffin wrote Walter Folger, Jr. (then in Boston), concerning "our Friends" who had recently left for Ohio. After quoting extensively from an enthusiastic letter written by Phebe Myrick, "who left this place almost broken hearted and her eyes full of tears," Coffin reported: "Such an account from the woman that left this place with so great reluctance appears to begin to work on many minds. . . . I begin to be apprehensive of being deserted by the major part of the middling class of townsmen with a great many of the more wealthy."

Coffin's fears were well-founded. The lure of the American West was so strong that even transplanted Nantucketers from as far away as Milford Haven were tempted by the promise of yet another new beginning. On September 25, 1818, a son of the bankrupt Benjamin Rotch wrote to his friend Gayer Starbuck, urging him to leave Wales and join him in Princeton, Indiana, where he was then living in his Nantucket uncle's cabin on the edge of a vast, lush prairie: "I wish a few of my industrious neighbors could find themselves suddenly translated from Milford to the prairie or, in other words, from a scanty and hardly earned pittance to a comfortable independent trade—for in this country obsequiousness makes no part of a man's stock in trade. . . . Every day I have reason to wish you were here." He may have taken a round-about route, but this removal was now back amid his Nantucket brethren, pushing west across the American heartland.

Although by this time Hudson, Dartmouth, Dunkirk, and Milford Haven had all fallen by the wayside, there was one Nantucket microcosm yet to be reckoned with. A year after returning to his native island, William Rotch, finding that his decade spent abroad had not exactly endeared him to the local populace, decided to relocate once again. This time he did not have to travel far—to what was then known as Bedford, Massachusetts, where in 1763 his father Joseph Rotch had started a small settlement on the mouth of the Acushnet River.

The "palmy days" to come would launch both New Bedford and what Melville called the "great original," Nantucket, on yet another roller coaster ride of prosperity. But as we shall see, the Nantucket of the nineteenth century would have less and less in common with the "great original" she had once been.

CHAPTER 14

A "Nest of Love" No Longer:
William Coffin and the Bank, Commons,
and School Wars

O N AN ISLAND OF Quaker whalemen, William Coffin marched to the beat of a different drummer. A self-described wig-maker and hair-draper, not to mention a Congregationalist, he was also Nantucket's first U.S. Postmaster. But more than anything else, it was Coffin's political affiliation that set him apart from the Quaker-whaling mainstream. Because on Nantucket, as was true throughout America in the years after the Revolution, party politics had begun to divide the people into two bitterly feuding camps.

On one side were the Federalists: generally well-to-do merchants and landowners who revered John Adams and whose international sympathies were with Britain. Most of Nantucket's modest Federalist population were either Congregationalists or, in Coffin's words, "Nothingarians." On the other side were the Democrats, otherwise known as Jeffersonians, Republicans, or, to their enemies, Jacobins. The Democrats were also the Quaker party on Nantucket, and in keeping with their high regard for Thomas Jefferson, their international loyalties lay with France, strengthened in many instances through service on Rotch whalers out of Dunkirk.

As an outspoken Federalist, William Coffin seems to have enjoyed (in the beginning at least) his role as an outsider. In a letter written in 1793 to a friend in Virginia, the thirty-seven-year-old Coffin mocked the calculated simplicity of the island's

Quaker merchants as well as their fondness for French revolutionary rhetoric: "[M]any of the owners themselves work in making casks in the absence of their ships, and on their return put on their frock and trousers, cart and cooper their own oil. If a Sans Culotte Frenchman was here, he would exclaim 'Ça Ira, Ça Ira—Liberté and Egalité en Perfection.'"

Whether or not he was whistling in the dark, William Coffin does not seem to have realized the seriousness of the growing rift between Federalists and Democrats on Nantucket, a "contention" that would ultimately "rage with pestilential fury" throughout the community, threatening to ruin the lives of not only Coffin but many of his friends. As with most deep-seated differences, it involved something more than mere matters of political opinion. Hidden beneath the Federalist-Democrat overlay was a battle over the very heart and soul of the island: Whether or not Quakerism would remain the dominant religious and social force on Nantucket in the century to come.

Prior to the Revolution, the Society of Friends had undergone a tightening of its Discipline, a process that turned into an outright purge during the war, when dozens of young men were disowned for sailing on privateers. Even after the war, the winnowing process continued as disownments were handed out to those who dared to inoculate themselves against small pox, join the Masons, wear fashionable clothes, update their hairstyles, attend dances or Congregational weddings, apprentice their children to non-Quakers, and, of course, marry outside the Friends.

By 1793, the religion that had once functioned as a much needed cohesive force was in danger of becoming spiritually and socially irrelevant. Although it still controlled most of the wealth and power on the island (accounting for approximately two-thirds of the population), the Quaker establishment found itself increasingly challenged by a new generation of Nantucketers who had little regard for the old way of doing things. Instead of relying upon the island's longstanding tradition of mediation, many of these men, with names like Coffin and Gardner (as opposed to Macy and Starbuck), often utilized an array of Kezia-like legal tactics to achieve their ends. They also had an inordinate amount of political clout (given their minority status on the island) since the Federalists were the ruling party throughout the rest of Massachusetts.

Among this group it is hard to conceive of a man whom the Quakers would have viewed with more suspicion than William Coffin—a Congregationalist, Federalist, and Mason who attended to people's vanity on a daily basis in his barbershop on Main Street. Even more alarming was his interest in progressive social reforms; indeed, Coffin was known to sermonize on the need for a free public school system on Nantucket—a horrifying prospect to a tight-fisted Quaker community that had chosen to ignore Massachusetts educational laws for more than a century.

As a portrait painted when he was an old man makes clear, William Coffin was no pushover. With a craggy brow, Karl Malden nose, and protruding jaw, he was as tough and hardbitten as any Quaker sea captain. But Coffin was no captain and he certainly was no Quaker. Here was just the man to drag Nantucket, kicking and screaming, into the nineteenth century.

~

On a foggy Saturday night in June, 1795, three men, using keys they had manufactured out of pewter spoons, broke into the newly opened Nantucket Bank on Main Street. It was exhausting, back-breaking work, but in a few hours they had cleaned out the vault of more than $20,000 in gold coins, lugging the clinking sacks through the black, unlit streets of town to a sloop tied up at the waterfront. By the time the break-in was discovered on Monday, the thieves were long gone.

A community that prided itself on the fact that most homes had no door locks was ill-equipped to deal with a robbery of this magnitude. (When told about the bank robbery, a Nantucketer in Hudson joked that "they must have left their latch string outside.") Although the robbery had occurred during the sheep shearing festival—an annual event that flooded the island with "strangers"—most Nantucketers were either unwilling or unable to believe that someone from the world beyond their own island could have stolen the money. And with no real evidence, each individual's opinion on the bank robbery became a litmus test for his or her political, religious, and personal loyalties as townspeople continued to "throng the streets" for days, speculating about who had stolen the money.

On July 9th, Joseph Chase, the bank's president, met with William Coffin, a fellow board member of the bank, at the lower section of town square. They had much to discuss as they strolled toward Old North Wharf. The first suspect to emerge from Chase's investigation into the robbery was the bank's cashier, Randall Rice, a Rhode Islander who had married a local girl and, besides working for the bank, owned and operated a slaughterhouse while also doing some legal work on the side. Rice had initially come under suspicion when Walter Folger, Sr. (a leading candle manufacturer, amateur phrenologist, and Democrat), claimed that Rice, a Federalist, "looked guilty." Now, as the two bank directors walked along the waterfront, Coffin was hopeful that Chase and his investigators had come up with something more substantial. He was to be rudely disappointed.

Not far from Rice's slaughterhouse at the foot of Old North Wharf, Chase turned to Coffin and said, "You are pointed out by Stafford, the conjuror, and by God I think you guilty." Dumbfounded, Coffin was initially at a loss to respond to the charge. But as he began to deny all connection with the robbery, it soon became clear that Chase had already made up his mind.

By August the president had consulted a Providence astrologer who described one of the four people who robbed the bank as "a quarrelsome fellow, a big bony man with rough face and sandy hair." This, Chase and the Democrat bank directors agreed, was William Coffin.

Although it was not much consolation, William Coffin was not alone. His best friend, Albert Gardner, a merchant and coasting captain (not to mention a Federalist), was also accused of taking part in the robbery. Rumor had it that Coffin and Gardner had planned to use the money to corner the whale oil market on Nantucket. The testimonies of astrologers and phrenologists were bolstered by a prostitute and a village idiot who claimed to have seen Rice, Coffin, Gardner, and assorted others at the scene of the crime. That the witnesses later recanted their testimonies did little to alter the perception that Coffin and company were guilty.

The Quaker Silvanus Macy (brother of Obed and grandfather of the future founder of Macy's department store) soon distinguished himself as the most calculating and underhanded of the bank directors. Throughout this period he corresponded regularly with William Rotch in New Bedford, keeping him up to date on the latest in the scandal and often seeking his advice, particularly when it came to Coffin and Gardner. Although Nantucket's original powerbase of Quaker whaling merchants was now scattered, it was still a force to be reckoned with.

At one point Macy offered one Henry Purrington $3,000 if he would stick by an earlier claim that not only Coffin, Gardner, and Rice but also Samuel Barker and Jethro Hussey were involved in the robbery. Hearing of Macy's dealings, Coffin accused him of being "a lying villain, a scandalous infamous felon," after which the pious Quaker complained to Rotch, "I am sure I ought to be above his slandering me with impunity."

Even after Purrington reported the bribe attempt to the

bank directors, Macy remained part of the investigation. In September, Coffin insisted that Macy come forward with whatever evidence he had. Macy replied that he needed a few more months to assemble his case; in December, Coffin appealed to what he recognized as the only real authority on the island—the Quaker meeting. In a carefully worded note, he explained that he was "ready to take any reasonable step although I . . . much fear his only aim is procrastination." There is no evidence that the Quakers (or Silvanus Macy) made any attempt to respond.

Certainly Coffin's impulsive nature made him an easy target, especially in a community in which public expressions of emotion were taboo. And as the pressures on him began to mount, Coffin seems to have had an increasingly difficult time controlling himself, becoming a kind of raging bull in a China shop of stolid Quakers. In the fall of 1795, he had an unfortunate run-in with the elderly Nathaniel Coffin. According to a letter Nathaniel wrote to an off-island paper:

> *I went into the U.S. Post Office here at Nantucket, and was quietly seated, waiting for my rotation to get a letter sent. The Barber, Deputy-Post-Master had been out. On his coming into the office, he took me by the collar and said, "Go out before I kick you." I said to him. "Oh no you won't." He replied, "I will," and added, "Don't come in here again." He did not let go his grab on me until he pulled me out. . . . By what the Barber said I was maltreated because I would not talk with him . . . about the Bank, hearing that he was suspected of being a pilferer, etc.*

Not long after this incident, Coffin became so frustrated by the bank directors' unwillingness to investigate any off-island leads that he decided to take matters into his own hands. Following up on tips that a suspicious sloop known as the *Dolphin* had left Nantucket within hours of the robbery, he set off on a desperate attempt to clear his name. After traveling to New Haven, New York, and Philadelphia, Coffin obtained warrants for "James Weatherly, John Clark, and one Johnson," and with the assistance of a constable from Philadelphia returned to New York where they searched the suspects' homes. On January 7, 1796, he wrote to his wife, "I am now in the most perplexing business I was ever in during my life. I would have left the matter and returned home before now was it not for the persons who are suspected at Nantucket who I believe to be as innocent as angels of knowing anything about the robbery."

Due to Coffin's efforts, Clark and Weatherly were finally brought back to Nantucket during the spring of 1796, with Clark admitting to the bank president Joseph Chase that he and two others had indeed robbed the bank. But Chase chose not to make the confession public, and the testimony was never used in court. Then in May, a guard at the Nantucket jail on High Street reported that Weatherly and Clark had admitted to robbing the bank. Rather than accepting the testimony, the bank directors fired the guard. Soon after that, Weatherly and Clark escaped under mysterious circumstances. Clearly, Chase, Macy, and the other like-minded bank directors were not out to discover the truth; they were out to destroy the reputations of Coffin and his fellow defendants.

The scandal pitted not only Quaker against Congregationalist, Democrat against Federalist, it also put members of the same family at each other's throats. At this time Phineas and Kezia Fanning were about as low as a couple could get; impoverished and with a growing family, not to mention maligned by most on the island, they were perfect candidates for Silvanus Macy's manipulative malevolence. In June of 1796, Phineas, who also happened to be Randall Rice's lawyer, was thrown in jail on trumped-up debt charges. It was made clear to him, however, that if he would testify that Rice had admitted to robbing the bank, he would become a free man. While in jail, Fanning had several detailed conversations with his fellow inmates, Clark and Weatherly, who may have told him where they buried the money. In any event, once he got out of jail in July, Fanning made a swift and mysterious trip to Long Island.

Meanwhile, Silvanus Macy and his fellow bank directors went to work on his wife Kezia who had publicly expressed her belief that Rice had indeed robbed the bank. According to her own written testimony, Macy appeared at her house and explained that he was part of a "Secret Committee [with] such power vested in us that we can be at any expense in getting at evidence . . . and are not obliged to be accountable to the bank and how and in what way we spend the money." After Kezia complained of being "destitute of money" and without a place to live, Macy offered to help, securing the Morris house on Main Street for the Fannings and Kezia's mother who was now living with them after her dispiriting experience in a Nova Scotia debtor's prison. As Macy told "brother Obed": "For Fanning wants us and we want Fanning."

But when Fanning returned from Long Island (apparently unsuccessful in his attempts to find the money), he proved frustratingly uncooperative, even though Macy and his "Secret Committee" insisted on visiting him every night for almost an entire week. At one point, according to Kezia, Macy "started out of his chair" and shouted: "It's enough to make a man eat red hot spikes! Why did thou come from Long Island to destroy our evidence?" Eventually Kezia would come to see the error of her ways, offering detailed testimony in Rice's defense that also provided a devastating look into the secretive and illegal practices of the Quaker bank directors.

It soon became apparent that the once idyllic community of Nantucket was in the midst of a cultural meltdown. In July of 1796 a handwritten notice appeared in town:

The Starbucks and others that are rich their property shall
be burnt the rich on this island ar a curse to the poor for they
do no regard their own kindred and they shall be destroyed
sooner or later

\REVENGE\

giving notice may seem strange but the motive is known to
myself

As the social fabric of their community threatened to unravel,
some Nantucketers looked to Siasconset, the remote fishing village on the eastern end of the island, as a summertime refuge
from the storm. Here, far away from the tumult to the west,
Nantucketers were free to live as they had in the old days: a
simple and self-consciously nostalgic way of life first popularized
in "The Laws of Siasconset," a ballad published at the height of
the bank scandal in 1797. A typical stanza reads:

> *Should party zeal the bosom rile,*
> *'Tis here nor felt nor seen sir,*
> *For chowder well corrects the bile,*
> *And dissipates the spleen sir.*
> *Then when with B**k the wild ear swells,*
> *Some Genius bids renounce it,*
> *For no revenge nor malice dwells,*
> *With thee, O Siasconset.*

Meanwhile, back in the real world, Nantucket's dark and
seamy underbelly was put on display for all to see in an agoniz-
ing series of legal battles staged in Barnstable and Boston courts.
Even though there was the same flimsy evidence against all
those accused of the bank robbery, only Randall Rice was found

guilty. By the time he emerged from a Boston jail—thanks to an executive pardon—he was a ruined man, and soon ended up in jail on Nantucket for debt. From the Quakers' point of view, even if the off-islanders had indeed stolen the money, it was Coffin and the others who had masterminded the job.

In 1805, ten long years after the robbery, William Coffin attended a meeting of the House of Representatives in Boston to promote the appointment of a second notary public on the island. At this time, Nantucket was represented by the seventy-one-year-old Micajah (pronounced "My-KAY-jaw") Coffin, a staunch Quaker. At one point in the proceedings Micajah—who had once used his political influence to change the venue of the bank robbery trials to the Democrats' advantage—asked a fellow representative if he knew who had put forward the request for an additional notary public on Nantucket. The representative pointed to William Coffin sitting in the audience. "What!" Micajah exclaimed, "that convict?" When the representative asked what he was talking about, the Quaker mentioned "the business of the Nantucket Bank"; after the representative protested that Coffin had been "honorably acquitted," Micajah insisted, "That did not make him the less guilty thee knows."

When Micajah and William Coffin ran into each other a few weeks later in the offices of the Nantucket Marine Insurance Company, William's temper got the better of him. After tweaking the elderly Quaker's nose—to the point that it bled—he called him "an old rascal." Their next confrontation would be in court, with Micajah suing for assault and battery while William claimed defamation of character. After several appeals, William was found guilty in the assault case and assessed damages of $15.00. Micajah, however, ended up the ultimate loser, as the court ordered him to pay William $2,500 for slander. Had it not been for his sons' financial assistance, Micajah would have lost his house on Pine Street.

The turmoil had an inevitable effect on the quality of daily life on the island. In 1807 James Freeman observed, "It seems to be universally allowed that [the Nantucketers] no longer retain their former purity of morals; but that during the last twelve years in particular, a spirit of bitterness has been introduced among them; that the people no longer live together like a family of brothers; but that they hate, and revile, and persecute each other. The causes of this melancholy change ought not to be mentioned." Many people simply left the island. Others began to reinvent themselves, breaking old alliances and forging new ones—particularly when it came to religion. Kezia Fanning, born and raised a Quaker and who later turned to Congregationalism when she married Phineas, became a Methodist as did a growing number of Nantucketers. William Coffin and a group of other Congregationalists, unhappy with their church's increasingly restrictive orthodoxy, began the Second Congregational Church on Orange Street, now the Unitarian Church. Meanwhile, Quakerism continued to self-destruct. Throughout the early decades of the century, more and more members were disowned (many of whom joined the new Congregational church), and then in the 1830s, what had once been the rock-solid foundation of the community would fracture into a group of bitterly feuding sects as the doctrinal controversies that were dividing Quaker communities all across the country inevitably came to Nantucket.

But the true deathblow to "Old Nantucket" would come from a different quarter. It was not just Quakerism and whaling that had defined colonial Nantucket. The common ownership of land also helped to create a sense of the community as one extended family. In 1781, a Quaker by the name of George Churchman visited the island and commented that this land-management system promoted a "social, friendly and commendable way of living." Unfortunately, this form of ownership was not particularly "friendly" to the land. Each year, the island's proprietors (of which there were approximately 300 by the turn of the century) would allot a different plot of land to its members for raising crops. In 1801 an observer claimed that "the tendency of this scheme to exhaust the land, is easily seen, as no possessor has an interest to give it any permanent improvements, but, on the contrary, to impoverish it as much as possible."

Most of the land was dedicated to grazing sheep, and here again, the system was not particularly fair or effective when it came to the resources involved. Even Obed Macy, who was one of the largest shareholders in the proprietorship, recognized its flaws, admitting that an inordinate number of sheep died in the winter due to a lack of care. According to Macy, the proprietors, "by long custom, have become so reconciled to the measure, that the thought of doing wrong has almost become extinct." There were proprietors, however, who were having second thoughts.

In 1810, a group composed chiefly of members of the Mitchell family but also including—you guessed it—William Coffin entered a petition claiming that they could not "possess, occupy, and improve" their portion of the land as long as it was in common ownership. As a consequence, they requested that portions equivalent to their shares in the proprietary be set aside and designated theirs.

This was, of course, heresy of the highest order. In May, 1811, an anonymous Nantucketer published a pamphlet called "A Nest of Love Disturbed, or, The Farmer's Dialogue" that defended the proprietary. Although the identity of the author has remained a mystery, it may have been Obed Macy. Indeed, the pamphlet reads like a warm-up for his *History* as it puts the current squabble in the larger context of the island's past. According to the writer, the beauty of the proprietary system is that there is no need for individual owners to fence off their land—an exceedingly expensive undertaking that would not be financially feasible for most "small proprietors," especially given the poor quality of the land. As it stood at that time, even those who were not members of the proprietary could pasture a cow for only three or four dollars per year. The Obed-like narrator goes on to claim that the common ownership of land is perfectly suited to a community whose "principal employment" is whaling and that the petitioners (being merchants rather than farmers) do not fully appreciate the ramifications of what they are proposing.

By the time "A Nest of Love Disturbed" hit the presses, the case was already in court. For an island still suffering from the aftershocks of the bank scandal, it was a painfully familiar scenario. Representing the proprietors was Silvanus Macy (who would make a total of nine trips to Boston during the proceedings); for the petitioners it was William Coffin. And once again it was a bitter and dirty battle as the two sides went at each other tooth and nail. In the midst of the court battle, Obed Macy wrote in his journal, "Could we all view these things as they are, how soon would we settle all things in dispute and become a family of Love." Contributing to the righteousness of Macy's despair was the court's decision in favor of Coffin and his fellow petitioners.

As if the tensions associated with this court battle were not already enough, the outbreak of the War of 1812 created yet another sense of déjà vu on the island. Fearing a replay of the Revolution, large numbers of families fled to the mainland as land values plummeted to next to nothing. Whereas during the Revolution Nantucketers had looked to Quaker whaling merchants such as William Rotch and Timothy Folger when it came to negotiating with British and American forces, the island was no longer able to present a united front. As a British gunboat patrolled the waters from Great Point to Tuckernuck Island and townspeople begged for food in the streets, Democrats and Federalists bickered over what the island's policy should be.

As was true in the bank and commons fights, William Coffin was once again a prominent figure. During a town meeting in May of 1814, Coffin and his fellow Federalists, fearful that the selectmen were jeopardizing the safety of the island because of their pro-French, anti-British leanings, became so "tumultuous and riotous" that the sheriff literally read them the riot act. According to one account of the meeting, "William Coffin observed that as the sheriff had read the riot act and commanded the people to disperse, he was of the opinion it was best to go and went out of the meeting, and many others followed. . . ." With a flair for the dramatic and the pugnacity of a street fighter, Coffin made it perfectly plain that in the war for Nantucket's future, the gloves were off.

And, in a remarkable turn of events, Federalists ultimately gained a temporary majority on Nantucket. Although all negotiations were conducted by a bipartisan committee, the island's inhabitants agreed to a private and highly controversial peace treaty with Britain: If the Nantucketers quit paying taxes to the U.S. government, the British would reestablish the flow of provisions to the island. As a consequence of this "separate peace," two British admirals, one of whom was of Nantucket descent—Sir Isaac Coffin—traveled to England's Dartmoor prison, where thousands of American seamen were being detained. Coffin made a point of assembling the Nantucket sailors together and assuring them that they would soon be released "on account of belonging to a neutral country." What Coffin and the others did not know was that a peace treaty ending the war had been signed less than a month earlier on December 24, 1814.

Whatever relief the Nantucketers felt concerning the end of the war (word finally reached the island on February 16th) was disrupted by the turmoil associated with what became known as the "Great Set-off," as a huge tract of land on the eastern end of the island became the property of the petitioners. Making it all the worse was the proximity of this embattled piece of land (known as Plainfield) to the hallowed soil of Siasconset. Soon the proprietary was swamped with additional requests for set-offs as the commons underwent a gradual process of disintegration not unlike what was happening to the Quaker side of Nantucket's identity.

By the early 1820s, the town was no longer the self-contained, almost pastoral community it had once been. First the New-town Gate at the end of Pleasant Street, where an "Uncle Cash" had collected tolls from those headed east out of town, was torn down. Then a year later the island's two sheep shearings—at Gibbs and Maxcey's Ponds—were consolidated into a single, much less intimate gathering at Miacomet Pond. Sheep and fences were still an omnipresent part of life on Nantucket, but the character of the place had been forever changed.

During this difficult, transitional time, William Coffin received information from the Keeper of the New York State Prison (whose name happened to be Alexander Coffin) that a prisoner had given a detailed account of the Nantucket Bank robbery. Here, at long last, was incontrovertible proof that it had been an outside job. So, in a few quick months in 1816, Coffin (with the assistance of his fellow accused, Albert Gardner) put together a pamphlet entitled "Narrative of the Robbery of the Nantucket Bank." Fired to an awesome eloquence, Coffin provides a passionate portrayal of a community in chaos:

> When it was publicly announced that the Bank was robbed, the inhabitants of Nantucket were seized with a consternation, that could not have been much exceeded had they been assured the dead had risen. . . . The atrocity of the act, and the darkness which enveloped the whole transaction had a powerful influence upon the minds of the inhabitants, not yet familiarized with crimes, to bring into operation a talent

for the marvelous, and the wonderful; and never, since the memorable times of the Salem witchcraft, did superstition and bigotry wave their scepter over the human intellect with such unlimited sway. . . . Our old men dreamed dreams, and our young men interpreted them. Madness was mistaken for inspiration, and the ravings of a lunatic were collected into form as the basis for a criminal prosecution. . . . The whole society was convulsed, with the action and reaction of the contending parties, till that peace and harmony, which once characterized the inhabitants, were destroyed, and fled forever.

Ultimately Coffin and Gardner's pamphlet failed to lay to rest the business of the Nantucket Bank scandal. For generations to come, families refused to forget the pain inflicted by the controversy. And then, to add insult to injury, other bank scandals (see Chapter 17) would rock the island in the years to come. Given the direct relationship that had historically existed between the community's dominant religion and its ability to turn a profit, it was perhaps inevitable that banking debacles would accompany Quakerism's gradual fragmentation and decline on Nantucket.

If Coffin and Gardner's 1816 pamphlet opened some old wounds (Obed Macy recorded in his journal, "Old Bank Fire is kindling again"), it also demonstrated the power of the written word to a Quaker community that had always discounted the need for anything more than a practical education. In a world in which words would become as important (if not more important) than deeds, the kind of eloquence (and education) Coffin displayed would become increasingly valued. And yet at this time Nantucket still lacked a public school system, leaving an estimated 300 children without access to any form of education. With no place to go, packs of boys roamed the streets, inevitably making a nuisance of themselves. Once again it was Coffin and his circle (especially his son-in-law, Samuel Jenks, editor of the *Nantucket Inquirer*) who led the fight for educational reform. After a long struggle against those who accused them of bringing "Boston notions" to the island, Coffin and Jenks's efforts finally forced Nantucket into compliance with state educational laws in 1827.

There was a fortunate subplot to the education controversy that began to heal some of the damage inflicted by Coffin's bruising battles with Silvanus Macy and others. In 1826, Sir Isaac Coffin, the British admiral who had treated the Nantucket prisoners with such kindness during the War of 1812, visited the island for the first time as the guest of William Coffin. With no family back in Britain to inherit his considerable estate, Sir Isaac hoped to "do something" so that his name would be remembered on Nantucket, a place for which he had maintained a life-long admiration. As might be predicted, William Coffin's son-in-law proposed that the Admiral build a free school for any child with Coffin blood in his or her veins, which, as it turned out, included just about everyone on the island. Thus was born the Coffin School, which still stands to this day on Winter Street, as well as the first training ship in America: an eighty-seven-foot brig known as the *Clio* that would take crews of young Nantucketers as far as Rio Grande, Brazil.

In the meantime, other forces were at work to help pull together a once divided island. By the 1820s, the old distinction between a Federalist and Democrat had, in the words of an *Inquirer* editorial, "ceased to exist" as another generation of Nantucketers began to take the stage. One of these was Coffin's only son, William, Jr. Although born at the height of the bank scandal, he proved to be a kinder and gentler version of his father. A schoolteacher, merchant, newspaper editor, cartographer, and eloquent temperance advocate, he helped achieve an extraordinary reconciliation when in 1834–5 he ghostwrote

Obed Macy's *History of Nantucket*, a partnership that was publicly announced in a long-running advertisement in the *Nantucket Inquirer*. Indeed, given the feuding of the past forty years,
it is hard to believe that the brother of Silvanus Macy would look
to the son of William Coffin for literary help.

This was probably not the younger William's first collaboration. He may also have been the coauthor of both Owen Chase's
Narrative of the *Essex* disaster, published in 1821, and William
Lay and Cyrus Hussey's *A Narrative of the Mutiny on Board the
Whaleship* Globe *of Nantucket*, published in 1828 (see Chapter
15), potentially making him the unheralded author of the three
most important books written on Nantucket in the nineteenth
century. When it came to his collaboration with Obed Macy,
William seems to have had a definite agenda. In the advertisement for subscribers that ran prior to the book's publication, he
makes it clear that facts—as opposed to the rumor and conjec-
ture that had once made his father's life a living hell—would be
the focus of the *History*:

> *I must own that I had some misgivings as to the value of
> any record that could at this period be made. . . . The only
> source, I thought, from which any amount of information
> could be collected was tradition; and consequently that the
> uncertainty of such authority must be too well known to give
> value to a work of the kind proposed. I need not express my
> surprise at finding not only a well written, but a connected,
> well authenticated, and, to myself at least, a very interesting
> history.*

Unfortunately, by the time of the book's publication, William
Coffin, Sr., was dead at the age of seventy-eight. And then, only
three years later in 1838, his son fell victim to a fatal attack of
pleurisy at the age of forty.

When recognized as the product of two very different authors, *The History of Nantucket* stands as a remarkable testament to the regenerative powers of time. Although Macy/Coffin do mention the ill-feeling that then existed between rival Quaker sects on the island, they speak only generally (when at all) about the bank robbery, commons fight, and public-education disputes. In fact, at one point they apologize for "the dull monotony" of their book since it only concerns "the peaceable settlement of a few enterprising families, and their slow progress in wealth and numbers, from the commencement down to the present moment." It may not have been an entirely true account of the island's history, but for Nantucketers finally emerging from close to half a century of economic, political, and social upheaval, its contrivances and omissions were necessary, even palliative, lies.

Many hands have been wrung over the tragic dissolution of Old Nantucket, but at this time in the island's (and the country's) development, the idyll of the "peaceable settlement" was proving ever-more difficult to sustain. Although there were some notable individual exceptions, vested interests rather than communal and spiritual ideals had become the driving force behind the proprietary and Quakerism on Nantucket. Indeed, it could be argued that more than anything else, Quakerism was what fouled the Nest of Love, as the religion that had once consolidated a community began to encourage a truly diabolical genius for character assassination. According to one observer, who had much to say about the "depravity" of the Nantucket Quakers: "Unfortunately, the anger which they are forbidden to express by outward actions, finding no vent, stagnates the heart, and, while they make professions of love and good will to their opponents, the rancor and intense malevolence of their feelings poison every generous spring of human kindness." It could also be argued that the effects of this attitude, combined with a knee-jerk economic and social conservatism, were what would ultimately doom the whale fishery to a premature death on Nantucket (see Chapter 18).

But this fate was still in the distant future. Throughout the 1820s and '30s whaling began to experience a remarkable resurgence as the Industrial Revolution took hold. Feeding the insatiable maw of the Machine Age with illuminants and lubricants, Nantucket whalemen led the charge into a new and inconceivably vast frontier: the Pacific Ocean. Here, not in the narrow streets of town, was where the action was.

CHAPTER 15

The Golden Boy and the Dark Man: Obed Starbuck and George Pollard

FATE, LUCK, or what-have-you always seemed to smile on Obed Starbuck. Born into a well-to-do whaling family, he set out on his first voyage to the Pacific in a brand-new ship built by his uncle. Captained by James Russell, the *Hero* returned in the winter of 1818 full of oil, and with prices at an all-time high. By the summer of 1819, she was once again headed for the Pacific, this time with young Obed Starbuck as her first mate.

While lying at the island of St. Mary's, a favorite gathering point for Nantucket whalers off the coast of Chile, Spanish pirates threatened to put an end to Obed's budding career when they captured the ship. With the captain and cabin boy imprisoned on shore, Starbuck and the rest of the crew were detained below-decks as the Spaniards looted the ship. When the pirates temporarily abandoned their plunder and rowed for shore, Starbuck broke down the door of his stateroom, freed the rest of the crew, and commanded them to set sail. Unfortunately, the breeze was distressingly light, and with the pirates in hot pursuit, it began to look as if the *Hero* might be overtaken by the gun-wielding buccaneers. At one point, several members of the *Hero*'s crew came aft and implored Starbuck to give up in hopes that their lives might be spared. But the twenty-three-year-old Starbuck was not about to surrender his uncle's ship, telling his crew: "Well, my lads, if any wish to remain and enjoy their clemency, they must take a plank and jump overboard. For my own part, the ship can't be stopped. If they shoot me, they must do it flying." With the help of a fortuitous puff of wind, the *Hero* made it safely out of the harbor. Although the captain and cabin boy were eventually killed, Starbuck and the rest of the crew arrived safely in Valparaiso.

Upon returning to Nantucket, Starbuck, not yet twenty-five, was given command of the *Hero*. His first voyage as captain was termed "most successful": after only twenty-five months at sea (the average voyage now took at least three years), he returned with a full ship. But this was just the beginning. His uncle next put him in charge of the *Loper*; this time he was back in only twenty months with a full ship; next voyage: eighteen months. Then, proving that three times is indeed the charm, the *Loper* had the voyage to end all voyages, returning to Nantucket after only fourteen months and sixteen days, with every inch of available space—including the deck—crammed with casks of oil. Even as they approached the island a whale was sighted, enabling them to anchor off the Nantucket Bar with their tryworks still blazing. Under the headline "Greatest Voyage Ever Made," the *Nantucket Inquirer* exulted:

> *This was whaling with a vengeance; and it must be that Capt. S. possesses the spirit of enchantment, which attracts the leviathans of the ocean around his ship. If this unparalleled success is the effect of superior skill in the art of whaling, would it not be proper for him to communicate it to others of the same profession, who are now three years in performing exploits for which he requires little more than one?*

On an island where whaling was not just big news, it was the only news, Obed Starbuck's feat was immensely exciting. Rumors circulated that at one point during the voyage there

were no fewer than fifteen dead sperm whales tied up to the
Loper, and then to arrive at the Nantucket Bar still trying out
a whale? Well, this was simply too much—"a glorious sight to
witness from the lookouts upon our houses," remembered one
Nantucketer. Enthusiasm ran so high among Starbuck's nearly
all-black crew that two prominent members of the island's
African-American community, Captain Absalom Boston (see
Chapter 16) and Samuel Harris, led a joyous parade through the
streets of town before all were treated to a gala dinner, replete
with hours of lengthy toasts (see Notes). According to the
Inquirer, "The occasion is said to have been one of great hilar-
ity and social enjoyment." And no wonder. The *Loper* had just
brought in 2,280 barrels of whale oil worth more than $50,000,
not only making the owners very happy men but enabling Obed
Starbuck to retire at the ripe old age of thirty-three. This was
Nantucket at its greasiest, culturally inclusive best.

Adding to the adventure and excitement of Starbuck's accom-
plishments was the fact that he and his fellow Nantucketers were
not just whalemen, they were also explorers, venturing out into
an unknown frontier that dwarfed that of the American West.
New islands were being discovered on an almost routine basis
(Starbuck named one of his "New Nantucket") as the whalemen often became the first white people the South Sea Islanders
had ever seen. Even though it was situated thirty miles off the
New England coast, Nantucket was a border town, a jumping-
off point into the vast Pacific, where the twin lures of money
and adventure fired the imaginations of the local populace long
before there ever was a Gold Rush. Whaling was no longer
something a Nantucketer did simply because it was all he knew
how to do; finally, after the interruptions of two catastrophic
wars, the Nantucket whale fishery was once again the envy of
not only America but the world.

Stories began to appear in newspapers around the country

commenting on the island's spectacular comeback. In May of 1825, the *Nantucket Inquirer* quoted from a story in the *Washington National Journal*, then gave its own assessment of the fishery's new strength, claiming that there were now at least sixty whaling vessels sailing out of Nantucket, of which more than forty were currently in the Pacific, with about twenty in port. These vessels employed 2,000 seamen, not to mention the "great numbers at home" (of a population of about 7,000) engaged not only in fitting out the whalers but also in the thriving coasting trade. According to the *Inquirer*, what made this fishery such an "effective nursery for bold and hardy seamen" was that Nantucketers, unlike "the ordinary Jack-Tars of many other places," were "continually stimulated by the most powerful of human motives—namely, a desire of promotion": "This honorable emulation is productive of the happiest effects—they soon become officers, and are even commanders at a very early age. After this period, the fruits of a few successful voyages banded with common prudence, enable them to become ship-owners, or manufacturers, and to settle down satisfactorily among their kindred, in the bosom of domestic life."

This was the blueprint by which Obed Starbuck led his life. After his profitable successes in the *Loper*, he would build a huge house on Fair Street, now known as the Ship's Inn, then retire (temporarily at least) to "every-day life" as a gentleman farmer with acreage in the Cato section of the island beyond Mill Hill. According to one Nantucketer, he was commonly regarded as "a marked man among us . . . who [brought] success to everything he put his hand to."

There was, however, another "marked man" on Nantucket, who as a young whaling captain had been just as ambitious and just as energetic as Obed Starbuck. But in the case of George Pollard, the pursuit of Nantucket's version of the American Dream would turn into a horrifying nightmare.

∽

We need look no farther than Owen Chase, Captain Pollard's first mate on the voyage of the ill-fated *Essex*, for a description of your average Nantucket whaleman in the 1820s. Not surprisingly, given the staying power of traditions on the island, he bears a decided resemblance to Ichabod Paddock of old. According to Chase, "The profession is one of great ambition, and full of honorable excitement: a tame man is never known amongst them; . . . and it has been truly said of them, that they possess a natural aptitude, which seems rather the lineal spirit of their fathers, than the effects of any experience."

Whether or not they possessed an inherent genetic superiority when it came to killing whales, these were tough, strong, and rigidly disciplined men, who were encouraged, virtually from birth, to whale "with a vengeance." One traditional anecdote tells of a nine-year-old boy who tied a kitchen fork to the end of his mother's ball of yarn and proceeded to "fasten" to the family cat. As the terrified pet let out a fearsome shriek, the boy's bewildered mother picked up the ball of yarn. At that point the boy is reputed to have shouted: "Pay out, mother! Pay out!! There she sounds through the window!"

On an island where "Oil! Oil! is the toast; and if it does not suit the delicacy of your ideas to live breathe and dream of oil, you are no Nantucket man," the whaleman was the center of attention. And according to some observers, the attention did not always bring out the best in a person: "A Nantucket man in any part of the world, may be known by the surly importance and glum dignity of his manner. . . . He considers it his business to draw the attention of every one to himself, and resents highly a want of peculiar respect and admiration for his own undeservings." Chase put it more diplomatically: "a Nantucket man is on all occasions fully sensible of the honor and merit of his profession," which involved nothing less than "an exterminating warfare against those great leviathans of the deep."

But if it was a war, it was an exceedingly one-sided conflict. As the whale did everything in its power to escape, the whaleman stabbed it with a harpoon and then as the terrified and wounded mammal dragged the whaleboat and its six occupants along on a "Nantucket sleighride," the boatsteerer hacked at the victim's vital organs with a lance until the whale "spouted blood" and went into its final, tail-lashing "flurry."

For the Nantucketer, the whale was not so much a living, breathing creature as it was, according to one commentator, "a self-propelled tub of high-income lard." Whales were described by the amount of oil they would produce (as in a "60-barrel whale"), and although the whaleman took careful note of the mammal's habits, he made no attempt to think of it as anything more than a potential prize that would add to his own personal glory and wealth. The whaleman was a hunter, pure and simple, and to concern himself with the feelings and motivations of his prey was unthinkable.

But on November 20, 1820, an event occurred that would require at least one crew of whalemen to begin to see it from the whale's perspective. The *Essex*, a converted sealer and China trader originally out of Salem, had a reputation as a lucky ship; that was one of the reasons why Thomas Nickerson, an orphan and not yet fourteen, decided to sign on, even though the "black and ugly" ship bore a disturbing resemblance, according to an account Nickerson wrote as an old man, to Noah's Ark.

Nickerson soon discovered that the average crew on a Nantucket whaler was not exactly a bold and hardy group of experienced seamen. Much had changed since the early days of the colonial fishery, when a Nantucket sloop was manned almost exclusively by sailors from the island. Now, with bigger vessels and only a handful of local Indians and blacks, Nantucket shipowners were forced to look beyond the island for crew members, actively recruiting "greenhands" who had no sailing experience whatsoever. In the case of the *Essex*, it was not until the arrival of a Boston packet containing seven African-American crew members that Captain Pollard was finally able to order his men to set sail.

Since only the officers (all, of course, Nantucket men) knew what they were doing, it was not a pretty sight. According to Nickerson, "All was bustle, confusion and awkwardness, that is, on part of the crew. The officers were smart active men, and were no doubt some [what] piqued at having such a display of awkwardness in full view of their native town. Nor was it until we had passed the eastern end of the island that our top gallant sails were set and all sails trimmed to the breeze."

It would not take long, however, before the crew of the *Essex* had become trained in not only how to sail their ship but also how to kill whales. In Nickerson's words, "experience has since taught me that a few months on board will make even the greenest capable of executing the general orders of the ship." This did not mean, of course, that all crew members were regarded as equals on a Nantucket whaler. Since only the island-born were destined to become officers, it was perhaps inevitable that an "us versus them" mentality typified crew relations. According to one commentator, "The honor of being a Roman citizen was not, in days of yore, so enviable a distinction, as it is on board one of these ships, to be a native of that sand bank yclept Nantucket." Indeed, among the crew of the *Essex*, the "honor" of being a native Nantucketer would soon prove to be a matter of life and death.

A little more than a year into the voyage, the *Essex* was approximately midway between the Galápagos and Marquesas Islands, a thousand miles from the nearest land. Two of the ship's whaleboats had fastened to whales while back on board the *Essex* the first mate, Owen Chase, directed the repair of his damaged boat in hopes of soon joining the hunt. Nickerson was at the helm when an eighty-five-foot sperm whale was sighted approaching the ship at approximately three knots. Once he became aware of the situation, Chase ordered the boy to "put the helm hard up," but the time for evasive maneuvers was past. Several members of the crew cried out that the whale was "coming afoul of the ship" just as it crashed into the *Essex*'s side, knocking the entire crew off their feet and shaking the ship "like a leaf." It was soon discovered that the whale had surfaced along the starboard side of the ship, providing the crew with an excellent opportunity to stab it with a lance. Chase, however, chose not to attack in fear that the whale might snap off the rudder with its tail. In hindsight, wrote Nickerson, this would have been the lesser of two evils.

Eventually the whale swam off about 300 yards ahead, turned quickly around and once again came at the ship, this time at twice its original speed. When it collided with the *Essex*, the whale's blunt head acted like a massive battering ram, easily smashing in the bow, and as the whale swam away to leeward, the ship began to fill up with water. Immediately, Chase ordered the crew to unlash the spare whaleboat as the steward went below to retrieve the captain and mate's chests as well as two quadrants and navigational guides. By the time the whaleboat was in the water, the ship had begun to go down; they were barely two boat-lengths away when it "fell over to windward."

In shock and amazement, they waited for the other two whaleboat crews to realize that something had happened to the ship. By the time Captain Pollard returned, the first mate "could scarcely recognize his countenance, he appeared to be so much altered, awed, and overcome, with the oppression of his feelings, and the dreadful reality that lay before him." Prior to this catastrophe, Pollard, although a first-time captain and "a man of few words," had demonstrated that he was perfectly capable of strong and determined leadership. At one point during the voyage when his crew complained about their provisions, he had flown into a rage, throwing down his hat and stamping on it before shouting, "I'll kill the whole bunch of you together and then bang up North-West and go home!" Although the expression was somewhat peculiar (Nickerson, for one, did not know what it meant), this was considered conduct perfectly becoming a Nantucket sea captain.

But now, as he looked upon the capsized wreck that had once been his noble command, Pollard was hardly the "spitfire" he had once been. He turned to the first mate and asked, "My God, Mr. Chase, what is the matter?" Chase's reply: "We have been stove by a whale."

For a Nantucketer, it was as if the whole order of creation had been turned upside down. Here was a whale—"proverbial for its insensibility and inoffensiveness," according to Chase—that had fought back with "decided, calculating mischief." How could this be? But the more Chase and the others thought about it, the more they became convinced that they had been the victims of "premeditated violence" on the part of the whale: "His aspect was most horrible, and such as indicated resentment and fury. He came directly from the shoal [or pod of whales] which we had just before entered, and in which we had struck three of his companions, as if fired with revenge for their sufferings." That a whale might not only think but also act as a man would do was terrifying to contemplate, especially since it was now obvious just how easily a whale could turn the Nantucketers' self-proclaimed "exterminating warfare" into a pitiful display of human frailty.

In any event, the crew of the *Essex* had been forced into a full retreat. But first they had preparations to make. In order to right the wreck, they chopped off the masts, enabling them to retrieve some casks of bread, water, and a few of the hundreds of turtles they had collected in the Galápagos Islands for meat. They also built up the sides of their three whaleboats to increase their seaworthiness while rigging two short masts and sails on each boat. By now the many casks of oil on board the *Essex* had begun to burst, sending out a vast slick of whale oil across the water. It was time to decide on a course of action.

According to Chase's account, he was the first one to bring up the matter with Captain Pollard, who seemed reluctant to abandon the ship. Chase also makes it sound as if the decision not to sail for the nearby Marquesas or Society Islands and go instead for the west coast of South America—a voyage of more than 3,000 miles!—was mutually agreed upon from the start. Nickerson, however, gives a different account. Writing more than fifty years after the incident, and without the perspective of a first mate attempting to put what would prove to be a bad decision in the best possible light, he claimed that Pollard initially proposed that they sail for the Society Islands (only ten days away) but that Chase and the second mate convinced him to sail instead to the east. The fear was that the islands to the west were inhabited by cannibals. As it would turn out, by deciding to go for South America, after first heading south to avoid what were known as the "kona" storms, the whalemen would be forced to act out their own worst fears more than twenty-five years before the Donner Party.

Although the officers of the *Essex* have had their apologists, who claim it was the only thing they could have done given their limited knowledge of the Pacific islands and the direction of the prevailing winds and currents, Nickerson was less sympathetic, attributing the decision to "gross ignorance or a great oversight somewhere," adding, "How many warm hearts have ceased to beat in consequence of it." Indeed, easterly winds and currents would push them so far south and west that after their first month of sailing they would be actually farther from the South American coast than when they had started!

Five days after leaving the *Essex*, Pollard's whaleboat was attacked at night by what they believed to be a killer whale. As the crew fought it off with their sprit poles (used to hold up the sail from the mast), the sixteen-foot whale smashed a hole in the fragile whaleboat's bow. Although they did their best to repair the damage, all three boats were in such bad shape that if they had been on Nantucket, Nickerson claimed he would not have felt safe sailing ten miles in any one of them.

Soon the men began to experience overwhelming pangs of thirst and hunger. But Pollard and his officers remained steadfast in their daily allotment of only a single "biscuit" (weighing a little more than a pound) and a half pint of water per man. In order to stay together, the three boats sailed in a line, raising up lanterns or shooting off pistols when they inevitably lost track of one another at night. During the day, the sun was almost unbearable, particularly in the frequent calms. When those who knew how to swim slipped over the side to cool themselves, they did not have the strength to get back into the boat and had to be pulled in by their companions. At one point a few flying fish fell into Chase's boat, only to be eaten whole—scales and all—by the starving crew.

Then on December 20th, after almost a full month, they sighted land—a small island that proved to be more of a tease than a salvation. After eating every bird and crab they could get their hands on and finally finding a source of water, they realized that the island could not support a population of twenty men for much longer, so they decided to push on, this time hoping to reach Easter Island to the east. But when it came time to leave, three of the men expressed their decision to stay on the island rather than risk another passage. Since this would give the others more provisions, it was readily agreed to, although emotions ran so high at the time of the whaleboats' leave-taking that the three remaining crew members—all of them off-islanders— elected not to come down to the beach to say good-bye.

With the wind howling from the west, the whaleboats were now making good time and in the right general direction; unfortunately, it soon became clear that they had missed Easter Island. They now decided to steer for the islands of Juan Fernán- dez and Más Afuera off the South American coast, more than 2,500 miles away. On January 10th, the second mate, Matthew Joy, who had been "not well" throughout the voyage, died. The next night Chase's boat was separated from the other two in a severe storm. Not long after that, Chase nearly shot one of his men for attempting to steal bread.

The Nantucketers now knew what it was like to be the prey in a vast, carnivorous ocean. At one point a large shark snapped at the steering oar of Chase's boat in "fearless malignity" but did no serious damage. Then a school of dolphins spent a day swimming beside their boat but not close enough to be caught. Nickerson's reaction: "Poor devils, how much they are now our superiors and yet not know it." Chase and his crew next found themselves in the midst of a pod of sperm whales, "foaming and thrashing past us in a most furious manner." No doubt remem- bering the incident that had brought them to this point, the whalemen were so fearful of these "intruders" that they thought about taking out their oars and rowing to safety but soon real- ized that they did not have the strength. The Nantucketers, proverbial for their courage and determination, could not help but lapse into despondency, knowing that they "might at any moment sink beneath this vast extent of ocean, leaving scarcely a momentary bubble."

Two days later, Richard Peterson, a sixty-year-old black sailor, died; on February 8th, more than two and a half months after leaving the *Essex*, Isaac Cole became delirious and then died in the midst of horrible convulsions. With their provisions about to run out, Chase proposed that they do the unthinkable— that they use Cole's body for food. So, after they had "separated his limbs from his body, and cut all the flesh from the bones," and then taken out his heart, which was "eagerly devoured," they buried Cole as "decently as we could." Nine days later, after subsisting on strips of Cole's cooked flesh, they sighted a sail and were saved.

Meanwhile, Pollard and crew had become separated from the third boat, which would never be seen again. They, too, resorted to cannibalism as four men (all of them black) died within the space of thirteen days. But by February 1st the four remaining crew members—Pollard, Owen Coffin (Pollard's much younger cousin), Charles Ramsdell, and Barzillai Ray (all Nantucketers)— were without anything left to eat. Pollard would later give this account of what followed next:

> *What could we do? We looked at each other with horrid thoughts in our minds, but we held our tongues. I am sure that we loved one another as brothers all the time; and yet our looks told plainly what must be done. We cast lots, and the fatal one fell on my poor cabin boy (Owen Coffin). I started forward instantly, and cried, "My lad, my lad, if you don't like your lot, I'll shoot the first man that touches you." The poor emaciated boy hesitated a moment or two; then, quietly laying his head down upon the gunnel of the boat, he said, "I like it as well as any other." He was soon dispatched, and nothing of him left.*

On February 10th, Barzillai Ray died and was also eaten, and then on February 23rd, almost within sight of the Chilean coast, Pollard and Ramsdell were finally saved. According to one account, "They were unable to move when found sucking the bones of their dead messmates, which they were loth to part with."

Eventually the three who had elected to stay on the island were saved, making them the only non-Nantucketers to survive the ordeal. Whether or not it was a question of "survival of the fittest," if you were not a Nantucket man (or boy), you did not make it out of the *Essex* whaleboats alive.

With the exception of the captain, the survivors returned to Nantucket on the whaleship *Eagle*; Pollard remained in South America to recuperate and then returned aboard the *Two Brothers*. Incredibly, almost all the survivors returned to the sea. Pollard, in particular, seems to have had the psychological strength to handle circumstances that might have easily unhinged a lesser man. Shortly after his arrival on Nantucket, he fulfilled his promise to Owen Coffin and went to the boy's mother (and Pollard's aunt) to inform her personally of the circumstances surrounding her son's death. According to Nickerson, "She became almost frantic with the thought, and I have heard that she never could become reconciled to the Capt.'s presence."

Not long after his return to the island, where he was almost universally "thought not to have dealt unfairly with this trying matter," Pollard was made captain of the ship that had brought him home, the *Two Brothers*. Given the horrific nature of his past experiences, he accepted this new command with remarkable optimism. During a gam off the coast of South America with the U.S. Navy schooner *Waterwitch*, he freely and "modestly" recounted the story of the *Essex* and then was asked "how he could think of again putting his foot on board ship to again pursue such a calling." According to the Navy midshipman with whom he was speaking, "He simply remarked that it was an old adage that the lightning never struck in the same place twice."

Unfortunately for Captain Pollard, lightning would indeed strike twice. On February 11, 1823, not far from the Hawaiian

Islands, the *Two Brothers* struck an uncharted reef and sank; this time, however, all the crew were saved after only a short time in their whaleboats. Although this was once again an unavoidable act of God, the thirty-one-year-old Pollard returned to Nantucket knowing that his whaling career had ended. At one point during his trip home he confessed to a fellow passenger, "And now I am utterly ruined. No owner will ever trust me with a whaler again, for all will say I am an unlucky man."

Pollard spent the rest of his days as a night watchman on Nantucket, living with his wife (they had no children) in their home on Center Street, now the Seven Seas Gift Shop. Beginning with Owen Chase's account of the disaster, published in 1821, the story of the *Essex* would gradually acquire national and even international fame, and for many the most intriguing figure in the drama was the star-crossed captain. In fact, when notables such as Ralph Waldo Emerson and Herman Melville visited the island, they often made a point of seeking out Pollard. In the back of his copy of Owen Chase's *Narrative* of the *Essex* disaster, Melville wrote, "sometime about 1850–3—saw Capt. Pollard on the island of Nantucket, and [exchanged] some words with him. To the islanders he was a nobody—to me, the most impressive man, tho' wholly unassuming even humble—that I ever encountered."

There were reasons why Pollard was a "nobody" on Nantucket. He represented the dark side of the Nantucket Dream—a "marked man" whose life had proven that the island's private frontier, the Pacific Ocean, not only was a place of opportunity and promise but also a place where the worst could happen even to the best of men. Among a people who were, according to Emerson, "very sensitive to everything that dishonors the island," the horrendous experiences of Pollard and the others were not to be discussed. In fact, when the daughter of an *Essex* survivor was asked about the disaster, she replied, "We do not mention this in Nantucket."

As far as Nantucketers were concerned, it was men such as Obed Starbuck who were the proper subjects of conversation, men whose lives proved that whaling was the noble and glorious pursuit it was supposed to be. Indeed, when examined in the context of the *Essex* disaster, two of the toasts delivered during the owner-sponsored *Loper* banquet are very revealing: "To War: that war which causes no grief, the success of which produces no tears—war with the monsters of the deep," and "Death to the living and long life to the killers— / Success to wives of sailors, / And greasy luck to whalers." The message was clear: whaling was a war without a down side, a field of bravery that ultimately enabled its heroes to "settle down . . . in the bosom of domestic life" just as Starbuck had done after his third *Loper* voyage.

This was the public side of the Dream, a side the Nantucketers guarded so jealously that when in 1822 an anonymous letter appeared in a Boston paper questioning the religious character of the island inhabitants, an irate Nantucketer responded, "We have a spy amongst us, who, like all other spies, sends abroad his cowardly reports where he thinks they can never be disproved. . . ." This kind of attitude meant that the seamier, less-than-glorious aspects of the whale fishery were rarely, if ever, mentioned. Up until only a few decades ago, there were island historians who claimed that the notorious abuses of the whale fishery (see Chapter 16) were the sole work of the New Bedford whalemen during the so-called Golden Age of Whaling (1830–60) and that the Nantucketers who preceded them in the 1820s were "a superior type of shipmaster," largely because of their Quaker upbringing.

Unfortunately, such a view does not fit the facts. Nantucket had its share of brutal and inhumane whaling captains. A "Captain Swain of Nantucket" gained a reputation as a drunken tyrant who delighted in playing mind games with his crew. One of his favorite tricks was to wait until his men had left on shore-leave, then set the ship's topsails, thus threatening to abandon them "after a long and arduous cruise." Captain William Worth of the *Rambler* was reputed to have killed several of his crew members, either through flogging or "harsh, unmanly treatment"; one Nantucketer described him as "a disfigurer of God's creation, . . . a monster dignified with not a manly virtue." In 1824, Samuel Comstock, who had received the benefit of the finest Quaker education the island had to offer, led the crew of the *Globe* in a bloody mutiny. But perhaps even more disturbing to the mothers and fathers of Nantucket were the stories of men such as David Whippey who, after a brief exposure to the drudgery and brutality of the whaling life, willingly joined the "cannibals," never to return to their native island.

Even our blessedly "marked man," Captain Obed Starbuck, was hardly beyond reproach. Just ask Moses E. Morrell, a greenhand from New York who shipped out with Starbuck in 1822 aboard the *Hero*. In a journal he kept of his voyage, Morrell described how Starbuck refused to pay what he felt was an exorbitant price for wood in the Society Islands, then headed for the frigid waters of Cape Horn "without wood sufficient to cook one meal a day." On November 28th Morrell wrote, "It is now 40 days since we were deprived of warm breakfasts and suppers. . . . Alas, alas, the day that I came a-whaling. For what profiteth a man if he gain the whole world but in the meantime starveth to death?" Stingy and hard-driving, Starbuck seems to have had an attitude typical of a Nantucket whaling captain in the nineteenth century. Certainly the contrast between Morrell's lament and Peleg Folger's references to the surfeit of good food and drink on board a Nantucket whaling sloop in the 1750s and '60s is dramatic. But as Morrell's journal also makes clear, there was yet another, far more shocking side to the life of a Nantucket whaleman in the Pacific.

Midway through the voyage, after 100 days of nonstop

whaling, the *Hero* sailed into the port of "Woahoo" in the Sandwich (now Hawaiian) Islands. Even before the sails were furled,
the ship was surrounded by a crowd of swimming native women,
known as "Whyhunas," who were eagerly invited on board.
Soon the *Hero's* decks were the scene of an all-out orgy, or as
Morrell put it, "every man took to himself a rib" for the price
of a "check shirt or an old handkerchief." According to Morrell,
who asked that his journal be destroyed after his friend in New
York had read it, "A smile or nod by the men was sufficient to
win [the women's] affections and obtain them for the time being
as a wife."

Needless to say, the logs left by the officers of Nantucket
whalers are without any mention of these kinds of scenes.
However, the last toast of the *Loper* banquet, delivered by an
African-American crew member and recorded in dialect in the
local paper, indicates that by 1830 the whalemen's debaucher-
ies in the Sandwich Islands were already public knowledge: "To
Woahoo—Glad he cant speak no cuckold telltale, den all our
captains go by him jus like ship *Loper*." For his part, Starbuck
seems to have adopted a strategy of silence when it came to reconciling his life as a whaling captain with his life as a husband
and father. According to his granddaughter, "Grandfather Starbuck never wanted to talk about his voyage[s]." Instead, Starbuck
left the talking to his friends, who cast him as the man "who
brought success to everything he put his hand to."

Unfortunately, even a man of Starbuck's mythic stature
proved to be only human when in 1843 he came out of retirement
for one last voyage as captain of the *Zone*. By this time the whaling grounds that had once served him so well—most notably
the "Japan Ground"—had become over-fished. After a voyage of
three years, he returned home with 1,226 barrels of oil, half of
what he had taken in the *Loper* in a single year. And then, to add
a disturbing end note to this disturbingly anti-climactic voyage,

Starbuck arrived on November 10, 1846, to find his home port in ashes, the victim of the Great Fire.

Perhaps on that bleak November day Starbuck thought back to a very different homecoming: that summer Sunday in 1821 when he returned as commanding officer and saviour of his first ship, the *Hero*; a day when, as fate would have it, another young captain returned to Nantucket but with a very different tale to tell. Many years later, an islander would remember:

> *We can never forget the Sunday, August 5th, 1821, the day the ship* Two Brothers *was announced in sight from the watch tower, for she had Captain Pollard as a passenger. In looking back to that day, with all its excitements, for there were full fifteen hundred people upon our wharves, we remember the interest manifested by our citizens for these afflicted men of the sea, suffering . . . as none had in any of our long career of whaling life. The same day . . . the ship* Hero, *Capt. Obed Starbuck, arrived without her captain, James Russell, who had been killed by the Spaniards. . . . This was of course adding to our excitements of the hour.*

From the "excitements" of this hour, Obed Starbuck and George Pollard went on to become the respective golden boy and dark man of the Nantucket whale fishery. With Starbuck as its standard-bearer, yet haunted by Pollard's sad and terrifying example, an island pursued its destiny.

Absalom Boston and Abram Quary: "Of Color" on the Grey Lady

THEIR PORTRAITS could not be more different. The first, painted around 1820, shows a prosperous sailing master: confident, substantial, with two gold earrings giving his otherwise formal appearance an exotic flavor of the sea. This is Absalom Boston, one of Nantucket's most prominent African-American citizens in the nineteenth century, a man so at ease with himself and his world that the only thing distinguishing him from a typical Nantucket whaling captain is the color of his skin.

The second portrait, painted in 1851, shows an elderly man sitting beside a basket of huckleberries. With his long, thinning hair neatly combed and his hands clasped politely in his lap, he has the dignified, somewhat threadbare grace of a banished courtier. Through the window behind him you can see the town of Nantucket in the distance: the church spires and a veritable forest of masts. When compared to the robust self-confidence of the Boston portrait, this is a marginal man: his narrow face sad and contemplative, his bare feet the only real indication of who he is: Abram Quary, the last Native American to practice traditional ways on Nantucket.

But for all their apparent differences, Boston and Quary shared a common ancestry. Quary, according to a variety of sources, was a "half-breed"; Boston, revered today as the island's "first African-American whaling captain," was also the son of a

Nantucket Indian by the name of Thankful Micah. But while Boston chose to participate in Nantucket's whaling economy, Quary retired to a two-room shack in Shimmo on what is still called today Abram's Point. There he made baskets and ship models, and at one point threatened to shoot a party of trinket gatherers who were digging up the Indian burial grounds near his home. When asked about his younger days (it was rumored that his father was Nathan Quibby, a notorious Indian hanged for the murder of a white man), his "already decided taciturnity [would] run into obstinacy" and he would refuse to speak. Two years after sitting for his portrait, his health had so declined that he was persuaded to move to the town's almshouse where he died a year later at the age of eighty-three. There is a photograph of him in extreme old age, perhaps taken in front of the almshouse, in which he appears to be setting forth on a fishing expedition, a long wooden rod in his hand, his lean body hunched and frail.

Whereas Quary remained faithful to the Native American side of his ancestry, thus isolating himself from the mainstream of nineteenth-century Nantucket, Absalom Boston identified himself wholeheartedly with the African-American side of his heritage. Unlike the situation of the Indians, conditions had been steadily improving for Nantucket's blacks, especially given the fact that they had first come to the island as slaves. Although the Nantucket Friends would eventually develop a nation-wide reputation for abolitionism, the island's first practicing Quaker, Stephen Hussey, was also one of its foremost slaveholders. In a will made up in 1716, he left "to my wife my Negro woman Sarah; to my son Silvanus the Negro boy Mark; and to my daughter, Theodate, my Negro girl Dorothy."

Boston's father, Seneca, a weaver, had been owned by William Swain, whose heirs were forced to free him when a 1773 court case resulted in the virtual elimination of slavery on the island. By this time, the Nantucket Friends had long since committed themselves to abolitionism, their position eloquently argued by the carpenter Elihu Coleman in the pamphlet "A Testimony Against the Anti-Christian Practice of Making Slaves of Men," published in 1733. In the years prior to the Revolution, it was the wealthy Quaker whaling merchant William Rotch who insured the freedom of Nantucket's remaining slaves by threatening to hire the noted Boston lawyer John Adams if the Swains did not agree to free Absalom's uncle, Prince Boston.

From 1770 to 1790, Absalom's father and uncles purchased land in the vicinity of what is now known as Five Corners at the intersection of Pleasant and West York Streets. As early as 1723, Africa, a black weaver, had purchased land in this part of town, then known as the West Monomoy shares, and as the Indian settlement in Miacomet began to disband in the aftermath of the 1763 plague, many Native Americans, their numbers bolstered, according to Crèvecoeur, by "removals" from the Vineyard, began to gravitate in this direction, ultimately becoming part of a community known as "New Guinea."

While the Nantucket Quakers had done their best to insulate themselves from the rest of the world, here was a community where a different attitude prevailed. Indeed, when viewed from the perspective of today's multicultural society, New Guinea, not the "Quaker Utopia" to the north, was the island's truly exemplary community. With its own stores, school, church, and graveyard, this was a place where Nantucket's men and women "of color" operated in a microcosm of extraordinary diversity that was knit together by family bonds which in the case of Absalom Boston extended back three generations.

Adding to New Guinea's mix of Native and African Americans was the arrival in the 1760s of Portuguese from the Cape Verde and Azores Islands as Nantucket whalers began to expand their operations to the west coast of Africa. Just as the Bostons were one of Nantucket's leading black families, the Williamses were an early Portuguese clan, and throughout the eighteenth century the two families would not only employ one another but also intermarry. By 1820, there were 274 people (approximately four percent of the island's population) who called New Guinea home.

Although members of the Quaker hierarchy on the island were against slavery, this did not mean that they thought of the residents of New Guinea as their equals. For those whose ships required cheap and bountiful labor, the growth of the black community was a matter of business rather than the result of lofty social ideals. With the dramatic decrease in the Indian population, they needed an alternative labor source, and the blacks were it. According to a visitor to Nantucket writing in 1807:

> *The Indians having disappeared, Negroes are now substituted in their place. Seamen of color are more submissive than the whites; but as they are more addicted to frolicking, it is difficult to get them aboard the ship, when it is about to sail, and to keep them aboard, after it has arrived. The Negroes, though they are to be prized for their habits of obedience, are not as intelligent as the Indians.*

There is evidence, however, that the expected "obedience" was not always forthcoming. During the summer of 1775, Abraham Williams of Sandwich wrote to Colonel Nathaniel Freeman in Watertown concerning "some particulars I have heard about Nantucket." First on his list was a "considerable riot and affray there between the Negroes and Portuguese on the one side and the inhabitants on the other; in consequence whereof many of our Indians and mulattoes are come off." Of interest is that four different terms (Negro, Portuguese, Indian, and mulatto) are used to describe those involved "on the one side" of the disturbance, corroborating Daniel Vickers's observation that blacks,

Indians, and Portuguese "came to be regarded by their English employers as a single, undifferentiated, subordinate caste." Also of interest is that the incident prompted a large number of them to leave the island, suggesting that at this stage, Nantucket was more of a way station than a home for seamen of color.

Inevitably, however, as the fishery began to stabilize after the shocks of the Revolution and the War of 1812, New Guinea began to acquire the look and feel of a settled community. Besides a group of houses and gardens, as well as pasture land, there was the African Baptist Church, erected in 1825. As it had been for the Indians in the previous century, this meeting house, which still stands at the corner of York and Pleasant Streets, was an important focal point for the community. Besides housing regular church services, the building was used as a school and may have been made available to the noted Native American author and itinerant minister William Apess, who came to the island in the late 1820s, "preaching the word wherever door was opened." Although Obed Macy commented that, like the Indians before them, the island's African Americans' "inebriety and want of economy kept them poor," by the 1830s New Guinea had reached the point that its residents considered it a "pleasant and healthy" village.

Throughout this period, Absalom Boston emerged as one of New Guinea's leading citizens. Although the town of Nantucket was a strictly segregated community (the Friends, despite their opposition to slavery, steadfastly refused to accept blacks into their Society), Boston enjoyed a very different environment while on board a Nantucket whaler, particularly in the early days of his career. The rigid discipline of shipboard life tended to treat each member of the crew in terms of his rank rather than his background. In the midst of a howling gale, a captain depended on the quality of his crew, not their skin color, and if a black seaman fulfilled his duties, he generally earned the same amount as his white counterpart. In fact, in the years after the Revolution, at least one all-black whaling ship may have sailed from Nantucket. In a tattered collection of letters and verse at the Nantucket Atheneum is recorded "The Arrivals of the Brazil Whalemen in the year 1788." Almost all the captains listed are from Nantucket's leading families; however, at the bottom of the list, recorded as arriving on the fifth of July, is a ship that has no specific captain named; instead it is referred to as "The Guine[a] Men."

Beginning around 1800, Absalom's career as a "Black Man Mariner" enabled him to put away enough money to allow him to obtain a license to run a public inn in 1820. Two years later, at the age of thirty-seven, he helped organize and finance an all-black whaling voyage on the *Industry*. Also serving as captain, Boston and his African-American crew departed from Nantucket in May of 1822. Unfortunately, the voyage proved to be a financial disaster. Six months later the *Industry* returned with only seventy barrels of oil, requiring that the ship be auctioned off. From that time forward, Boston seems to have remained on island, opening a store while buying and selling land in and around New Guinea.

According to the Nantucket abolitionist and women's rights activist Anna Gardner, Boston was employed at one time by her grandfather, Francis G. Macy, "to do outdoor work," and because of his contact with the Macy household, he became "quite domesticated," i.e., educated. Boston was one of the island's first subscribers to William Lloyd Garrison's anti-slavery paper *The Liberator* and frequently visited Gardner's mother to discuss the issues of the day.

By 1830, his stature in New Guinea had reached the point that when the *Loper* and its nearly all-black crew returned in record time, Boston and his friend Samuel Harris were the ones who directed what would become not only the celebration of a voyage but an expression of the pride and aspirations of their community. In a series of "volunteer toasts" (recorded in dubious dialect in the *Inquirer*), Boston raised his glass and proclaimed, "To Misser General Lafayette—He freed de poor Frenchmen—hope he come 200 years ago and free poor darky to de South." After a burst of shouts and applause, he continued, "To Peoples of Color—May de enemy of our celebration and of African freedom, hab 'ternal itch and no benefit of scratch so long as he lib." And finally, "To City of Boston—Where seed ob liberty come from—Washington plant him, Lafayette till him, may African reap him." In this last toast to his namesake, Boston made it clear that as far as the country's African Americans were concerned, the full benefits of the American Revolution were yet to be realized.

Meanwhile, the whalemen's activities in the Pacific Ocean were bringing them in regular contact with yet another people of color, and by March of 1822, a handful of Hawaiians had made their way to Nantucket. In April of that year, the *Inquirer* reported that seven of them were attending Sunday school at the First Congregational Church. Soon a story appeared in a Boston paper under the headline "Heathen School in Nantucket": "The place has long been the resort of youths from pagan countries. . . . [T]here reside there twenty Society or Sandwich Islanders who on stated evenings when the sky was clear, assembled in the streets, erected ensigned idols, and in frantic orgies paid their homage to the Host of Heaven. No Barnabas or Paul running among them, saying, 'Why do you do such things?'"

As was to be expected, this inspired an immediate response from a Nantucketer who did indeed "recollect seeing the tawny youngsters alluded to in merry gambols." Rather than apologizing for his fellow townspeople, the respondent applauded the fact "that nobody disturbed them while they worshipped the Host of Heaven." He then concluded by suggesting that the "disinterested missionaries" currently at work throughout the Pacific could do with some of the Nantucketers' tolerance for foreign cultures.

By 1825 the *Inquirer* estimated that there were "more than fifty natives of the South Sea Islands employed on board the whaleships belonging to this port," and that "many are now on the island. They are extremely tractable, free and ingenuous—and if they become vicious the fault is not their own." Where these Polynesians lived while on Nantucket is difficult to determine. Few, if any, of them seem to have settled permanently on the island; no South Sea Islanders are specifically mentioned in the census rolls. Some may have stayed in Absalom Boston's boarding house between voyages. In any event, if we recall the scene aboard the *Hero* in Oahu (see Chapter 15), the treatment of these Sandwich Islanders seems to have been of an entirely different order from that experienced by their sisters.

By 1830, the year of the *Loper* banquet, things had begun to change within the Nantucket whale fishery. A dramatic increase in the number of Portuguese sailors, as well as an ever-expanding pool of South Sea Islanders, resulted in a gradual decrease in the number of African and Native Americans employed on Nantucket whaleships. Throughout this period (1830–60), working conditions and pay on board the whalers went from bad to worse. In fact, the pay on a Nantucket whaler gradually became so low that many a greenhand discovered that when the voyage was over and the cost of his clothing (provided from the ship's "slop chest") was subtracted from his "lay," he actually owed the owner money! Reuben Delano, for example, tells of returning home from his first whaling voyage only to realize he was forty dollars in the red. His response was fairly typical: Get drunk and go to sea again, thus entering the same vicious circle that had been a Nantucket tradition ever since the first days of Indian debt servitude in the seventeenth century. Now, however, the circle had widened.

But as the circle widened, Nantucketers turned increasingly inward, jealously guarding their privileged status as ship's officers with a truly clannish intensity. Although all off-islanders or "Coofs" were outside this charmed circle, Nantucket whaling captains were by no means color-blind in their abuse of off-island crews. According to one observer, "an African is treated like a brute by the officers of their ships. Should these pages fall into the hands of any of my colored brethren, let me advise them to fly Nantucket as they would the Norway Maelstrom." Thomas Nickerson also mentions the Nantucket whaling captains' reputation as "Negro drivers," and in the case of the *Essex*, all six of her off-island African-American crew members died, whereas seven out of fourteen white crew members survived.

Whether or not a man's color had any direct bearing on his chances of surviving the *Essex* disaster, Herman Melville, who may have been one of the island's biggest fans, recognized that its whaling captains could be racists of the highest order. In an article entitled "The 'Gees" (in reference to "an abbreviation, by seamen, of Portugee, the corrupt form of Portuguese"), he satirizes the attitudes that were then prevalent toward Portuguese sailors. After specifying the traits that distinguish the 'Gee as an "inferior (though hardy) race," whose main attraction is that they will work "for biscuits instead of dollars," Melville points to "old Captain Hosea Kean, of Nantucket" as the world's leading expert in procuring 'Gees. This is a man whose appetite for cheap labor has made him a veritable 'Gee connoisseur: "Like the Negro, the 'Gee has a peculiar savor, but a different one—a sort of wild, marine, gamy savor, as in the seabird called haglet."

Underlying Melville's bitter satire is the fact that while island Quakers enjoyed an ever-increasing reputation as high-minded abolitionists (Frederick Douglass would begin his career as an orator during an anti-slavery meeting at the Nantucket Atheneum in 1841), they showed little interest in addressing the problems in their own backyard. The irony was not lost on J. Ross Browne, who wrote in 1841: "Massachusetts being largely interested in the whale fishery, has constantly before her practical demonstrations of the horrors of slavery. The philanthropists of that state will, it is to be hoped, make some grand efforts in behalf of the seamen employed in their whaling fleet, as soon as they dispose of the African race."

Meanwhile, back on the island itself, the disparity between Nantucket's public reputation as an abolitionist stronghold (a "refuge of the free" according to the Quaker poet John Greenleaf Whittier) and the reality of being a nonwhite Nantucketer was becoming disturbingly apparent. In 1840, Eunice Ross, a seventeen-year-old student at the African School on York Street was denied entry into the town's all-white high school, even though she had passed the entrance exam. During the next six years, attempts to change Nantucket's segregated status quo were met, for the most part, with strong opposition. In 1842, it was reported that town officials had allowed pro-slavery rioters to harass an abolitionist meeting, while selectmen and school committee members led a continuing battle to keep African Americans out of their high school. One Nantucketer, David Joy, became so disillusioned with his native island that he moved to Northampton, Massachusetts, where he reported, "there is less bitterness and determined pro-slavery."

There was another Nantucketer, however, who refused to give up the fight to open the school system to African Americans. In 1845 Absalom Boston filed suit against the town so that his seventeen-year-old daughter, Phebe, could attend the high school. Finally in 1846, after a major shake-up in the composition of the school committee, the system was integrated, allowing not only Phebe Boston but also Eunice Ross, who was now twenty-four years old, to continue their educations. Three years later the pride that Boston must have felt over this dramatic turn of events changed to sorrow when Phebe suddenly died of dysentery.

For Boston, this was only one of many personal losses. By the time he died in 1855 at the age of sixty-nine, he had been preceded by two wives and five of his children. Abram Quary, it was said, lost not only his wife but also all his children prior to taking up residence in Shimmo. Although members of the Boston family would remain on the island into the twentieth century, Quary's death in 1854 marked the symbolic, if not the literal, end of Native Americans on Nantucket.

Quary's race was not the only native culture to endure devastating changes as a consequence of their contact with white Nantucketers. As we have seen, by the 1820s the whalemen's attention had turned to the peoples of the South Sea Islands, known collectively as "Kanakas." If the men proved "tractable" whaling hands, the women were just as easily coerced into prostitution. Of all the island whaling ports, the worst, according to the historian Ernest Dodge, was the Bay of Islands in New Zealand, with which Nantucket had an extremely close connection (see Chapter 18). Whereas most Nantucketers had at least a modicum of respect for the Sandwich Islanders, many dismissed the Maoris of New Zealand as "cannibals." The whaling captains' fascination with the Maoris' skill in manufacturing shrunken heads created a black market in these artifacts that encouraged rival tribes to war against each other so as to acquire more heads for the illicit trade. Indeed, if a whaling captain saw a native whose facial tattoos especially appealed to him, he "might order a head on the hoof, so to say," and when he returned on his next voyage, the shrunken head would be waiting for him.

Prostitution also flourished on the Bay of Islands. In Dodge's words, an extremely "lucrative business" centered on "supplying the captains—more fastidious than their crews—with temporary wives." Meanwhile the captains' ships became what the second American consul at the port described as "floating castles of prostitution." Due to the effects of disease and the shrunken-head market, the Maori population was cut in half by 1839, a pattern that was repeated wherever the whalemen roamed throughout the Pacific.

As early as 1825 the *Nantucket Inquirer* commented: "Thus the benefits as well as the evils of civilization are gradually spreading throughout these remote regions—leaving the question still undetermined, whether savage or cultivated man be most capable of enjoying happiness." By the 1840s, when Herman Melville saw these islands firsthand, it was no longer an open question. In a lecture entitled "The South Seas," first delivered in 1858, he claimed that "the whalemen of Nantucket" had, with "those brutal and cruel vices which disgust even savages with our manners," spearheaded the transformation of "an earthly paradise into a pandemonium."

Late in life Melville would meditate in verse on how the whalers he had once glorified as "so many Alexanders" in *Moby-Dick* might also be considered "pirates of the sphere . . . who in the name of Christ and Trade" (read: Quaker whalemen) "dispossessed . . . the Indians East and West" while "Deflower[ing] the world's last sylvan glade." If a temporary window of opportunity opened on Nantucket for African Americans such as Absalom Boston, it must be placed in the context of what happened to these "Indians East and West." On the island today, the human cost of the Nantucketers' remorseless hunt for whales can still be seen in the sad, mournful eyes in the portrait of Abram Quary.

CHAPTER 17

Maria Mitchell,
the Provincial Cosmopolitan

I N ONE SENSE, Nantucket was an island of astronomers. The whalemen depended on stars for navigation; stars were also the one thing the whalemen still shared with their wives and children even though they might be separated by two oceans and a continent. Just about every house had a roof walk (no one on Nantucket referred to them as "widow's walks"), and with ship's telescopes as common as umbrellas are today, it was only natural that Nantucketers took more than an ordinary interest in the heavens.

In 1829, when Maria (pronounced "Ma-RYE-ah") Mitchell was only eleven years old, the editor of the *Nantucket Inquirer*, Samuel Jenks, attended an astronomy lecture delivered by her father and then wrote an eloquent editorial on the importance of the science to all members of the Nantucket community—not just to both landsmen and sailors but to women as well as men: "Are the imaginations of women less vivid than those of men? If not, why should their minds be denied the privilege of contemplating the countless orbs of argent light that roll in silent magnificence through the deep illimitable expanse?" Although this opinion may have made perfect sense to most Nantucketers, it would have struck many off-islanders as a shocking outrage. Even after she had made a name for herself in the world's astronomical circles, a "learned" gentleman asked Maria if the delicate constitution of a woman made it difficult to stay up late watching the stars. "Sir," she responded, "my mother had more night work than astronomy will ever demand of any woman. She brought up eight children."

As Crèvecoeur had observed back in the eighteenth century, the whale fishery tended to foster a more independent breed of women; also at work among the islanders was Quakerism's belief in the spiritual and intellectual equality of the sexes. With their husbands away for extensive periods of time, Nantucket wives were required not only to manage the household but also in many instances to run their own businesses so as to keep money coming in. The women also maintained an active network of social ties, visiting each other on what Crèvecoeur described as an "incessant" basis. When a husband returned from a voyage, he joined his wife in the socializing, an unheard of practice on the mainland where women and men traveled in entirely different social spheres. Commented Lucretia Mott, who was born and raised on Nantucket before moving to Philadelphia, "How odd it would seem to the natives [of Nantucket] for husbands to not be as ready as wives to visit."

But for those of us from the twentieth century looking to Nantucketers such as Mott and Mitchell as prototypes of the modern woman, it is easy to romanticize the island into a utopia it never was. Nantucket women were, for the most part, independent out of necessity, not out of choice. Loneliness and the nagging fear that their husbands might never return were a constant part of life on Nantucket. In a letter written by the wife of the whaleman Peter Folger, a sense of frustrated longing underlies what is an otherwise extremely level-headed (and very Mary Starbuck–like) communication:

> *Loving Husband, I write these lines to let you know that we are all well at present, and I hope this letter will find you the same. I lack for nothing this world affords but only your good*

company. I hope it won't be long before I have your company.
I want to hear from you very much. I would not have you
think it strange that I sent no letter by Barzillai Folger. At
that time I had neither pen, ink, nor paper.

In her comments concerning her brother Jonathan, Mrs. Folger offers insights into the difficult, even desperate process by which two young Nantucketers found the time and opportunity to fall in love: "Jonathan came here . . . and is now gone again. . . . He sailed 20 days ago for the Davis Straits. Jonathan went upon Town almost every night. He would have married before he went away [but] Father would not consent to it yet."

The cumulative pressures of such a life inevitably took their toll. Whether or not opium was as widely used by Nantucket wives as Crèvecoeur claimed, large numbers of opium bottles have been found amid the buried refuse of the Great Fire of 1846. The long stretches without a sexual partner (while their husbands were amid the notorious temptations of the South Sea islands) must have also been difficult to bear (see Notes). In any event, the three-years-away, three-months-at-home cycle of the Nantucket whale-men, while it may have produced its share of "superior wives," was not without its emotional, psychic, and physical costs.

And even though women were given a remarkable amount of responsibility and independence on Nantucket, married couples did not necessarily enjoy an equal partnership. He may have been almost always gone, but the husband still ruled the roost. In the late eighteenth century a young Nantucket woman addressed a poem to a friend who had just been married:

> *Small is the province of a wife*
> *And narrow is her sphere in life*
> *Within that sphere to move a right*
> *Should be your principal delight.*

For all their "peculiarities," Nantucketers were also very much a product of their times.

To a certain extent, the young Maria Mitchell enjoyed the benefits of Nantucket life while remaining insulated from many of its drawbacks. On an island where most children grew up barely knowing their fathers, Maria's childhood was dominated by the presence of William Mitchell—a remarkably capable and broadminded man, who worked as (among other things) a farmer, teacher, and bank cashier. By the time Jenks's editorial about astronomy and women appeared, the eleven-year-old Maria was already assisting her father in his astronomical observations. The whaling captains on the island brought their ship's chronometers to William Mitchell to be "rated" (calibrated), and it was not long before Maria was able to perform the service, making observations with a sextant from the backyard of the family house on Vestal Street.

Although he dabbled in various business ventures associated with the whale fishery, William Mitchell was most interested in other things. One of Nantucket's foremost educators, he ran several schools on the island until he accepted a job as cashier at the Pacific Bank. The position not only provided a steady source of income, which the perpetually cash-strapped Mitchells sorely needed, but also gave them housing in the living quarters on the bank's second floor. Here, in a large room overlooking Main Street, which William called the "Hall," the Mitchells would gather among their chronometers and books. On the bank's roof they constructed a cupola-like observation booth for "sweeping the skies."

The Mitchells were part of a long line of primarily self-taught "scholars" on Nantucket that dated back to the illustrious Peter Folger. In the tradition of their forebear Benjamin Franklin— whose mother was, after all, a Nantucket Folger—the family had produced accomplished writers (à la "Uncle Pillick") as well as amazingly proficient experimental scientists. Walter Folger is said to have locked himself in his room until he came up with the secret to manufacturing spermaceti candles. His son, Walter, Jr., continued the scientific tradition, to the point that his wife is reputed to have said to a neighbor, "Why, sometimes I almost wish he didn't know any more than thy husband."

Maria seems to have been deeply impressed by this short, eccentric Benjamin Franklin look-alike, who published widely on "the dismal science of mathematics" while devising a clock that besides telling the time (from second to century) displayed the phases of the moon and tides, as well as the position of the sun. When she was not visiting Folger's fascinating, book-crammed home on Pleasant Street, Maria spent time with another role model, the elderly and mathematical Phoebe Folger, who, according to Maria, "taught navigation to her husband, and he became, in consequence, the captain of a ship."

With mentors and influences such as these, Maria quickly developed into a world-class astronomer. Although astronomy was the passion that dominated her life, it was, by no means, the only thing in her life. After a stint as a schoolteacher, Maria became the librarian at the Nantucket Atheneum, a post she maintained for almost twenty years. It was a job that gave her plenty of time for her astronomy (the Atheneum was open only on weekday afternoons and Saturday evenings) and also placed her in an important position within the island's cultural life. According to her sister Phebe Kendall, "Her visitors in the afternoon were elderly men of leisure, who enjoyed talking with so bright a girl on their favorite hobbies. When they talked Miss Mitchell closed her book and took up her knitting, for she was never idle. With some of these visitors the friendship was kept up for years."

She also formed lasting relationships with the girls and boys who came to the Atheneum. According to her sister, "the young girls made her their confidante and went to her for sympathy and advice." In her diary she recorded what seems to have been a fairly typical encounter with a local boy just back from the Pacific: "A young sailor boy came to see me today. It pleases me to have these lads seek me on their return from their first voyage, and tell me how much they have learned about navigation. They always say, with pride, 'I can take a lunar, Miss Mitchell, and work it up!'"

Throughout this period, Maria lived at home, taking an active part in the household chores. Although Quakers, the Mitchells worked against the type. In the front hall of their living quarters was a very un-Quakerly piano. When an elder from the Society suggested that William remove the instrument from his home or risk disownment, Maria's father mildly reminded the old man that as cashier of the bank he held the mortgage for the Friends meeting house. The piano stayed.

By the 1830s and '40s, the religion of Mary Starbuck had become something of a moral and spiritual dinosaur on Nantucket. In 1845, a letter appeared in the *Nantucket Inquirer* that declared, "It is a well known and lamentable fact that for many years the Society has been too much under the control of those who have but little, except their wealth to recommend them." In 1849, a visitor to the island attended a Quaker meeting with her friend Mrs. Folger and reported, "After sitting half an hour we were entertained for three-quarters of an hour by two old women and one man who repeated over and over again what Mrs. Folger says they have for twenty years." By the time she turned twenty-five, Maria had decided that Quakerism was not for her. According to the Society's "Book of Objections," "Maria Mitchell daughter of William had neglected the meetings. She told the committee that her mind was not settled on religious subjects and that she had no wish to retain her right in membership. Disowned 8–31–1843."

Quakerism was not the only aspect of island life in which Maria chose not to participate. Even though Nantucket was without many of the "amusements" in which young people indulged off island, there was still a very active social life, heightened no doubt by the island's reputation for producing beautiful women. According to one male observer, "it is almost impossible to avoid falling in love on Nantucket. The girls are so plentiful, and so pretty, that if the hearts of the men did not palpitate at the sight of them, the very grindstones would turn around with ecstasy." Given the island's communal lust for "Oil! Oil!" it is perhaps not unsurprising that courting rituals revolved around the whale fishery. Dancing parties on Nantucket were "very select," with "no youths being admitted except those who have struck a whale." Harpooners, who decorated their lapels with chock-pins (used on whaleboats to keep the line from tangling), were the most eligible of bachelors—not in the least because they were on the fast track toward officer and eventual captain's status.

Traditional Nantucket social circles were clearly not for Maria Mitchell. According to her sister Phebe, "She cared but little for general society, and had always to be coaxed to go into company." Self-consciously plain, with a dark complexion and deep voice (on an island where the girls were famous for their blond hair and black eyes), Maria dedicated herself to her science with a single-minded intensity rivaling that of the Nantucket whalemen. As a young woman, virtually all her evenings were spent with her astronomy; if the weather was bad, there were always calculations to perform. According to Phebe, "No matter how many guests there might be in the parlor, Miss Mitchell would slip out, don her regimentals as she called them, and, lantern in hand, mount to the roof."

Certainly Maria would not have been the astronomer she was if she had fit more comfortably into Nantucket social and spiritual circles. Indeed, despite its world-wide reach, Nantucket was a remarkably static place, where ancient customs and out-worn creeds must have felt stultifying to a woman whose ambitions did not involve winning a whaleman for a husband. (In 1840 Audubon observed that most islanders "know little more than the value of dollars.") Inevitably, she yearned to see the world beyond the island, just as had generation after generation of Nantucket men. In 1844, she wrote a whimsical poem concerning the legend of Maushop's moccasin that ended with this rather plaintive stanza:

> *Ill-judging Sachem! would that you*
> *Had never shaken here that shoe;*
> *Or, having done so, would again,*
> *And join Nantucket to the main!*

In 1852, a year after publishing *Moby-Dick*, Herman Melville came to Nantucket for the first time and spent an evening at the Mitchells' residence above the bank. Many years later he would publish a poem in which a female astronomer, after years of dedicating herself to the stars, seeks the affections of a man who remains oblivious to her. Entitled "After the Pleasure Party," the poem probably is as much about Melville's relationship with Nathaniel Hawthorne (whom both Melville and Maria knew) as it is about Maria Mitchell. Nonetheless, if Melville's portrait of "Urania" is any indication, Maria's life on Nantucket was not without its frustrations. In 1853, a year after meeting Melville, she complained in her diary about the limitations placed on a woman by society, declaring that "the needle is the chain of woman, and has fettered her more than the laws of the country." After mentioning the importance of education, she indignantly wrote, "I would as soon put a girl alone into a closet to meditate as give her only the society of her needle. . . . A woman is expected to know all kinds of woman's work, and the consequence is that life is passed in learning these only, while the universe of truth beyond remains unentered."

By this time forces were already in motion that would forever change not only Maria but also the island of her birth. Although the whaling business was booming in the rival ports of New Bedford and Sag Harbor throughout the 1840s, Nantucket found itself in the midst of a disturbing decline. On July 1, 1846, under the headline "Emigration from Nantucket," the *Nantucket Inquirer* reported on the large number of families being forced to leave the island in search of new opportunities. Unlike the emigrations of the Revolution and the War of 1812, this one was not of the rich, but of the lower and middle classes. The increased length of the voyages meant that there were fewer ships to fit out each year, providing fewer jobs to the "mechanics" living on the island. Also, improvements in manufacturing the "casks, pails, ironwork, etc." required for a whaling voyage had increased the profit margin for the shipowner while reducing job opportunities for the mechanics. According to the *Inquirer*, "Times may be good, capitalists may grow rich, but the mechanics cannot get employment." The writer went so far as to blame these "capitalists" for not investing in other on-island endeavors that might employ the dispossessed workers: "But our capitalists have been appealed to, and they will do nothing,—so that the only remedy which remains for the present over-population, is emigration." On an island gradually running out of economic steam, those who retained power only held it more closely to themselves.

And then, less than two weeks after the *Inquirer* made these comments concerning "capitalists" and "mechanics," came the "point from which all events are reckoned": the Great Fire of 1846. At this time the town was without a municipal fire department. Instead, privately organized "fire companies" were relied upon to respond to the alarm, connecting their hoses to giant cisterns underneath the surface of Main Street, then directing hand-pumped streams of water at the blaze. When smoke was spotted at William Geary's hat store and the alarm went out at around eleven o'clock at night, two fire companies arrived on the scene simultaneously. Although, according to one eyewitness, "a good smart stream of water at this juncture would have quenched the flames," the two companies began to argue among themselves about who should have the honor of putting out the fire.

Unfortunately, the island had been without rain for weeks, and the tinder dry structure was soon engulfed in flames. As other companies arrived, the fire spread from roof to roof, the crackling sound of burning wood gradually building to a deafening roar. The immense upward flow of heat created its own wind currents that circulated along the narrow, densely packed streets, spreading the fire in all directions. The center of a huge, swirling fire storm, Main Street became impassable as windborne fire brands flew through the air only to land on faraway roofs and burn down houses that had been assumed safe. The intense heat generated by the holocaust reduced iron safes to puddles of melted slag.

In a desperate attempt to stop the fire in its tracks, buildings were dynamited, the explosions adding to the terrifying confusion of the night. At one point, the fire wardens determined that the Methodist church (beside the Pacific Bank on Center Street) must also be blasted. In a tradition that may be too good to be true, Maria Mitchell was supposedly the person who rushed to the building's defense. The argument was that the swirling convection currents created by the fire at the head of Main Street would blow the flames away from the church. What is perhaps one of the town's most magnificent buildings still stands today as proof that the argument—whoever presented it—was a good one.

Although Maria may or may not have saved the Methodist

church, her roof-top observatory was almost completely destroyed before she and her father could put out the flames. Soon the same hot winds that saved the church proved to be the Atheneum's undoing. The Episcopal church that used to stand beside the present-day Jared Coffin House also succumbed to the flames. And then, after most of the commercial district of town had been lost to fire, it was the waterfront's turn. Warehouses packed to the rafters with casks of whale oil burned so hot that not even cinders remained the next morning. As the casks burst and the burning oil poured across the wharves and into the water, the harbor became a scalding sheet of flame. It made more than a few observers think of Sodom and Gomorrah.

Much has been written about how the islanders courageously banded together and rebuilt their town in a matter of months. A new Atheneum would be standing by February, even though the trustees' president, William Mitchell himself, had neglected to renew the building's fire insurance policy. But there was another side to the conflagration that would make it difficult for some Nantucketers to look each other in the eye after the smoke had, quite literally, cleared. A committee headed by Samuel Jenks reported that although many of the women in town "rendered more efficient service than could be obtained from the usually stronger sex," most town residents were guilty of an "appalling" lack of civic responsibility. Instead of pulling together to put out the fire, it had been a case of, in Jenks's words, "Save himself who can." After enumerating how "these facts reflect a measure of dishonor upon us," he reserved his strongest criticisms for the island's upper classes, bestowing "a sentence of censure upon those individuals, who possessed of wealth and influence, pressed into their private service large bodies of dependent laboring men— in effect hiring them to surrender the residue of the town to its fate—who, otherwise, without reward or incentive, could have wrought successfully against the desolating elements. . . ."

Even after the flames had died out, leaving the town a charred wasteland, it was still every man for himself. One townsperson told Ralph Waldo Emerson, who visited the island in May to help dedicate the new Atheneum, "At the fire they pilfered freely as if after a man was burnt out his things belonged to the fire & everybody might have them." Only a few days after the fire, another alarm was sounded, and Maria, perhaps fearful that her private papers might be subjected to the looting, destroyed all her diaries and letters. (According to her biographer, Helen Wright, "In those few tragic moments the early record of a remarkable life was lost forever.") In any event, it was now shockingly clear that the familial, virtually classless Utopia of "Old Nantucket" had vanished (if it had ever truly existed) long before it could be swallowed up in flames.

And yet the Great Fire of 1846 was not without its positive effects. Chastened by the events of that terrible summer night, the selectmen adopted measures to insure that it would never happen again, including a revamped system of fighting fires. The new town had wider, more sensibly laid-out streets. The most important changes to the town, however, were not in its physical structure and organization. The social fabric of the place was changing, as well as its cultural and commercial life. Although most accounts of Nantucket in the aftermath of the Fire make it sound as if the island plummeted headlong into ruin, such was not the case. Even amid the devastation of the Fire and the decline in whaling, the boom times of less than a decade before had a certain momentum; otherwise the town would have never been able to rebuild itself so quickly. Although three years later the California Gold Rush virtually evacuated the island of able-bodied men, many of the older and wealthier shipowners and merchants stayed on (according to Emerson, only "50 persons owned 5/7 of all the property in the island"), insuring that at least the upper stratum of the community remained relatively intact well into the 1850s.

In 1852 the trustees of the Coffin School built a new and dramatic brick structure on Winter Street; meanwhile, a long line of distinguished speakers—including Emerson, Thoreau, Frederick Douglass, Horace Mann, and many others—came to the new Atheneum, where Maria added steadily to the library's collections. Although not as prosperous and commercially alive as it had been in the "Great Days of Whaling," the island became a much more interesting place in which to live as the self-imposed blinders of the whale fishery were gradually removed. Nantucket's schools, by almost all accounts, had become first rate. And according to Theodore Parker, who lectured on the island, it was Nantucket's women who were the most deserving of praise: "I think there is no town in New England where the whole body of women is so well educated." Agriculture on the island experienced a resurgence as more than a few husbands returned from whaling voyages to discover that their wives had made more money on the family farm than they had made at sea. Inspired by this phenomenon, the ardent feminist Anna Gardner included these lines in her poem, "Nantucket Agricultural Song":

> *And the Goddess, fair Ceres benignant,*
> *When all undisputed her reign,*
> *Will scatter rare blessings abundant,*
> *O'er hill-top, and valley, and plain!*
> *Exotics may blossom in beauty,*
> *Where fallow-lands stretch to the shore,*
> *And each son of toil may make duty*
> *A pleasure he ne'er felt before.*

Just as the island entered into this post-Fire, post-boomtown mentality, Maria Mitchell made a discovery that was not without a certain irony, given the fact that a comet is traditionally regarded as the harbinger of, not the follow-up to, a natural disaster. In 1831 the King of Denmark had offered a gold medal to "the first discoverer of a telescopic comet," and in 1847, just over a year after the Great Fire, Maria made the sighting that qualified her for this coveted award. Her sister Phebe has left us with this account:

> *On the evening of Oct. 1, 1847, there was a party of invited guests at the Mitchell home. As usual, Maria slipped out, ran up to the telescope, and soon returned to the parlor and told her father that she thought she saw a comet. Mr. Mitchell hurried upstairs, stationed himself at the telescope, and as soon as he looked at the object pointed out by his daughter declared it to be a comet.*

The discovery soon gave her world-wide attention, and in 1848 she became the first female member of the American Academy of Arts and Sciences. The following year she was asked to become a paid "computer" for the American Nautical Almanac, as well as for the United States Coastal Survey. In 1855, after attending an annual convention of the Academy in Boston, she recorded in her diary, "It is really amusing to find one's self lionized in a city where one has visited quietly for years; to see the doors of fashionable mansions open wide to receive you, which never opened before. I suspect that the whole corps of science laughs in its sleeves at the farce."

Maria's commitments had reached the point that by 1854 she had "determined not to spend so much time at the Atheneum another season, but to put some one in my place who shall see the strange faces and hear the strange talk." She also wanted to travel, and in 1857 a wealthy Midwestern banker asked her to chaperone his daughter on a tour of the Southern states and Europe. While in Liverpool, England, Maria and her charge received word that the girl's father had lost his fortune in a nation-wide financial panic, requiring that the girl return home immediately. Maria, however, decided to stay on, ultimately traveling with the family of Nathaniel Hawthorne through France and Italy. Of the noted author, she wrote, "His hair stands out on each side, so much so that one's thoughts naturally turn to combs and hair-brushes. . . ."

Hawthorne's young son Julian was, according to Maria, "in love with me," and later in life he would record his impressions of the Nantucket astronomer and traveling companion: "There was a simplicity and a dry humor about this lady; . . . as if a bit of shrewd, primitive, kindly New England were walking and talking in the midst of the gray antiquity of Europe." Although now a world renowned astronomer, Maria was first and foremost a Nantucketer: witty, intelligent, and extremely down-to-earth. In fact, if anything, the European tour increased her appreciation for her native island. In 1859 she wrote to a friend on Nantucket:

> *Even in Rome, and after eight months in Europe, I think our Nantucket people are bright. . . . If I think well of the Nantucketers intellectually after "seeing the world," I must think well of them morally. I really believe there are few communities in the world to compare with it in this respect, and out of New England, I am afraid there are none. So you see, I shall not come back despising the sea-girt isle, if I have looked upon sunnier ones.*

Ultimately she would become a professor of astronomy at Vassar College, a post she would hold for twenty years. But this part of her life, in which she employed some relatively radical teaching techniques (many of them inherited from her free-thinking father), is beyond the scope of this volume.

To return to the island of her upbringing (where Maria

Mitchell is buried within sight of an observatory owned by the Maria Mitchell Association), it is safe to say that there was probably no other town in nineteenth-century America that could have produced a woman of Maria's remarkable character and abilities. But perhaps Nantucket's greatest gift to the young astronomer was that it instilled in her a need to one day venture beyond the confines of her "sea-girt isle." In the true Nantucket tradition, Maria Mitchell, though a product of a tiny, often ingrown community, had been destined to become a woman of the world.

CHAPTER 18

F. C. Sanford, the Mythmaker

B Y THE 1860s AND '70s, Nantucket's glory days as the
whaling capital of the world were a distant memory.
Although efforts had been made to point the economy
in a different direction (silk, shoe, and straw-hat manufacturing were all attempted), they were doomed to failure. If it did
not involve a harpoon, few on this island of defunct whalemen
wanted anything to do with it; in fact, it was said that most
Nantucketers displayed a decided "lack of cooperation" whenever these newfangled enterprises were proposed. According
to Alexander Starbuck, "It was difficult to lead them into new
and strange channels. A people cannot change in a day the habits that have become inbred by two centuries of activity in one
direction."

Given the island's remoteness and spectacular summertime
climate, it was generally agreed that Nantucket's only hope was
to attract vacationers. As early as 1845, the *Inquirer* had predicted, "Every day's experience convinces us that our little island
is destined to become *the* watering place of the country, to which
the wealthy, and fashionable, and health-seeking thousands . . .
will fly, for relaxation or pleasure during the summer months."
But here, once again, there was resistance from the Nantucketers. For a people who had once fished for the "salt-sea mastodon,"
fishing for tourists was a major indignity. As Mary E. Starbuck
wrote, "It is not entirely in accordance with our 'druthers' that

our island has become within a few years a fairly popular summer resort." For Starbuck it was particularly wrenching to see the old whaling captains—"upright, chivalrous, kindly if humorously tolerant"—subjected to the fatuous scrutiny of summer folk. Wrote Starbuck, "We rise to protest. We are islanders, and our island has an illustrious past." To see the island degenerate into a carnival show for Coofs was more than any self-respecting Nantucketer could rightly stand. As Alexander Starbuck correctly predicted, only "with the passing of the last of the generations of whalemen" would the island be able to turn successfully to "new enterprises."

In the meantime, Nantucket slipped into its darkest and most listless days. By 1870, the island had "not a ship, bark, brig, or vessel of any kind, suggestive of the vast amount of business done in the past." By 1875 the population had dwindled to just over 3,000 souls (compared with 10,000 at the peak of the island's prosperity). Beyond the "lethargic old wharves," where "a few battered and dismantled hulks of whaleships" rotted silently, lay a virtual ghost town. One visitor in the early 1870s wrote, "Here, indeed, was the town, but where were the people?" According to another, "Nantucket now has a 'body-o'-death' appearance such as few New England towns possess. The houses stand around in faded gentility style—the inhabitants have a dreamy look, as though they live in the memories of the past." The "idleness" that had been in Crèvecoeur's day "the most heinous sin that can be committed in Nantucket" had become a way of life. Even Mary E. Starbuck admitted, "we seem quite content to sit still and let things happen."

The truly amazing thing was how quickly Nantucket had fallen. Men who had made whaling history in the 1820s, such as Obed Starbuck and George Pollard, were still walking the town's streets in the 1870s. With little in the present to occupy the attention of contemporary Nantucketers, the focus of the island inevitably turned backward, toward these men and their glorious past. And as each year brought the passing of yet another one of these whaling captains, Nantucket watched its connection to this heritage fade gradually away. Unless something was done about it, Nantucket, once the great "Mother Ship" of the American whale fishery, would be cast adrift, her cable to the past cut forever.

Answering this need to fill up the emptiness of the present with the heroic ghosts of a vanished era was Frederick Coleman Sanford, a retired merchant and shipping agent, who lived out the last years of his eventful life not only as president of the Pacific Bank and a gentleman farmer but also as a widely published author. From the memories of his youth and the stories he had been told, he would write a series of fascinating reminiscences about a time when Nantucket was "the Chief in the World!"—a romantic vision of the island that is just as captivating today as it was 100 years ago.

Listen now to F. C. Sanford as he replaces the preternatural silence of Nantucket's decaying waterfront with the "multitudinous din" of the 1820s, when more than a thousand workmen hurried down to the waterfront each morning:

I love to stand now on the wharves where the huge oil-blackened hulls of the whalers once swung, and recall the scene. Heavy-timbered three-storied warehouses filled the heads of the wharves, beside which half a hundred vessels would lie, discharging or taking in cargo. Overhead were the sail-lofts, with the riggers and sailmakers busy sewing the white canvas or shaping spars. Then there were the blacksmith shops, where the ironwork for the ships and tools used in fishing were made; and the cooper shops, that turned out their hundreds of butts and casks per day, and the huge ropewalks, seven in number, where men spun, walking to and

fro, all the cordage used in shipbuilding and for repairs. It
was indeed a busy scene.

The central figures in this drama were, of course, the whaling
captains, "knight-errants of the world," whom Sanford dubbed
the "Sea Kings." There was Captain Edmund Gardner, permanently disfigured by his experience in a sperm whale's mouth: one
hand gone and an "indentation in his head deep enough to hold
an egg." There was Captain Obed Fitch, "a fine, majestic figure
over six feet tall," who could lift up a barrel of water "as easily as
an ordinary seaman a bucket." And there was Captain Benjamin
Hussey, his huge head containing "a half-bushel of brains," whose
last voyage would be to the Greenland fishery. As the rugged captain guided his ship through the ice floes, a chunk of ice "crushed
against the rudder and threw him over the wheel, breaking his
ribs." Captain Hussey ultimately died of these injuries at the age
of eighty years and five months. Challenged Sanford, "If you can
show me anything like this I will come down a peg."

Although these "large and noble figures" were all revered
by Sanford, they were part of a larger, and even nobler social
phenomenon: the "most enterprising and dauntless community
on the face of the Earth," whose commercial ambitions extended
far beyond the selling of whale oil. For, as Sanford repeatedly
pointed out, Nantucket also had ships that sailed to China
and India. In fact, as a boy it had been not so much the life
of a whaleman as the exotic goods of the Orient—"liquorice,
spices of India and Ceylon, and tea-chests covered with strange
hieroglyphics"—that had captured his imagination. Nantucketers still talked about the day in December of 1807 (two years
before Sanford's birth) when the Cantonese trader Punqua
Wingchong (whom Sanford recorded as "Wing Ling") and
a fellow merchant, both wearing "caps with red buttons upon
the top," arrived in Nantucket on the ship *Favorite* (Jonathan

Paddack, Master) to see the owner Paul Gardner. This was during the days of the Jeffersonian Embargo, and when Gardner failed to act upon Wingchong's request for a trading permit from Washington, the door was opened for John Jacob Astor in New York, who ultimately cleared (according to Sanford's not always reliable memory) $500,000 in a single shipment of tea. It was a lesson in the need for decisive action that the young Sanford would never forget.

Combining a risk-taker's boldness with a truly visionary sense of his own destiny, Sanford would one day become the island's leading merchant, with control over a quarter of the entire Nantucket fleet. Even as the island fell into a precipitous decline, Sanford demonstrated a remarkable talent for turning a "Proffit" (which he always spelled with two f's for emphasis). By the time of his retirement in the 1850s, he was poised to begin what would become a thirty-five-year project: the redemption of Nantucket's nearly static present through the evocation of a ceaselessly heroic, ever-glorious past. To this day, it is a vision of the island's whaling heritage that Nantucketers are loath to part with.

✎

Like most Nantucket boys, Sanford went to sea at the age of fourteen, shipping out with Captain Joseph Barney on the *Equator.* But when he returned home from the Sandwich Islands at the age of seventeen, he discovered that his father had died, requiring that he remain on island with his mother. So he took up the trade of watch repair, quite a comedown for a Nantucketer with the sea in his blood. As if to announce to the world that he would one day prevail, Sanford had a remarkable set of business cards printed up. Emblazoned across a magnificently drawn ship are the words "Never Despair," as an idealized woman sits upon a shore-side rock, her finger pointed toward the motto. Bordering this scene are the words "All Kinds of Watches and

Clocks Repaired. By Frederick C. Sanford, Nantucket, Massachusetts." Here was displayed a talent for self-promotion and hype that would serve both Sanford and his island extremely well in the years to come.

By 1830, the twenty-one-year-old Sanford had become a partner in the business of "Easton and Sanford" situated next door to the Manufacture and Mechanics Bank on Main Street, where the Hub is now located. Sanford's store specialized in upscale goods: "fine cutlery; gold and silver watches; gilt and fancy goods; silver spoons; jewelry, watch trimmings, etc." But Sanford, whose father had come from a long line of traders and merchants in Newport, had not entirely left the whaling business. Like many a Nantucket merchant, he also invested and traded in whale oil. Just down the street from Easton and Sanford was the "House of Lords," at one time the counting house of Zenas Coffin, where owners and shipping agents met every business day at 11:00 (while the captains convened at the Rotch Counting House) to find out the latest news.

Capitalizing on the contacts made here, he invested in several whaleships, two of which, the *Charles Carroll* and *Lexington*, were built at a local shipyard on Brant Point. Gradually, Sanford's wheeling and dealing in whalers had become so profitable that he withdrew from his partnership with Easton to concentrate on trading. By this time, the Panic of 1837 had set in, which was, according to William C. Macy, "one of those financial revulsions, which, in addition to immediate disaster to many of our merchants, entailed upon the town and its people, a series of misfortunes . . . which continued their havoc through many years thereafter." Amid these grim economic times, Sanford, keeping true to his motto, "Never Despair," forged ahead. While other owners put up their ships for sale, Sanford bought two ships "on the wing," and both of them would return with what were described as "glorious results."

Contributing to the glory of these results was the fact that Sanford utilized his ships not only as whalers but also as trading vessels. By this time he had established a profitable link with James R. Clendon in the Bay of Islands in New Zealand, a popular gathering point for whalers through which as many as seventy-five ships passed in a single week. Sanford would typically load his outgoing whalers with tobacco, shoes, and cigars for the Bay of Islands, thus insuring a profit margin beyond what he received from the whaling side of the voyage.

Sanford apparently had a very close relationship with Clendon, who became the Bay of Island's first U.S. consul as a result of Sanford's efforts. In fact, in 1838 he set out as a passenger on one of his newly acquired ships, the *Rambler*, for a ten-month "voyage around the world." First stop was the Bay of Islands where Sanford "hoisted the first American ensign upon that island." As we have seen, according to at least one historian, Clendon presided over the "worst" port in the Pacific, a place where corruption and abuse of the native population, the Maoris, ran rampant (see Chapter 16). Since these conditions only enhanced his ability to profit from the Bay of Islands, Sanford (who dismissed the Maoris as "cannibals") does not seem to have taken much notice.

More than anyone else of his generation on Nantucket, Sanford was a driven man. Whereas his noble Quaker predecessor William Rotch (whom Sanford greatly admired) had claimed that he accumulated his enormous wealth "while thinking all the time of the life hereafter," Sanford had a more personal motivation: righting a wrong against his beloved mother, Peggy. It went something like this: Even before Frederick was born, his mother and father moved from Newport to Nantucket so that Peggy could tend to her failing mother, who eventually died. When her father remarried, Peggy's loyalty to her mother seems to have gone unappreciated, with the ancestral home (which had been promised to her) going to her siblings. From that day forward, Frederick determined that he would set things straight. One day he would buy back not only the Barnabas Coleman House but the entire block on which it stood (where the Town Building and police department are now located).

Accumulating the wherewithal to make this purchase would take more than fourteen years, during which time his mother moved to Indiana to live with Frederick's two older brothers and their families. When Sanford left for his voyage around the world in 1838, it appears that his own wife and children also moved to Indiana. Sanford himself spent at least some time in the Midwest, as four of his children were ultimately born in Indiana. During this period, the man who would eventually become one of Nantucket's biggest boosters seems to have had a less than firm attachment to his native island.

By 1846 the only thing between Sanford and his ancestral house on Nantucket was Sally Coleman's one-third interest in the property, giving her the right to inhabit the house for as long as she lived. Then came the Great Fire. While other Nantucketers were wiped out by the conflagration, Sanford's dreams were ultimately realized because of it. With the old house in ashes, Sanford now had the opportunity to rebuild. So on this fire-blackened blank slate, Sanford constructed the home of his dreams, hiring his uncle, Frederick Brown Coleman, architect of the Methodist church and Nantucket Atheneum, to design a building with which he might announce to the world that Peggy Coleman Sanford had finally gotten her due. With a noble, pillared entrance and a grand central staircase, the home stood beside what is now a memorial for war veterans at the corner of Federal and Broad Streets. Behind the main house was an elaborate garden as well as a stable and a residence for Sanford's "hired man."

But if Sanford had finally "arrived" on Nantucket, he was

also about to leave. On January 16, 1849, he wrote a hurried, almost panicked letter to Captain David Bunker in command of Sanford's favorite ship, the *Lexington*, then in port in South America:

> *There has sprung up a new business—viz. the "California Gold Fever." Every ship is taken from the business of whaling as fast as they come in, to go to California. The Aurora sailed last week with passengers from here, Seth Swain, Master, and 100 ships from other ports. . . . All things look black here for us. Not a bright place in the horizon. . . . I talk some of going to California myself, so don't be surprised, but you keep clear of there by all means, or you will not have a crew to bring you out.*

By 1849 it had become clear, to Sanford at least, that the end of the line had been reached for Nantucket. It was not the rise of petroleum that killed Nantucket (whaling would be carried on in New Bedford and California for another fifty years), it was the sandbar at its harbor mouth. As the ships got bigger, the bar that had simply been a nuisance in the old days became a major obstacle to prosperity, requiring that ships regularly go to Edgartown to off-load their oil—an expensive and time-consuming process. In 1828 a half-hearted attempt was made to dredge a channel, but it only filled in again; then in 1842 Peter Folger Ewer designed and built two 135-foot "camels"—forming a floating drydock—to carry the whaleships over the bar. Contrary to what some have insisted, these mammoth water wings proved remarkably successful. For example, forty-five out of the fifty-seven ships that crossed the Nantucket Bar in 1845 made use of the camels.

But as Sanford would recognize late in life, "commercial affairs always centralize themselves," meaning that New Bedford, with its deep port and access to the railroad system, was destined to take over Nantucket's portion of the whaling business. The age-old conservatism of the Nantucketers also hastened their decline. While whalemen in the rival port of Sag Harbor on Long Island moved from the sperm to the bowhead whale in the North Pacific, and thus pioneered a new and profitable era in the fishery, "it was difficult," according to William C. Macy, "for the people of the island to relinquish their old hunting ground."

As he hints in his letter to Captain Bunker, Sanford—along with many other Nantucketers—had decided by 1849 that it was time to head west. With the help of his life-long friend, R. B. Forbes (whom he first met during his one and only whaling voyage as a teenager), Sanford secured a position as the representative in San Francisco for A. A. Low Brothers. The magnificent clipper ships of this New York–based shipping firm were the envy of the world, carrying tea and other China goods to America in record time. For Sanford, who had always been fascinated with the Orient, this was the culmination of yet another early dream, and he would later call his five years in San Francisco "the pleasantest" of his life.

With the advent of "Gold Mania," the clipper ships began to make San Francisco a regular stop, discharging high-priced cargoes for the miners before continuing on to China and Japan. Sanford quickly established a reputation as a tough and demanding agent in what was a very tough and demanding town. Captain Charles Low would never forget bringing the clipper ship *N.B. Palmer* into San Francisco on her maiden voyage, completing the passage from New York in 107 days, then a record. When the pilot refused to bring the ship into the wharf, Sanford, whom Captain Low described as "a regular driver, a Nantucket man," told him that no matter what the pilot said, "the ship must come up to the wharf." So the captain shrugged and told his crew to set sail, ultimately bringing the gigantic craft into the wharf with "every stitch of canvas on her." According to Low, "A great crowd on the wharf cheered me most heartily. Mr. Sanford cried out, 'Well done!'"

But if San Francisco marked the beginning of an era, it also offered stirring testimony to the end of another, as the harbor's mudflats became the graveyard for hundreds of old ships—many of them whalers—abandoned by their crews for the gold fields. Wrote Sanford, "Within the Golden Gate of San Francisco, I saw in 1852 1,000 ships, few of which ever went to sea again. . . . [T]he ships thus left were converted into stores, piers, and dwellings, some allowed to decay and wash to pieces about the rivers and bays, while a part . . . were broken up for the metal that was in them." Late in life, he would equate this sad end to some of Nantucket's "most majestic ships" with the Great Stone Fleet of the Civil War—a group of old whalers purposely sunk in Charleston Harbor by Union forces in a vain attempt to block Confederate shipping.

But if their ships were no longer needed, the skills of Nantucket's seamen were still in demand. In 1854, Mr. Low back in New York asked for Sanford's recommendation regarding a Nantucket whaling captain who might take over as master of his original clipper ship, the *Houqua* (pronounced "HU-kwa"), named for a leading Chinese merchant. Sanford proposed Captain Henry Coleman, who had already retired to his two farms on Nantucket. In the tradition of island whaling captains, Coleman was an extremely earthy, no-frills fellow, and when he went to New York for the interview, Mr. Low, who happened to walk through the reception area, asked his clerk, "Who is that dirty man out there with trousers tucked in one boot and loose over the other?" Despite this first impression, Coleman got the job.

Through his connection with Coleman and other clipper ship captains, Sanford procured a stunning collection of Chinese art, including ship portraits and scenes of Houqua's gardens on

Honan Island, now on display in the Nantucket Atheneum. By 1855, the frenetic pace (and profitability) of life in San Francisco had begun to slacken, and Sanford started to make plans for his permanent return to Nantucket. But first the Low company had one more job for him: arranging shipment of the French army's horses and heavy equipment to the Crimean War via the *Great Republic*, the largest clipper ship ever built—325 feet long and 3,357 tons displacement. This final deal seems to have capped Sanford's already considerable fortune, and in 1855 he returned to Nantucket.

Once again, however, he was forced to resort to his old motto, "Never Despair"; for in June of that year, his only son Herbert, eleven, fell from the mast of a ship at the Nantucket wharf and died. Yet another death, that of an old friend, opened the door to a new life on the island, when he bought a 300-acre farm from the friend's widow. Sanford would ultimately own three farms— Beechwood, Spotswood, and Norwood, all in the Polpis area of the island. Here he ran a state-of-the-art operation, crossbreeding cattle, experimenting with the use of sea kelp as fertilizer, and constructing a high-tech brick dairy that produced as much as 2,500 pounds of butter in a single year. Wrote one visitor, "It is one of the richest treats to visit a farm like this, whose owner is so full of enthusiasm and so heartily enjoys his occupation."

Despite this new life as a gentleman farmer, Sanford never lost his interest in the sea—an omnipresent reality on Nantucket, no matter how moribund its commercial life had become. Even though its harbor was now virtually empty, the island was almost constantly surrounded by ships. Indeed, for us today it is difficult to appreciate the sheer volume of shipping that passed by the island in the nineteenth century. In 1843, for example, the lightship anchored off the Nantucket shoals reported that 151 ships, 1,194 brigs, 8,228 schooners, and 3,525 sloops had passed through Nantucket Sound in a single year. In the 1870s a visitor approaching Nantucket on the steamer *Island Home* reported, "As far as the eye can discern, the fleet that passes almost without intermission is hurrying up and down the Sound."

When the weather turned bad, the shoals around Nantucket inevitably claimed more than their share of wrecks, and it was Sanford who spearheaded efforts to save as many lives as possible. Through his affiliation with both the Humane Society and Coast Guard, he supervised the construction and maintenance of lifesaving stations and "humane houses" for the benefit of shipwrecked seamen. In a fierce gale in April, 1880, no less than thirty-eight vessels were sighted from the tower of the First Congregational Church, many of them foundering on the shoals surrounding the island.

One of the island's most dramatic shipwrecks was that of the *British Queen* in 1851, when 226 Irish emigrants were saved through the courageous efforts of island residents. From this group came the man who supervised Sanford's farming operations, Robert Mooney, whose descendants still live on the island today. Yet another wreck survivor who would one day owe a debt of gratitude to Sanford was Robert Ratliff. After being wrecked on the island in 1820, Ratliff shipped out on several whaling voyages, eventually earning the right to marry a local girl and settle down permanently on the island as a prominent rigger. Unfortunately, Ratliff, a veteran of the British Navy who had been among the crew that delivered Napoleon to St. Helena, lost everything in the Great Fire and ultimately ended up in the town's poorhouse. Sanford wrote several articles for Nantucket and Boston papers concerning Ratliff's situation, ultimately securing a government pension for the veteran that enabled him to live out his life in dignity.

Through articles about not only Ratliff but a wide assortment of Nantucket whaling captains and ships, as well as a regular stream of obituaries whenever yet another "Sea King" was buried on Prospect Hill, Sanford left a rich and detailed account of the old whaling days on Nantucket. Within the snug comfort of his study, surrounded by his books and paintings, Sanford also read voluminously, scribbling his comments in the margins of his books. As Irene Jaynes Smith, a former librarian of the Nantucket Atheneum, wrote, "Many of these notes show him to be a man of strong convictions with little patience for the misguided, and none at all for the misinformed. An error in statement which concerned Nantucket's history, or the whaling industry, caused him to dip his pen in vitriol."

As to be expected, Sanford was not about to take Crève-coeur's claim about Nantucket wives and opium sitting down, terming it "A lie. Without a shadow of foundation." However, when it came to adding to the glory of his native isle, Sanford was perfectly willing to be a little loose with the facts. In the pages of James Fenimore Cooper's *The Pilot*, he declared that one of the novel's heroes, the Nantucketer Long Tom Coffin, was based on Reuben Chase (1754–1824): "I remember him well, just such a man as Mr. Cooper describes, over six feet tall, boney and angular, very powerful. He fought on the *Bonhomme Richard* in September, 1779, with the Heroic Paul Jones in North Sea, and it is here Cooper was made acquainted with him." Unfortunately, Cooper did not enter the Navy until 1808, and Chase, although he did serve as midshipman with Jones, had been transferred to another ship by the time of the historic sea battle.

When it came to his beloved China trade, Sanford was will-ing to believe almost anything if it fit his conception of Nan-tucket as the maritime leader of the western world. In 1884 he signed an affidavit testifying to the authenticity of a letter dated September 20, 1735, telling the story of what became known as "The Nantucket Tea Party." This charming tale describes how Nathaniel Starbuck, Jr. (son of the "Great Woman"), returned from a voyage to China with the first box of tea "ever landed upon the island." At that time, however, tea was no novelty in the colonies, having been sold in Boston as early as 1690. Certainly, a voyage to China in 1735 would have placed Starbuck at the very vanguard of the trade in America, but at that time he was a sixty-seven-year-old blacksmith, sheepherder, and store owner. Despite these and other inconsistencies, Sanford remained convinced of the letter's veracity. In any event, "The Nantucket Tea Party" was reprinted many times in local and national newspapers and magazines, providing just the kind of exposure that Sanford felt was Nantucket's due.

Sanford was generally recognized as the island's leading public personage. When President Grant visited the island in 1874, he rode in Sanford's carriage; at one point the horses bolted and might have carried the President over the edge of Steamboat Wharf if Sanford had not coolly steered them into a tree on Broad Street. In 1882, President Arthur also visited Nantucket and addressed the public from the steps of Sanford's house on Federal Street. If some called Sanford the "King of Nantucket," he seems to have conducted himself with all the swagger and grace of true nobility. One islander recalled, "He used to wear a silk hat, drive a fast horse, and walk about with one hand in a coat-tail pocket." Certainly Tristram Coffin, our country squire of old, could not have played the part any better.

And, indeed, with F. C. Sanford, the process that Coffin had originally set in motion with the purchase of the island back in 1659 had finally come full circle. But whereas Coffin had started something new, Sanford presided over a community whose best days were behind it. To insure that those days might never be forgotten became his life's work.

But if Sanford's message lives on, the memory of the messenger has been almost altogether lost. Although his Chinese paintings and portrait (by Eastman Johnson) can still be seen in the Nantucket Atheneum, his magnificent home is now gone.

In 1966, it was tragically bulldozed to make room for the brick Town Building. He also owned a cottage in Siasconset known, appropriately enough, as the Frederick C. Sanford House, but it, too, has disappeared. Even his family plot in the Prospect Hill cemetery has no marker to show where he or any other member of his family is buried. Just like the Native Americans, first settlers, and Quakers before him, F. C. Sanford has vanished, almost without a trace.

Epilogue

On July 8, 1891, the brand-new, 203-foot steamer the *Gay Head* chugged into Nantucket Harbor for the first time. Before the docklines could be secured on Steamboat Wharf, an eager crowd of islanders began to leap onto the *Gay Head*'s decks, curious to see the latest in the New Bedford, Martha's Vineyard and Nantucket Steamboat Company's new line of elegant and speedy vessels. Inside, the gawking Nantucketers found an immaculate Neapolitan-style interior, featuring gold trim and cherry-wood seats with maroon velvet upholstery. Besides a fifty-foot social hall finished in black walnut and maple, the *Gay Head* boasted ten private staterooms, where passengers could relax amid a luxurious ensemble of specially crafted willow furniture.

The new ship was not an acknowledgment of Nantucket's central place in the world of commerce; quite the opposite, in fact. As the nation's economy surged ahead in the decades after the Civil War, Nantucket's viability as a commercial community had, as we have seen, declined with equal rapidity. But as we have also seen, it was not long before a new trend began to bring at least a hint of vitality to the island's economy. The invigorating summertime climate and picturesque seaside haunts of Old Nantucket now made her, in a most New England way, a mecca for the wealthy and powerful in their quest for high-class R and R. The Grey Lady began to exchange her Quaker bonnet for a bathing costume; her chowders were no longer just the staple food of simple fishermen but a revitalizing nectar for the white-collared gods of American business as well as a handful of painters and writers.

But these tycoons, middle managers, and artists were not the first to recognize Nantucket's potential as a harbor of refuge. If the truth be told, Nantucket's whaling captains were its original tourists. In between voyages, they inevitably spent as much time as possible in a recreational mode, getting to know their wives and children on "squantums" (the Nantucket equivalent of a picnic) or heading out to Siasconset with a few of their pals to fish, drink, and generally have a good time.

In fact, the ramshackle collection of fishing shacks at Siasconset has been called America's "first summer resort." As we have seen, by the bank scandal of the 1790s it was already a well-established haven from the cares of the world, where a "plain simplicity" prevailed and where the unencumbered view of the ocean offered a balm to the soul. Prior to the Revolution, the islanders also entertained themselves in another outlying village—Polpis, where what Crèvecoeur described as a "house of entertainment" gave them the opportunity to "throw the bar" (the eighteenth-century equivalent of tossing horseshoes) and indulge in an "exhilarating bowl" of their favorite beverage before heading back to town. The island's many ponds provided Nantucketers with yet another diversion. According to one account, many a whaling captain "had transferred his affections from the cable and harpoon to the hair-line and hook, . . . pursuing perch in a pond half a mile in circumference."

Even Nantucket's last practicing Native American, Abram Quary, was part of this recreational trend, earning a reputation as the "Prince of Nantucket caterers." In his later years, Abram would fly a flag whenever he had a pot of chowder on the stove. Easily seen from town, this signal inevitably brought a group of picnickers, who either walked, drove, sailed, or rowed to Abram's house in Shimmo, where his table was always set with an immaculate white cloth. By the time his guests arrived, Abram would be gone, although it was expected that "a good sum of money" would be left on the table for his return.

Seasonal celebrations such as today's Daffodil Weekend and Christmas Stroll were anticipated by the sheep shearing held every year around June 20th. As early as 1801 a visitor to the island gave this report: "Not only great numbers come from the continent as shearers, but multitudes of hucksters and traders flock to the island at this time to buy wool and vend their wares; so that shearing-time, on Nantucket, is a sort of fair, resembling in everything but splendor and literature a Cambridge Commencement." Rather than being the victims of the tourist industry, it might be argued that the Nantucketers were the ones who invented the concept.

Since the island's past is such an important part of its present-day appeal to summer people, pressures have inevitably come to bear on how that past is perceived. With F. C. Sanford leading the way, Nantucket's history has been cast, for the most part, as a nostalgic roll call of heroic whalemen. And, as we have seen, since the Nantucketers of old did everything in their power to suppress all that might "dishonor" the island, this is just the way they would have wanted it.

This impulse is by no means limited to Nantucket. As John Steinbeck, who summered on the island in the 1950s, once remarked, "There is a tendency among many American towns to make museums of themselves and to celebrate an illustrious past they never had." Certainly the realities of Old Nantucket bore little to no resemblance to what we experience today: a whaling Williamsburg of boutiques and ice cream shops. We have already seen that the chaste, gray-shingle-and-white-clapboard look is not precisely as it was in the beginning for Nantucket's townspeople. Indeed, there is more than a small bit of Disney in the diligent—some would say fanatical—efforts of "historical preservationists" to standardize modern Nantucket's look and feel.

If we seek to experience Nantucket at her most timeless, we must look not among the Federalist houses along Main Street or the artifacts in a museum; instead, we must venture to that most elemental yet ephemeral of common grounds: a Nantucket beach.

Crèvecoeur stood on a beach at Siasconset, and as he watched the waves crash against the sand, he felt an almost overpowering sense of his own frailty: "How diminutive does a man appear to himself when . . . standing as I did on the verge of the ocean!" Seventy-five years later, Ralph Waldo Emerson saw a similar spectacle but had a very different response: "On the seashore at Nantucket I saw the play of the Atlantic with the coast. . . . Ah what freedom & grace & beauty with all this might. The wind blew back the foam from the top of each billow as it rolled in, like the hair of a woman in the wind. . . . We should not have dared to believe that this existed. . . ."

Well, it does exist (and probably will for at least another 400 years) much as it did when Bartholomew Gosnold first ventured in the island's direction. Whether it overwhelms or inspires us, Nantucket is still a nation to itself, "away off shore."

Notes

Specific references are given in order of appearance in the chapter.

Abbreviations

HN—*Proceedings of the Nantucket Historical Association and Historic Nantucket*

MR—"Miscellaneous Records, 1659–1823" at the Registry of Deeds Office in the Nantucket Town and County Building

NA—Nantucket Atheneum

NHA—Nantucket Historical Association

NI—*Nantucket Inquirer* and *Nantucket Inquirer and Mirror*

NP—*Nantucket in Print*, ed. Everett U. Crosby (Nantucket, 1946)

Preface

The epigraph referring to the island as being "away off shore" appears in the "Nantucket" chapter (14) of *Moby-Dick*. Burke's comments appear in his speech "Conciliation with the Colonies," delivered in the House of Commons a few days after Burke talked with Benjamin Franklin, who knew more than most (being a "cousin" of the Folgers of Nantucket) about the island. Emerson recorded his remarks in his *Journals*, ed. Merton M. Sealts, Jr. (Cambridge, 1973), during a week-long stay on the island in 1847 when he delivered a series of lectures in the newly rebuilt Atheneum.

Obed Macy speaks of the island's "peaceable settlement" in his *History of Nantucket* (1835; rpt. Ellinwood, 1985). Alexander Starbuck's reference to "historical idols" appears in his *History of the American Whale Fishery* (Waltham, 1878). For a discussion of Nantucket's cherished image in the nineteenth and twentieth centuries, see my "'Every Wave Is a Fortune': Nantucket Island and the Making of an American Icon," *New England Quarterly* (September, 1993).

1. An Island and Its Altar

Preston Morris in "Interesting Landmarks on Nantucket," NI (August 19, 1922), speaks of Altar Rock being holy to the Indians. My account of Nantucket's geological origins owes much to Robert N. Oldale's *Cape Cod and the Islands, The Geologic Story* (East Orleans, 1992) and Barbara Blau Chamberlain's *These Fragile Outposts* (Garden City, 1964). The comments concerning the lack of stones on the south shore are in "A Journal of Nantucket by Zaccheus Macy—1792" in NP.

For an analysis of the vegetative history of the island, see Peter W. Dunwiddie's "Postglacial Vegetation History of Coastal Islands in Southeastern New England," *National Geographic Research* (6[2] 1990). The reference to Coatue's trees comes from the Town Meeting Records in the Town Clerk's Office of the Nantucket Town Building. Obed Macy speaks of oak trees not only in his *History of Nantucket* but also in an unpublished volume in the NHA with the heading "Copied from a book of Obed Macy's writing when he was an old man: 'If ever my *History of Nantucket* is republished in a second edition some of the following anecdotes may be found useful.'" Portions of these "Anecdotes" have been reprinted in Alexander Starbuck's *The History of Nantucket* (1924; rpt. Rutland, 1969). In "Anecdotes," Macy states, "My ancestors have often told me that from the best information they could obtain, the island was originally covered with woods." During the Revolutionary War, when Nantucketers were reduced to digging peat for fuel, they discovered, according to Macy in "Anecdotes": "a hard bottom of sand below the peat" on which were found "many large stumps and roots of trees . . . burnt to charcoal." Audubon's letter to his son concerning his trip to Nantucket is in NHA Collection 153, Folder 1.

For information concerning early Native American culture in the Northeast, see Howard S. Russell's *Indian New England Before the Mayflower* (Hanover, 1980). The reference to the island's sterility comes from St. John de Crèvecoeur's *Letters from an American Farmer* (New York, 1981). Information concerning the island's Indians as well as its climate comes from "Notes on Nantucket, by the Reverend James Freeman, August 1st, 1807," in NP. Also see Elizabeth A. Little's excellent series of monographs, *Nantucket Algonquian Studies #1–12* at the NHA (in which she discusses the lack of evidence for the cultivation of corn by island Indians), as well as M. M. Brenizer's *The Nantucket Indians, Legends and Accounts Before 1659* (Nantucket, 1976). In a personal correspondence (May, 1992), Peter Dunwiddie, an island scientist with the Audubon Society, states that the Indians "simply lacked the numbers, and often, the means to desecrate their environment as badly as we have." A chip of deer bone found at an archeological dig in Quidnet was dated between A.D. 460 and 155 B.C.; see Little's "Locus Q-6, Site M52/65, Quidnet, Nantucket," *Massachusetts Archaeological Society Bulletin* (45[1] 1983).

For the early evolution of Nantucket's English community, see Henry B. Worth's indispensable *Nantucket Land and Land Owners*, HN (1901). The reference to killing dogs is in MR. The snake anecdote appears in Macy's "Anecdotes." A 1684 Indian deed (reprinted in Starbuck) mentions "Shawkenes or the snake place." The reference to the Indian-English trench at Long Pond is in MR.

The story of Love Paddack and Lily (originally Wesco) Pond appears in Macy's "Anecdotes"; in May of 1967, after eight inches of rain fell in seven hours, Lily Pond was temporarily refilled; see photos in HN (April, 1968). The loss of Lily Pond may have contributed to the shoaling of Nantucket Harbor. According to Edmund Gardner writing in 1872 (whose information came to him "by tradition from my father"), "after the Lily Pond was tapped, it spoiled the inner harbor for small vessels. . . . The water being drawn off, the land came up"; in NI (May 7, 1910).

I am indebted to Helen Winslow Chase for pointing out the impact of losing Lily Pond on Love Paddack's father. John W. McCalley writes insightfully about Nantucket's water-power problem and its impact on sheep-raising in *Nantucket, Yesterday and Today* (New York, 1981). Even as late as 1770, the proprietors were still casting about in search of new sources of water power, ordering "a dam to be made at Shawkemo to see if we can raise a head of water in order to place a fulling mill" (Proprietors' Book I, Nantucket Registry of Deeds).

According to a story in NI (October 29, 1822), a family of runaway slaves hid from the authorities in the "vaults" of the peat-diggers. Alcon Chadwick describes the old peat beds as wet swamps in "Reminiscences of Old Podpis [the original spelling of what is now Polpis]," HN (1922); he also gives a detailed description of how the peat was prepared and dried in "Peat Houses" resembling slatted corn cribs.

Obed Macy gives the corn statistics in his *History*; Crèvecoeur's remarks concerning sheep fertilization come from the French version of his *Letters*; this translation appears in NP. According to a visitor quoted in NI (October 15, 1831), "The sheep that was 'bred and born' on Smith's Point, will in a very few hours, although it is eight miles from the place of shearing, find the way to his native soil, and the resident of Siasconset may be seen wending his way thitherward, with an assiduity that forbids his stopping for refreshment. A few years since, when a fence was erected around the town, and the sheep that had lived in the town as well as the rest were excluded, the obstinacy of this habit was so inveterate that the town sheep came to the fence and persisted in staying there, until numbers actually died of starvation."

Emerson's account of the island's outlying areas appears in his collected *Letters*, ed. Ralph L. Rusk (New York, 1939); Thoreau recorded his observations in his *Journals*, ed. Francis H. Allen (New York, 1962).

For an account of the town's growth, see J. Christopher Land and Kate Stout's *Building with Nantucket in Mind* (Nantucket, 1992). The Bocochico Lots were named, according to Obed Macy (in "Anecdotes"), for "a Dutch vessel cast away at the east end of the Island." The description of what the town looked like from the harbor is in Joseph Sansom's "A Description of Nantucket," which first appeared in 1811 and is in NP.

Whale oil was not the only thing that stank in and around Nantucket Harbor; there was also the inevitable water pollution. In 1801 Josiah Quincy stayed at a boarding house along the waterfront that "was accompanied by a considerable dock effluvia" (in NP). According to an observer writing in the *Hampshire Gazette* in 1825, "The sand is so deep that [the calashes] pass through the streets without making the least noise" (in NP). Joseph Sansom made the observations concerning the town's "tranquility" in 1811. "Town sheep" are discussed in a letter to the editor in NI (August 27, 1831).

Phebe Folger's watercolors appear in an article by Katherine Seeler in HN (October, 1966). In an article in NI (November 7, 1825), a visitor remarked, "A singular taste exists among the people in the color of paint on their houses. The chameleon in its most changing moments never exhibited such variety. Every possible shade from the jet black to the white may be seen."

The reference to how close to town most Nantucketers kept is from William Coffin's 1793 letter in NHA Collection 150, Folder 78. An account of the two lost boys (one of whom died) is in the *Nantucket Journal* (September 14, 1827).

Daniel Webster's reference to Nantucket as an "Unknown City" is cited in Emil F. Guba's *Nantucket Odyssey* (Waltham, 1965). The list of businesses comes from G. W. Jones's "Nantucket's Busy Days 150 Years Ago," HN (April, 1981). Edouard Stackpole in *Rambling through the Streets and Lanes of Nantucket* (Nantucket, 1951) describes the different sections of town in the nineteenth century.

Articles concerning the dangerous darkness of Nantucket's streets are in NI (October 18, 1828, and October 3, 1829). See Michael Hugo-Brunt's "An Historical Survey of the Physical Development of Nantucket: A Brief Narrative History and Documentary Source Material," an unpublished study sponsored by Cornell University in 1969 (at the NHA), for the nuts-and-bolts of the town's development—health care, sewer systems, etc. The reference to "drunkenness and debauchery" appears in *Wanderings and Adventures of Reuben Delano* (Boston, 1846).

John Woolman's reference to the Nantucket Bar appears in his *Journals*, reprinted in NP. A story in NI (February 27, 1841) mentions the clay basis of the Nantucket Bar. Samuel Adams Drake in *Nooks and Corners of the New England Coast* (New York, 1875) makes the reference to the pitch pines. Wesley N. Tiffney, Jr., former Director of the University of Massachusetts Nantucket Field Station, provides a detailed scientific analysis of the past, present, and future of the island's heathlands in "Human Land Use History and Nantucket's Coastal Heaths: Origin, Development, Loss, and Conservation," an unpublished manuscript. The 1891 Committee on Sanitation Report is cited in Hugo-Brunt. The reference to Easy Street as "The Dump" is from Merle E. Turner's "Nantucket Streets and Lanes," HN (1929). In a personal communication (August, 1993), Tiffney provides this analysis of the island's erosion rate: "Much of the south shore loses about 15 feet/year. Increase that by times three (45 feet) to bring it in line with the 3X increase in sea level expected over the next 100 years, then divide that into the average width of the island (about 18,000 feet), and I get 400 years."

2. Native Origins: Maushop, Roqua, Wonoma, and Autopscot

My account of the various Indian myths relies heavily on Brenizer's *The Nantucket Indians, Legends and Accounts Before 1659* (from which the myths of Roqua and Wonoma and Autopscot come), as well as James Freeman's 1807 "Notes on Nantucket" and the writings of Zaccheus Macy, both in NP. Crèvecoeur also talks about "ancient" customs of the Nantucket Indians. Edward Byers in *The Nation of Nantucket, Society and Politics in an Early American Commercial Center, 1660–1820* (Boston, 1987) speaks of the high density of Nantucket's Native American population prior to the arrival of the English. Elizabeth Little's "Indian Politics on Nantucket," *Papers of the Thirteenth Algonquian Conference* (Carleton University, 1982), analyzes many of these myths with reference to known records. Dr. Little's work on Nantucket Indians is unmatched for its scope and scholarly rigor, and I am indebted to her in this and other chapters concerning the island's Native Americans. For a guide to the many articles she and others have written on this subject, see her "Bibliography for Historic and Prehistoric Nantucket Indian Studies," *Nantucket Algonquian Studies #8* (NHA, 1990).

Little and John Pretola in "Nantucket: An Archaeological Record from the Far Island," *Bulletin of the Archaeological Study of Connecticut* (51, 1988), discuss the effects of the island's remoteness on Indian culture. Obed Macy speaks of Gosnold's sighting Nantucket on his way to Virginia; unfortunately, there is no historic evidence that Gosnold ever even saw Nantucket Island. Several years later George Weymouth did see the white cliffs of Sankaty Head but did not land on the island. See Captain John Lacouture's "The Voyage of Captain Bartholomew Gosnold in 1602 to Cape Cod and the Vineyard," HN (July, 1987). For an account of the Pilgrims' haphazard voyaging around the Cape, see Bradford's *History "of Plimouth Plantation"* (Boston, 1898).

In "Sachem Nickanoose of Nantucket and the Grass Contest,"

Little recounts the tradition concerning the Massachusetts seal. Paul Dudley made a report concerning the New England whale fishery to the Royal Philosophical Society of London in 1725; his description of the sweat houses comes from a clipping dated 1724 in the "Indian" Folder at the NA. Throughout this chapter I have also depended on Russell's *Indian New England Before the Mayflower*, which contains an interesting account of the role of the sexes in Indian culture.

In his "Anecdotes," Macy tells the tale of an Indian boy's capture during an attack in the Madaket section of the island and the revenge he ultimately exacted at a much later date. Russell describes the often elaborate burial techniques of many New England Indians, in which the head of the dead person was directed to the "Happy Hunting Ground" to the southwest, while the body was surrounded by objects that would prove useful in the hereafter. Little has found no evidence of ceremonial Indian burials on Nantucket; however, white Nantucketers of the nineteenth century are known to have repeatedly "pilfered" Indian graves in Shimmo and Miacomet and may have been responsible for the lack of artifacts. If, as Little points out, the myth of Wonoma and Autopscot is actually the myth of Askammapoo and Spotso, then Nickanoose—not Wauwinet (who was Nickanoose's son)—is a better candidate for the eastern sachem in the tale. See Russell for an account of the plants used by the Indians for healing. Sansom (in NP) mentions the dependence of Nantucket doctors on "the simples which were used by the Indian natives."

The Indian burial ground in Miacomet is not far from the site of the annual sheep shearing in the nineteenth century. NI (June 18, 1842) reported that many of these graves had been repeatedly violated by amateur phrenologists in search of skulls. Most recently the burial ground was unwittingly disturbed by a backhoe breaking ground for an affordable housing project; see Little's "History of the Town of Miacomet," *Nantucket Algonquian Studies #12* (NHA, 1988).

3. Thomas Macy's Great Escape

Perhaps no event in the history of the island (outside its whaling heritage) has received more attention through the years than the voyage of Thomas Macy and his family to Nantucket, where they established

the first permanent English settlement in 1659. In his very popular poem
"The Exiles" (first published in 1840), the Quaker poet John Greenleaf Whittier transformed the story of Macy's journey into an Indiana
Jones–style escape sequence, with Macy barely eluding the clutches of
a Puritan sheriff and minister before setting off for Nantucket in the
name of religious freedom. Although we know precious little factual
information about Macy's voyage to Nantucket, we do know that Whittier inevitably simplified and misrepresented what actually happened
in order to make a better story of it. Unfortunately, Whittier's account
has taken on a life of its own, with otherwise dependable historians
such as Samuel Eliot Morrison in *The Maritime History of Massachusetts, 1783–1860* (Boston, 1921) relying on it as historically correct. This
chapter is an attempt to retell the story in the context of what we know
about the facts without completely gutting the traditions of their narrative impact.

Obed Macy in his *History* refers to the Macys' vessel as an open
boat. For an account of the incredible fecundity of New England coastal
waters in the seventeenth century (and the havoc Nantucketers and
others wreaked on not only whales and fish but also seals and birds),
see Farley Mowat's *Sea of Slaughter* (Boston, 1984). Most accounts
of Macy's journey have him sailing all the way around Cape Cod.
Throughout the seventeenth century, however, it was common for small
vessels to sail through a passage across the Cape that eventually became
known as "Jeremiah's Gutter"; see Chamberlain, *These Fragile Outposts*.
Emil Guba in *Nantucket Odyssey* refers to Daggett as acting as a pilot
for Macy from the Vineyard to Nantucket while Zaccheus Macy (in
NP) refers to a Daggett who spent that first winter with the Macys as a
"boarder" for "the sake of gunning." Both Guba and Edouard Stackpole
in *Life Saving Nantucket* (Nantucket, 1972) agree that the Macys did
not sail directly to Nantucket (as Obed Macy maintains) but (in Stackpole's words) "actually chose the more logical route by way of Martha's
Vineyard."

Concerning the Daggetts, records in the Edgartown Town Hall
from 1658–9 have many references to the dispute between the Daggetts
and the town; for example, one entry speaks of four people being
selected (two by the town and two by Daggett) to choose "an umpire
to settle the Controversy"; see also Charles Edward Banks, *History of*

Martha's Vineyard, vol. 2 (Boston, 1911). My account of the tradition concerning the storm and Macy's words to his wife (which would have her "going below" in an open boat, leading one commentator to suggest that he may have actually told her to go "somewhere else") comes from Silvanus J. Macy, *Genealogy of the Macy Family* (Albany, 1868).

Thomas Macy's land grant to start his sawmill in Salisbury gave him use of all available wood except for the oak trees, which the grant designated as being used to make canoes. Could an Indian-style dugout canoe have been the "open boat" Macy sailed to Nantucket? It would have meant the literal fulfillment of Roqua's prediction, with Macy not only arriving in a storm but also in a canoe. Joseph Merrill's *History of Amesbury* (Haverhill, 1880) provides valuable information concerning Macy's life at Salisbury.

In the Edgartown Town Records is this entry: "The request of Peter Foulger granted Touching the Laying Down of his Creed By the Major Part of the Freeman acted and voted the same. 4th Oct. 59." Interestingly, the Edgartown records also include Thomas Mayhew's deed of Tuckernuck Island to Tristram Coffin and sons; the deed is dated October 10, 1659. The text of the early Nantucket land deeds with Mayhew and the Indians is reprinted in Lydia S. Hinchman, *Early Settlers of Nantucket* (Philadelphia, 1901). Although James Coffin's arrival on the island with the Macy party cannot be documented by a specific primary source, tradition tells us he was there.

Henry Forman's *Early Nantucket and Its Whale Houses* (1966; rpt. Nantucket, 1991) contains a sketch of "Uncle Black's Cave, Tuckernuck Is., 1829" that Forman describes as a "probable type of seventeenth and eighteenth century dug-out on Nantucket." The account of Starbuck and Macy's encounter with the Indian pow-wow comes from Sansom in NP. According to what is probably an apocryphal article in NI (November 12, 1831), Macy and Starbuck agreed prior to landing on Nantucket that Starbuck would fake insanity so as to prevent the Indians (who were thought to be wary of the mentally infirm) from attacking them. Freeman (in NP) speaks of the Indians' early relations with the English, especially their interest in firearms.

Information concerning Isaac Coleman's parentage comes from *The Coleman Family* (Detroit, 1898). The reference to Isaac and the dog committee is in MR (February 15, 1667). The canoe incident is recounted in Macy's "Anecdotes"; references to the circumstances of the deaths of Coleman and the Barnards is in "Births, Marriages, Deaths, 1662–1835," Nantucket Town Clerk's Office.

4. Tristram Coffin, Country Squire

The passage from the Newbury Town Records describing the incident involving the Coffins and their beer-making is quoted in Will Gardner's introduction to *The Coffin Family*, ed. Louis Coffin (Nantucket, 1962). Why Tristram Coffin decided to migrate to America is uncertain. Although there is no direct evidence, Will Gardner hypothesizes that he was a Royalist who had become dissatisfied with inroads made by the Puritans in England. (Why then was one of his descendants named Cromwell Coffin?) For an account of the dissatisfaction settlers from the West Country of England commonly experienced in Puritan New England, see Byers's *Nation of Nantucket* and DavidHackett Fischer's *Albion's Seed* (New York, 1989). Byers compares the Nantucket proprietary to its counterparts in New England while providing a detailed analysis (to which I am indebted) of its development throughout the seventeenth century.

Tristram's eldest son Peter Coffin was what we could call today a leading "player" in colonial New England. In 1668, on behalf of the General Court of Massachusetts, he presented a shipload of masts to the King, for which he received close to 250 acres of land in what is now Mendon, Massachusetts; see Elizabeth Little and Margaret Morrison, "The Mendon-Nantucket Connection, 1708–1737" (NHA, 1986). Peter Coffin's trade agreement with the town did have one qualification, however, in that it allowed "Nat Davis [who had a house near the harbor in the vicinity of present-day Federal Street] to trade 100 bushels of corn when he comes or sends together his Debts" (MR, October 13, 1664). The original assignment of lots is in MR (May 10, 1661); as early arrivals, Thomas Macy and Edward Starbuck also received their pick of land, with Macy settling to the east of Capaum and Starbuck building his house near the English-Indian border at Waqutaquaib Pond. Coffin's land deed is in MR (June 15, 1677). Byers compares the settlement pattern on Nantucket with that of a typical New England village.

Hummock Pond was still horseshoe shaped until 1978 when a

winter storm cut what was once a single pond into two separate entities. The deed describing the feeding rights is in MR (May 10, 1660). The half-share accommodations can be traced throughout MR; by 1670 the proprietary consisted of twenty-seven shares upon which all subsequent land titles were based.

For an analysis of stinting rights on Nantucket and their relationship to English-Indian relations, see Little's "Grass Contest." In 1672 the town made the decision to move from cattle to sheep, and throughout these early years measures were passed to keep not only horses and cattle but also pigs and goats from interfering with the growing flock. As mentioned in Chapter 1, dogs were a persistent problem. In 1672 it was ordered that "all dogs more than four months old shall wear a sufficient muzzle" to keep them from killing lambs (MR). Coffin's earmark as well as those of all proprietors are listed in the Proprietors' Book I, Registry of Deeds. The description of the sheep pound appears in MR (1669). Florence Bennett Anderson's *A Grandfather for Benjamin Franklin* (Boston, 1940) describes how Coffin consciously attempted to evoke his native Devon on Nantucket. References to the mill on Wesco Pond appear throughout MR: June 10, 1667; March, 1668; October 28, 1672. The early population records are in "Births, Deaths, and Marriages," Nantucket Town Clerk's Office. The number of Coffin descendants comes from Gardner's introduction in *The Coffin Family*. Z. Macy's reference to old Tristram appears in NP.

The 1680 law against Sunday vagrancy appears in Franklin B. Hough's *Papers Relating to the Island of Nantucket* (New York, 1856). See William F. Macy's *The Nantucket Scrap Basket* (Boston, 1930) for a discussion of the term "rantom scoot." The reference to Mrs. Folger's walking with a chair comes from an undated and unsigned scrap in NHA Collection 118, Folder 34.

Sarah Neeffeld is mentioned in MR (November 10, 1679). Nantucketers remained jealously protective of their island community throughout the eighteenth century as the town selectmen issued a regular series of warrants demanding the eviction of specific individuals who "may be of bad consequence to the town if not removed." For example, in May of 1763 a warrant was issued for the removal of a goldsmith by the name of Samuel Barros "of Boston," the reason being that "we are not in want of any such tradesman." The community that Crèvecoeur described in the

1770s as a well-ordered "beehive"—where the men filled up their idle hours by obsessively whittling while the women spun their wool—was achieved only through constant and careful vigilance.

The tribute of codfish to New York appears in MR (1671); the half-share accommodation to J. Gardner is in MR (August 5, 1672), as is mention of his home site (MR, 1673). The reference to Mrs. Cottle appears in MR (September 5, 1673).

5. "An Island Full of Indians": King Philip, John Gibbs, and Peter Folger

Governor Winthrop made the statement "Nantucket is an island full of Indians" in 1634; cited by Little in "Indian Horse Commons at Nantucket Island, 1660–1760," *Nantucket Algonquian Studies #9* (NHA, 1990). Through deed records (see Little's "Sachem Nickanoose of Nantucket and the Grass Contest") and tradition (much of it coming from Zaccheus Macy in NP), it is possible to reconstruct at least partially who lived where on the western end of the island before the arrival of the English. Wesco (where today's town now stands) was divided among Tequamomamy, Mekowakima, and Francis, a sachem from Cape Cod. The Hoites lived in the area that Thomas Macy would call home between Washing and Reed Ponds (known as Wannacomet or "the pond field") while the Jafets preceded the Coffins at Capaum. In and around Hummock Pond lived Nanahuma, Jonas Harry, and Lemmo, with today's Ram Pasture being claimed by a Martha's Vineyard sachem by the name of Pakepenessa. Then there were Peteson, Mr. Larry Akeramo, and Obadiah, who claimed that the Khauds had no right to sell their land.

That at least some of these western "Taumkhods" did not go willingly is indicated by a law (in MR) stating that any Indians remaining "after the 14 day of October, 1662, shall pay to the English 5 shillings per week. . . ." Worth speaks of the Native Americans' concept of ownership in *Nantucket Land and Land Owners* HN (1901). Zaccheus Macy claims that Attapehat was a warrior in NP. The request for setting up a court on Nantucket was made in June, 1671 (in MR) and prefaced by the statement, "seeing the Indians are numerous among us. . . ."

The joint Indian-English trench/weir proposal is in MR (1665). Throughout the 1660s and '70s committees were organized on a virtually annual basis to "go among the Indians and see what stray there is done in their corn by the English cattle and to agree with them in point of satisfaction . . ." (MR, August 16, 1671).

Gookin left his account of Nantucket's Indians in *Historical Collections of the Indians in New England* (Towtaid, 1970). The fears both English and Indian Nantucketers felt over the murders on Coatue must have been exacerbated by the knowledge that thirty years earlier a similar event (the murder of a white man by an Indian) on Block Island had initiated the Pequot War. Worth's account of Nickanoose's response to the murders appears in MR (June 11, 1709); the reference to Indian hangings in 1665 also appears in MR. Little's "Indian Politics on Nantucket" places these references in the context of Indian-English relations throughout this period. My account of King Philip's appearance on the island is based primarily on Macy's *History*.

Zaccheus Macy records a somewhat different version of the King Philip incident: "In about the year 1669 King Philip came to the island to kill an Indian whose name was John Gibbs for speaking or naming the name of the dead which we suppose was one of his nigh connections, for it was a sort of a law they had then that no one was to speak the name of the dead, and when the said Philip came he landed at the west end of the island intending to travel along shore under the bank to the east part of the island where said John lived so as not to be discovered. But an Indian happened to know his business and ran and told said John the plans, and John ran to town and went to Thomas Macy and got him to hide him. The English held a parley with said Philip and it took all the money they could muster to satisfy the said King. The above story we have handed down to us from our fathers so that we do not doubt the truth of it and so the said Philip went off satisfied" (NHA Collection 96, Folder 44).

Josselyn's description of Philip appears in Russell Bourne's *The Red King's Rebellion* (New York, 1990). Robert F. Mooney and Andre R. Sigourney in *The Nantucket Way* (New York, 1980) touch on Indian versus English law in their account of Philip's visit. According to Macy's "Anecdotes," Gibbs was found by Philip's men in the swamps surrounding Gibbs Pond. The reference to Attapehat and the Taumkhods vowing their allegiance to the English is in MR.

Peter Folger describes his role as Indian interpreter in his March 27, 1677, letter to Governor Andros in Franklin B. Hough's *Papers Relating to the Island of Nantucket, Martha's Vineyard and Other Islands Adjacent, Known as Dukes County While under the Colony of New York* (Albany, 1856). Some details about Peter Folger: At the age of twenty he sailed for America on board the *Abigail* and during the voyage he fell in love with Mary Morrill, the servant of the famous preacher Hugh Peters. Not until nine years later would they be married, when Folger was finally able to save up the twenty pounds required to free Mary from her indentures. According to tradition, he later referred to it as "the best money" he had ever spent. After living in Dedham and Watertown, Peter moved to Martha's Vineyard, where he was referred to as the "English schoolmaster that teacheth the Indians and instructs them on Lord's Day." But Folger did not move directly from Martha's Vineyard to Nantucket. Soon after asserting his Baptist beliefs, he relocated to the more tolerant town of Portsmouth, Rhode Island, then in 1663 accepted the offer of a half-share grant on Nantucket. As the "scholar" of the island, Folger would remain a leading religious figure. The strength of his beliefs is suggested by a passage from a letter to his son-in-law: "The world can willingly part with you, and it is high time for us to be more willing to part with it."

While Macy's *History* contains parts of Peter Folger's "A Looking Glass for the Times," the most complete and accessible version of it is in Anderson's *A Grandfather for Benjamin Franklin*. Folger's poem was not published until 1725 and then again in 1763; the 1763 version was reprinted in 1883 by Sidney S. Ryder as No. 16 of *Rhode Island Historical Tracts*; the NHA also has a very early holograph manuscript of the poem. Benjamin Franklin (whose mother was Folger's youngest daughter Abiah) quotes extensively from the poem in his *Autobiography*, ed. Leonard W. Labaree et al. (New Haven, 1964).

Francis Jennings provides a moving and often horrifying account of Indian-English relations in seventeenth-century New England in *The Invasion of America: Indians, Colonialism, and the Cant of Conquest* (New York, 1975). The 1675 Indian loyalty oath to the English is in MR (August 5, 1675).

The biblical account of Jonathan and Saul is in 1 Samuel 14; during the seventeenth century it was common for the English—particularly the Puritans—to find parallels between their contemporary situation and events from the Bible: "a private typology of current affairs" according to the literary critic Sacvan Bercovitch in *The Puritan Origins of the American Self* (New Haven, 1975). Little speaks of the Indians' use of "dramatic landscape features" (such as rocks and hills) in "Indian Politics." Although Edouard Stackpole insisted that the name "Altar Rock" was invented by "a 'Sconseter" in the twentieth century (stated in a private conversation; October, 1991), F. C. Ewer's famous map of the island (published in 1869) indicates Altar Rock. According to an article about Altar Rock in NI (August 19, 1922), "When war raged between the tribes, and prisoners were taken, they were brought to this rock, which was supposed to be holy, and their lives sacrificed. The rock has a large cross upon it." Although Saul's Hills may have been named for "old Saul, a very stern looking old man" in Wanackmamack's bounds mentioned in Zaccheus Macy's list of notable Indians (in NP), this reference was made in 1792, more than 100 years after Peter Folger. Also, Ewer's map includes a Saul's Pond in the old section of town (across Madaket Road from where Peter Folger's house was located)—nowhere near Wanackmamack's bounds. Was this pond also named for Philip? Both Obed and Zaccheus Macy's accounts have Philip coming to the English settlement, and we do know for a fact that he attended a town meeting.

Philip's Run would later be used in the spring to drain the cranberry bogs that had been flooded in the winter with water from Gibbs Pond. According to J. Franklin Chase (and communicated to me by Helen Winslow Chase), the Commonwealth of Massachusetts installed a marker at sea level in Gibbs Pond as a warning not to pump it out below that level.

The first to deal with the subject of Indian debt servitude (or peonage) on Nantucket with genuine sympathy for the Indians' plight was William Root Bliss in his deceptively named *Quaint Nantucket* (Boston, 1897); Bliss relied heavily on town and court records, from which the examples of debt servitude are taken. Daniel Vickers in "The First Whalemen of Nantucket," *William and Mary Quarterly* (1983), offers a detailed analysis of the workings of Indian debt servitude in the following century once whaling had emerged as the driving force behind the island's economy; also see Byers.

Zaccheus Macy speaks of Corduda in NP. Mayhew's statement concerning the lack of justice for Nantucket Indians is in Starbuck. The law against taking Indian servants off the island is in MR (July 8, 1670). The reference to Tuckernuck Island as an Indian refuge is from a request to have the island placed under the jurisdiction of Nantucket so that these Indians could be brought to justice; the petition also claims that "Indians from Rhode Island and the mainland carry over liquors and strong drink to them [on Tuckernuck], when they get drunk and fight and make great disorder" (in Bliss).

The account of the French privateer raid and the help that the Indians provided was written by le Sieur de Villebon, Governor of Acadia, on September 10, 1695, and is in the Archives Nationales of Paris (Colonies C11d2); I thank Gasser Jacques for bringing the account to my attention and Thomas L. Philbrick for translating the passage. On May 3, 1695, John Gardner wrote officials in Boston: "This night the French landed on our island[;] plundered [a] house and carried away four men and are now about the island of what for I know not. It is but a small vessel, they said at the house. There was two more of which we know not" (in Starbuck). Corroborating the French governor's statements concerning the Indians' questionable loyalties during the raid (also see Chapter 8), James Coffin petitioned the Massachusetts General Assembly concerning the island's status as "being on the frontier of this province" and spoke of "the necessity of liberality to the Indians in drink and provision" during times of threatened attack. By this stage in the game, the only way the English could count on the loyalty of the Indians was to provide them with rum.

Z. Macy speaks of the "good fashion" of many Indians in NP. Crèvecoeur in his *Letters* describes the Nantucketers' shouting "Awaite Pawana" when first sighting a whale. William Comstock in *A Voyage to the Pacific, Descriptive of the Customs, Usages, and Sufferings on board of Nantucket Whale-Ships* (Boston, 1838) compares Nantucket's Indians to snow melting in the sun. In his "Anecdotes," Obed Macy describes a meeting house "near the east end of Gibbs swamp" and gives the following account of the structure: "The meeting house was built of wood, according to the common practice of building at that time. But at what time it was built, or by whom, is not known. . . . About the year 1770, Peleg Swain removed it to town and occupied it as a dwelling house, for which purpose it has been used till the year 1838 when it was taken down." John Cotton's reference to Nantucket Indians and the Baptists is in Gookin. Z. Macy's description of Indian worship is in NP. Gardner's description of the state of Indian affairs in 1694 appeared in Cotton Mather's *Magnalia* and is cited in Starbuck.

6. Gardner versus Coffin: The Revolt

The circumstances surrounding Peter Folger's imprisonment are described in his letter to Governor Andros, dated March 27, 1677, in Hough's *Papers Relating to the Island of Nantucket*; this useful collection of correspondence and court records from the New York archives in Albany is probably the best source of information concerning the Half-Share Revolt. References to town meetings come from MR; Henry Barnard Worth's *Nantucket Land and Land Owners* also serves as an excellent source of information concerning this controversial period in Nantucket's history. The best blow-by-blow account of the Revolt is in Byers. Interestingly, Macy and Crèvecoeur make no mention of this early period of conflict.

What happened to Folger's court book remains a mystery. Since Folger does not explain why he went to Gardner's house in his letter to the governor (in Hough), I think it a reasonable explanation that he did so to make sure the court book did not fall into "enemy" hands. Although the court book's fate has been the subject of some rather romanticized speculation, the town records that do exist for the years prior to 1677 (in MR) suggest that if it was not eventually "found" after the Half-Share Revolt, large portions of the book were copied down elsewhere prior to its disappearance. Indeed, when one compares the state of Nantucket's town records from the seventeenth century with those of Edgartown, the two are remarkably similar in their general state of incompleteness and disorder.

My account of grass rights and Indian-English relations is based largely on Little's "Sachem Nickanoose of Nantucket and the Grass Contest." The town's attempt at a final offer concerning Indians and horses is in MR (January 29, 1673). The Earl of Bellomont's account of his calling the winter-grass deeds a "circumvention and fraud" is in Starbuck.

The measures against Gardner and Folger can be followed in MR (March 16; April 14, 1677). The English half-share men were not the only ones displaying disrespect for island authority in June of 1677. Later that same month, the minor sachem Obadiah and several of his men attempted to rescue an Indian who had been sentenced to be whipped. A scuffle broke out in court as Obadiah, "using reviling speeches and speaking opprobrious words against the members of the court," was ultimately sentenced to be fined three pounds and whipped twenty stripes (MR, June 26, 1677). If the full-share men saw this confrontation as evidence that Gardner was indeed guilty of fomenting insurrection among the Indians, it seems to have been, in reality, more of an isolated incident than part of any organized attempt by the Indians to overthrow English authority. Later that year, Gardner himself, the supposed upholder of Indian interests, was the victim of an Indian break-in. According to court records, Jack Never "went into Captain John Gardner's house in the middle of the night and took out of Mr. Gardner's pocket by the bedside five shillings in money and also opened a case and carried away a bottle with one pint of liquor in it."

Although Folger was technically imprisoned for more than a year, it is doubtful that he spent the entire time in jail, especially given "the fire" his initial imprisonment had ignited. Documents concerning the 1680 salvaging case against Tristram Coffin are in Hough. See Little's "Grass Contest" on the town's attempt in 1682 to reach a compromise solution with the Indians. For more information concerning the Oldest House, see Helen Winslow Chase's *Jethro Coffin House Chronology, 1686–1986* (NHA, 1986).

The comments concerning Nantucketers being a "band of brothers" were made by Sansom (in NP); Walter Folger's remarks also appear in NP. Without records of birth defects and mental retardation, the question of inbreeding on Nantucket awaits the analysis of genealogical records by a trained geneticist. For example, in 1682 Elizabeth Starbuck, daughter of Nathaniel and Mary (Coffin) Starbuck married Peter Coffin, Jr., son of Peter and Abigail (Starbuck) Coffin, meaning that the father of the bride was the brother of the groom's mother, while the mother of the bride was the sister of the groom's father. According to Lydia Hinchman, by the nineteenth century "nearly all natives of Nantucket were cousins through a common ancestry." Although Quakerism encouraged a certain insularity (since Friends were expected to marry within the fold), it mandated against the marriage of first cousins. Guba has a chapter about inbreeding on the island, although he makes the mistake of linking Nantucket with the Vineyard, where, as I point out in the text, conditions were very different. The poet and translator Mary Barnard in *Nantucket Genesis, The Tale of My Tribe* (Portland, 1988) has a good, brief discussion of inbreeding on the island. Matthew Folger's comments concerning inbreeding are in Starbuck.

William F. Macy in *The Nantucket Scrap Basket* defines "Seeing the Look." There are several mammoth genealogical compilations (such as the Barney [NHA Collection 186] and Pollard [NA] Genealogies) based on information garnered from specific family censuses. There are several versions of Fanning's poem concerning Nantucket families; for example, in one variation the Gardners are described as "plodding" instead of "plotting"; the version that I have quoted is, according to E. K. Godfrey in *Island of Nantucket, What It Was, and What It Is* (Boston, 1882), the correct one. Fanning's poem was written in the midst of what might be termed the Half-Share Revolt II—the bank scandal of the 1790s (see Chapter 14).

7. The Whaling Legacy of Ichabod Paddock

The whale jackknifing is described in the *Boston News-Letter* (October 4, 1744) and is cited in Alexander Starbuck's definitive *History of the American Whale Fishery*. What little solid information there is concerning Ichabod Paddock is recorded in Robert Joseph Curfman's *The Paddock Genealogy* (Fort Collins, 1977). The transgressions of various Paddocks in the eighteenth century are recorded in the "Quaker Committee Book of Objections" (NHA Collection 35, Box 4, Book 9). As Henry Forman points out in *Early Nantucket and Its Whale Houses*, the Jethro Coffin House, commonly known as the Oldest House, should be rightly referred to as the Paddock House since Paddocks bought it from the Coffins in 1708 and lived in it from generation to generation until 1840. Paddocks also lived in the house across the street, making Sunset Hill a kind of Paddock family compound.

The merman and mermaid anecdotes appear in B. A. Botkin's *A Treasury of New England Folklore: Stories, Ballads, and Traditions of the Yankee People* (New York, 1947). The Ichabod Paddock legend is recorded by Jeremiah Digges in *Cape Cod Pilot* (Provincetown, 1937); an excellent children's story based on this account is Anne Malcolmson's *Captain Ichabod Paddock, Whaler of Nantucket* (New York, 1970).

Macy describes the islanders' first encounter with a whale in his *History*. The reference to whales around the *Mayflower* is cited in Edouard A. Stackpole's *The Sea-Hunters: The New England Whalemen during Two Centuries, 1635–1835* (Philadelphia, 1953). The reference to Gardners, Indians, and whales is in MR, as is the reference to James Lopar. Zaccheus Macy is the one who claimed Ichabod Paddock introduced the Nantucketers to the art of whaling; there is no mention of him in town records, which is not surprising, considering the fact that (unlike his brothers) he seems to have maintained his connections with the mainland.

Elizabeth Little mentions the change in tax law associated with the island's jurisdictional change in "The Indian Contribution to Along-Shore Whaling at Nantucket," *Nantucket Algonquian Studies #8* (NHA, 1981). The reference to whaleboats and Coatue cedar is in MR. Is the "green pasture" anecdote in Macy's *History* a kind of folk-tale pun on the name of the island's first professional whaleman—Paddock, which means "a small pasture"?

Little makes the estimate regarding the number of Indians and English involved in the whale fishery in "Along-Shore Whaling." Macy's account of Indian-English cooperation in the fishery is in his "Anecdotes." Little speaks of the relative earnings of an Indian whaleman in "Nantucket Whaling in the Early 18th Century," *Papers of the Nineteenth Algonquian Conference*, ed. William Cowan (Ottawa, 1988). Vickers's very different account of Indian earnings in the eighteenth century is in "The First Whalemen of Nantucket."

For an authoritative account of the genesis of the American whaleboat, see Willits D. Ansel's *The Whaleboat* (Mystic, 1978). The sketch in the Proprietors' Book was used by Forman in his architectural analysis of Siasconset. The account of saving the whale comes from Macy's *History*. In "Along-Shore Whaling" (in which she also mentions the irony of the term "saving the whale"), Little speaks of the development of the lay system and its similarities to the way in which Indians divided up drift whales; but as Marcus Rediker in *Between the Devil and the Deep*

Blue Sea: Merchant Seamen, Pirates, and the Anglo-American Maritime World, 1700–1750 (Cambridge, 1987) points out, the "share system" for the payment of seamen (used by eighteenth-century pirates and privateers) dated back to the Middle Ages.

Z. Macy (in NP) speaks of the remarkable safety record of Nantucket's shore fishery. O. Macy's reference to weather conditions in the eighteenth century is in his "Anecdotes." The worth of a whale to the oarsman of a whaleboat is estimated by Daniel Vickers in "The First Whalemen of Nantucket." The data concerning 1726 is in Macy's "Anecdotes"; he speaks of the first sperm whale in his *History*. Samuel W. Bryant in *The Sea and the States* (New York, 1967) describes Hussey's historic harpooning of a sperm whale; although by tradition it was Christopher Hussey who killed this whale, genealogical records indicate that his first name must have been Sylvanus, Bachelor, Daniel, or George (sons of Stephen, the original Quaker) who were all between the ages of eighteen and thirty in 1712. The switch to half-shares is described in Vickers's "Maritime Labor in Colonial Massachusetts," Ph.D. Dissertation (Princeton, 1981), and Byers. The statistics concerning the growth of the Nantucket whale fishery were provided by the Congregational minister, the Rev. Mr. Shaw, in NP. Macy's story concerning the shooting of a whale by an Indian is in his "Anecdotes." Z. Macy's anecdote concerning Indian-English whalers caught in a storm is in NP. In 1791 Walter Folger spoke of the use of Wampanoag phrases by Nantucket children (in NP). The description of Nantucket whalemen as "free Indians" appeared in the *New York Enquirer* and was reprinted in NI (February 14, 1829).

In the novel *Lila* (New York, 1991), Robert M. Pirsig argues that the "cultural values of America" come from the "assimilation of Indian values": "The early frontiersmen such as the 'Mountain Men' deliberately and enthusiastically imitated Indians. They were delighted to be told that they were indistinguishable from Indians. Settlers who came later copied the Mountain Men's frontier style but didn't see its source, or if they did, denied it and credited it to their own hard work and isolation." In many ways the Nantucket whalemen's interaction with island Indians anticipated the process Pirsig describes. Indeed, as I imply later (Chapter 15), the Nantucketer might be termed America's first "Marlboro Man": Instead of the cowboy's six-shooter and horse, the Nantucketer had a harpoon and whaleboat; and before the buffalo, there was the whale.

8. Mary Starbuck, High Priestess of the Company Store

For information concerning Quakerism in New England, see Arthur J. Worrall's *Quakers in the Colonial Northeast* (Hanover, 1980); H. Richard Niebuhr's classic *The Kingdom of God in America* (Chicago, 1937) offers penetrating insights into the theological similarities between Quakerism and Puritanism. The reference to Quakerism's relationship to business is from another important work, Frederick B. Tolles's *Quakers and the Atlantic Culture* (New York, 1960). Byers also has a good chapter on the rise of Quakerism on Nantucket.

Nathaniel Starbuck's "mark" appears on a will and codicil from 1716/17 in Nantucket Probate Records, vol. 1; his run-in with the law is recorded in MR. The tradition concerning Mary's reference to her husband when expressing her opinions in town meetings is in Gardner's *The Coffin Family*. For a detailed analysis of Starbuck's account book, which emphasizes the potential "benefits of the English economic system" to the island's Indians, see Elizabeth Little and Marie Sussek's "Index to Mary Starbuck's Account Book with the Indians," *Nantucket Algonquian Studies #5* (NHA, 1981).

According to a story in NI (June 10, 1843), Nathaniel Starbuck, Jr., once pointed to Waqutaquaib Pond and said to his grandson, "In this pond, through blind zeal, Peter Folger dipped my mother. . . ." Throughout this chapter I have drawn upon the published accounts of the Quaker ministers Thomas Story, Thomas Chalkley, and John Richardson—all reprinted in Starbuck. It must be remembered that these accounts were originally published after Nantucket had become a well-known Quaker success story, suggesting that a retrospective attempt to magnify the role each individual minister played in bringing Quakerism to the island may be informing these narratives.

Given the fact that Stephen Hussey's father Christopher is reported to have been "eaten by cannibals" on the coast of Florida (not to mention the eventual fate of the crew of the *Essex* in the nineteenth century), Hussey's conversation with the Quaker minister about gnawing flesh takes on a weirdly ironic dimension. The house that Story describes being raised that day in 1704 would become known as the Swain-Sevolle-Smith dwelling and would remain a famous Nantucket landmark until it was tragically burned at the beginning of the twentieth century; see Forman, who also cites the Probate Record's reference to Swain's still house, which was left to his wife.

In his "Anecdotes," Macy tells the story of the arrival of the French privateer in 1695. Besides the story concerning Swain's loss of his money, Macy also tells about how the privateer threatened to disrupt a Hussey marriage celebration (Macy mistakenly says it was Stephen's wedding, when it must have been his eldest daughter's)—an event that seems to have resembled Swain's house-raising in that Indians and rum were also involved.

The progress of Stephen Hussey's eventual disownment can be traced in the "Quaker Committee Book of Objections" at the NHA. For a profile of Nathaniel Starbuck, Jr., and his dual role as clerk of both the town and the Friends Meeting, see Robert Leach's three-part series, "Nantucket's First Man of Wealth," in NI (November 9–23, 1966). See Starbuck and Byers for the specifics of Quakerism's growth on the island. Byers speaks of the importance of the Macy-Starbuck alliance while also citing Fothergill concerning the attractions of Quakerism from an economic point of view.

That Crèvecoeur may have exaggerated the decorum of the Nantucket waterfront is suggested by a 1764 letter to the Browns of Rhode Island from grog shopkeeper Mary Pinkham requesting "what is due in New England rum at the first opportunity [as] I expect the whaling men every day and I must have some to welcome them" (cited in Byers). The account of watching "First Day" from a ship anchored off the bar appears in William Root Bliss, *Quaint Nantucket*. Several copies of Mary Starbuck's letter are at the NA.

9. Richard Macy, the Master Builder

Most of this account is based on "A Short Memorial of Richard Macy, Grandfather of Obed Macy" in Macy's "Anecdotes." The wheat-stacking anecdote comes from the *Macy Genealogy*. The best discussion of Nantucket's early architecture is in Forman, who also discusses the island's mills. Contrary to what is sometimes claimed, Straight Wharf was not the first wharf on Nantucket. According to town records, in 1716 Joseph Coffin was granted the right to build "a wharf at the old landing forty feet wide." My description of the construction of Straight Wharf is based on a HABS account quoted in "A Waterfront History, Nantucket, 1870–1970," an unpublished study compiled by Martha R. Boynton for Sherburne Associates in 1974 ("Harbor" green-dot file, NHA). Macy's wharf would prove to be remarkably durable. In fact, when the wharf was rebuilt in the twentieth century, the original logs were extracted from the mud in an excellent state of preservation and were subsequently used to fill in marshy areas in the neighborhood of the Creeks near Marine Lumber (personal communication with Albert F. Egan, Jr.—February, 1993). The references to patrolling the wharf are in the record of Town Meetings, 1696–1783, in the Town Clerk's Office.

Another important structure built during this period was the first lighthouse on Brant Point in 1746. By the time of the Revolution, there were a total of four mills built along the ridge of what was then known as the Popsquatchet Hills. The single mill that remains today, known as the "Old Mill," was constructed in 1746 by Nathan Wilbur, a Nantucket sailor who based its octagonal design on the mills he had seen in Holland. According to tradition, this mill was hit by a cannon ball (which reportedly passed completely through it, narrowly missing the miller's head) during the Revolution.

In Macy's daybook are the following dimensions for a whaleboat: "The beginning of the head from the end of the keel: to the first bend—3′8″; to the next bend—3′3″; to the next bend—5′3″; to the next bend—3′5″; then to the end of the keel—4′1″." As Little points out, this adds up to 19′8″ which corresponds very closely to another contemporary account of the whaleboats being about 20′. In their later form in the nineteenth century, the whaleboat would approach 30′. In the 1750s, Richard's son Zaccheus provided 78 whaleboats to James Otis "for King's service for raids on Canada" (in Byers).

The court case involving Zaccheus and Richard Macy and the Indian Panjame is in Book I of the Superior Court Records. For an account of bookkeeping barter as it applied to Nantucket, see Little's "Nantucket Whaling in the Early Eighteenth Century." Lydia

Hinchman's description of the Macys as a "close corporation" is in *The Early Settlers of Nantucket*. An account of the exchange between Macy and his son Caleb comes from William F. Macy's *The Nantucket Scrap Basket*.

In his old age, Richard Macy appears to have been part of an island-wide phenomenon; after his visit to the island in the 1770s, Crèvecoeur claimed, "You will hardly find anywhere a community . . . exhibiting so many green old men who show their advanced age by the maturity of their wisdom rather than by the wrinkles of their faces. . . ." Richard's apology to the Friends Meeting appears in the "Quaker Committee Book of Objections." The Elihu Bunker letter is in NHA Collection 3, Folder 33; Richard Macy's deeds and wills are in NHA Collection 96, Folder 35.

10. Of God, Indians, and Getting By: The Hireling, Timothy White

Although Congregationalists and Presbyterians shared the same beliefs, in terms of governance the Nantucket church was Congregational; the island's Quakers, however, often referred to them as Presbyterians. Helen Winslow Chase's "First Congregational Church and Old North Vestry," a 19-page memorandum written for the Church, provides a chronology and history of Congregationalism on the island. In 1764 the original meeting house near No-Bottom Pond was moved to Beacon Hill overlooking Center Street and Nantucket Harbor where it became known as the Old North Vestry; in 1795 what would become a famed tower was built on the south side of the vestry, providing an excellent view of the town and harbor; in 1800 a bell was hung in the tower; and in 1834 the vestry was moved back on the lot to accommodate a much bigger church building. Danforth's description of Nantucket as a godless "frontier" is cited in Byers.

The letter from Prince appears in Henry J. Cadbury's "Nantucket and Its Quakers in 1722," HN (1946). Where not otherwise stated, all references to White's correspondence, sermons, and memorandum books come from NHA Collection 129—almost all of which appears in HN (1898) entitled "Timothy White Papers, 1725–1755," ed. Myron Samuel Dudley—and NHA Collection 299 ("White Family Papers," from Dover, New Hampshire). It is from this last collection, relatively little of which has previously appeared in print, that most of my quotations come.

White was one in a long line of distinguished Nantucket schoolteachers. In 1716, Eleazer Folger became the town's first official schoolteacher but seems to have quit after a year due to a lack of interest (in Starbuck). According to Obed Macy's "Anecdotes," another early teacher was a shadowy figure by the name of Collings who kept a school on Pleasant Street in a "very old shattered building with diamond cut glass windows." Although a man of "ability and good learning," he left the island suddenly, handing over the school to Benjamin Coffin. It was later rumored he was a pirate who had come to Nantucket to avoid arrest. Another schoolmaster by the name of "little Draper" kept school in a meeting house that stood not far from Maxcey's Pond. According to Macy, it was the "first building that was burnt down on Nantucket that I ever heard of." White's letter to Colman is cited by Byers. The letter from Governor Belcher appears in HN (1900).

In his "Anecdotes," Macy describes the corrosive effects of drink on the Indians: "When they were furnished with strong drink, they would leave town at night and proceed towards their home until the effect of the poison would cause them to drop by the way, exposed to the inclemency of the weather. It often happened in these cases that they were found dead, and not much care was taken to carry them to any particular burying ground but were interred where they were found, which sometimes happened several days afterwards." Macy in his "Anecdotes" describes "the principal or last [Indian] meeting house" as situated within "a short distance" of the Indians' final burying ground in Miacomet, and claims that it "was standing until about the year 1782." This structure was built in or before 1732 when Judge Benjamin Lynde recorded that "Mr. White preached very well at the new built Meeting House" (cited in Chase's "First Congregational Church").

Byers refers to the Indian churches as "a buffer" and also cites the Indian petitions (which are reprinted in Starbuck). While Byers and Vickers paint a picture of Indian exploitation on Nantucket, Little is quick to point out that island Indians enjoyed a level of participation in the English whaling economy that was without precedent in New England.

Her analysis of eighteenth-century account books causes her to dispute claims that most Indian whalers on Nantucket were indebted servants, while she reminds us that the lay system enabled an Indian to make more than a decent wage in the whale fishery. In "Along-Shore Whaling" she states, "English-Indian relations [on Nantucket], while certainly not perfect, have to be considered among the best in America." Unfortunately, however, even though Indian-English relations on Nantucket were about as good as it got, it was still essentially a slave-master relationship. Even Nathaniel Starbuck, Jr., son of the "Great Woman," would will several of his Indians, as well as his "Indian debts," to his heirs (in Starbuck).

The references to Abraham Monkey and Cromwell Coffin appear in Book 1 of the Nantucket Court Records. The Indian petition quoted here is dated July 14, 1747, and appears in Starbuck. The reference to the potential Indian uprising is in Macy's *History*; the *Boston News-Letter* report is cited in Starbuck's *History of the American Whale Fishery*. Eliza Mitchell recorded in a notebook of reminiscences in 1894 (NHA Collection 23) another account of the Indian uprising. As an eight-year-old girl, Mitchell heard the tale from a woman "between eighty and ninety years of age," whose account was later confirmed by the famed Siasconset genealogist and historian Benjamin Franklin Folger (see Chapter 12). According to Mitchell, after learning of the Indians' plot, the English families "gathered their little ones close around them, club'd together," while the men set out "through fog and darkness" only to find "not the least indication of any disturbance." It turned out that the informer had come up with the story of the plot just to get some rum from the English. When the Indians were told of the "culprit's" tale, they demanded that he be punished at the whipping post that then existed near where the Civil War monument now stands on Main Street. According to Mitchell, this was the last Indian whipping to be performed on Nantucket. Although the fears of a rebellion were apparently groundless, the behavior of the English clearly indicates that they were well aware (and leery) of Indian discontent.

Macy speaks of the English and Indians having the equivalent of a final legal showdown concerning the Indians' claims that their lands had been taken through nefarious means. According to Macy, the decision was in favor of the English, with the Indians resigning themselves to their situation from that point forward. Although Macy dates this turning point as 1753, Starbuck claims that it was actually in 1758, five years before the plague.

That White had a lot to learn about the coasting trade is suggested by a letter from one of the leading merchants of the day, Joseph Rotch, who complains about White's instructions concerning a shipment from Philadelphia: "As for sending orders for such things it is not the way amongst merchants. When I sent Capt. Chase last year I never had any agreement with any man but sent him to John Misslen and desired him to load his bark. . . . Thou must trust to me and my friend to fill the vessel up."

Macy's *History* contains an account of the Indian sickness, as does Eliza Mitchell's notebook of reminiscences, which focuses on the role played by Zaccheus Macy, who attended the sick on a daily basis. According to Mitchell, he provided them with broth while keeping "the Indians to the leeward of himself" so as to avoid infection. If Timothy White failed to be the Peter Folger of his day, the title probably should go to Zaccheus Macy, who according to Mitchell "was the only person of that time who understood the Indian dialect. He could converse freely with them [and] consequently could influence them in many ways for their good." Perhaps more important, Z. Macy (unlike White) had the financial means to devote extensive time and energies to the Indians. According to Mitchell, "He was considered wealthy in his time because it took so few thousand dollars in his day, as compared with this, to make the fortunate quite independent." Macy's altruism did not stop with the Indians; he also became known as the primary bonesetter on the island, performing his services free of charge.

11. Peleg Folger, the Poet Whaleman

Peleg Folger's original log is at the NA. On the inside cover is written, "The property of Sam'l Swain, Nantucket"; beneath that: "To F. C. Sanford, 1885." An incomplete nineteenth-century transcription of Peleg Folger's log is at the NHA, Log #318.

William Root Bliss was the first to quote generously from Folger's log in *Quaint Nantucket*. Edouard Stackpole relies almost exclusively on Folger's journal for information concerning eighteenth-century whaling in *The Sea-Hunters.* In *And the Whale is Ours: Creative Writing of American Whalemen* (Boston, 1979), Pamela Miller provides a sampling and literary analysis of nineteenth-century logs, but, to my mind at least, Peleg Folger's eighteenth-century log beats them all hollow.

The specifications of a typical whaling sloop come from *The Sea-Hunters* and Douglass C. Fonda, Jr.'s monograph, *Eighteenth Century Nantucket Whaling* (Nantucket, 1969), a distillation of information gleaned from logs and journals in possession of the NA and NHA. The rig of a typical whaling sloop included a gaff-rigged mainsail (which when reefed was referred to as a "balanced mainsail"), a squaresail set on a short topmast above the main, a trysail just forward of the mast, and a jib set on a bowsprit.

According to tradition, Nantucketers sometimes used the taste of the sea bottom to help them determine their location. An old Nantucket anecdote describes a trick played on a captain when the crew substituted the contents of a flowerpot for the soundings he had been using to plot their course through a thick fog. After tasting the soil, the Captain shouted, "Nantucket's sunk and here we are right over Old Marm Hackett's garden!" Two versions of this anecdote are cited in William F. Macy's *The Nantucket Scrap Basket*; a third is entitled "A Cruise Along Shore in the Seventeenth Century" and contained in *Sailor's Magazine* (November, 1848) and reprinted in Roger Duncan and John Ware's *A Cruising Guide to the New England Coast* (New York, 1983). There is also a Down East "Bert and I" version of this tale.

That sociability was expected among whalemen is indicated by this entry in Folger's log: "In the morning we spied a sail and drew up with him but the clown would not speak with us, steering off about SE." When Folger refers to whalers from "Cushnet," he is talking about the Acushnet River on which the whaling village of Bedford (eventually New Bedford) would soon be founded by the Nantucketer Joseph Rotch.

Peleg's "bogtrotters" were not the only ones who did not appreciate the dead whales left by the Nantucketers. By 1765, the governor of Newfoundland had issued an order that required whalemen to "carry the useless parts of such whales as they may catch to at least three leagues from shore . . ."; also of interest is this directive: "In all dealings with the Indians, to treat them with the greatest civility: observing not to impose on their ignorance, or to take advantage of their necessities.

You are also on no account to serve them with spirituous liquors"; from Starbuck's *History of the American Whale Fishery.*

For an account of the racial make-up of colonial whaling crews, as well as how the technological advances of whaling reduced the whalemen's quality of life, see Vickers's "Maritime Labor in Colonial Massachusetts." The text of the 1758 exemption for Nantucket Quaker whalemen (in Starbuck) reads in part: "Inasmuch as the inhabitants of Nantucket most of whom are Quakers are by law exempted from impresses for military service. And their livelihood entirely depends on the whale fishery—Advised that his Excellency gives permission for all whaling vessels belonging to said island to pursue their voyages, taking only the inhabitants of said Island and said vessels. . . ." Even if the Quaker whalemen did not fight against the French, they were inevitably caught up in the conflict. According to Starbuck, six Nantucket vessels were lost at sea in 1755–6, while another six were captured and burned by the French.

From Folger's log: "In Straits St. Davis are several things remarkable: 1. A right whale is a very large fish (for the most part) they are somewhat hollowing on their backs, being all slick and smooth and having no hump at all as other whales. Their bone (of which is made stays and hooped petticoats) is grown in their mouth, the under end or butt growing in the gum of the upper jaw. Their tongue is monstrous large and will commonly make a tun of oil. Their bone is from 3 to 12 feet long according to the bigness of the whale and is all the teeth they have. They have two spoutholes and make a forked spout whereby they are distinguished from other whales at a distance. Blubber, lean, and fluke of a young right whale is good food. 2. A spermaceti is a large whale. They will make from 10 to 100 barrels of oil. They have no bone in their head and their brains is all oil. They have a hump on the after part of their back: one spouthole. Their under jaw is full of hard ivory teeth and tongue very small. 3. A humpback hath a hump differing from a spermaceti—that being hooking and this straight. They have bone like a right whale only tis short and good only to make buttons."

When the *Greyhound* spoke with a Dutch ship, they discovered a unique passenger: "They had an Indian and his canoe on board and intended to carry him to Holland and bring him back next year." Obed Macy in his *History* has this to say about the difference between the whale fishery and the "cold-blooded butchery" of war: "For deeds of true valor, done without brutal excitement, but in the honest and lawful pursuit of the means of livelihood, we may safely point to the life of a whaleman, and dare the whole world to produce a parallel."

Macy quotes from Folger's poem "Dominum Collaudamus [Let Us Praise the Lord]" while providing a brief description of his character: "His general deportment was serious and contemplative. It was rare that he indulged in levity, but he was free and sociable in conversation on useful subjects, whether moral or religious." Macy also describes the circumstances of Folger's death: "For several days previous to his departure, he appeared to have a satisfactory presentiment of his approaching end, and that the sting of death was entirely removed. He had much to say by way of advice to his friends and neighbors, who visited him in his last moments."

The poem about "Uncle Pillick" is in Macy's *Scrap Basket*. Folger's workbook (kept from 1758 to 1762) as well as the log-like group of stitched-together papers that comprise his later journal are in NHA Collection 88, Box 23, Book 57, and Collection 118, Folder 37.

The quote from Emerson concerning Nantucket captains comes from his *Journals*. Any discussion of eighteenth-century whaling on Nantucket would not be complete without the inclusion of "The Whale-List" by Thomas Worth (cited in Starbuck's *History of the American Whale Fishery*):

> *Out of Nantucket there's Whalemen seventy-five,*
> *But two poor Worths among them doth survive:*
> *There is two Ramsdills & there's Woodburys two,*
> *Two Ways there is, chuse which one pleaseth you,*
> *Folgers thirteen, & Barnards there are four*
> *Bunkers there is three & Jenkinses no more,*
> *Gardners there is seven, Husseys there are two*
> *Pinkhams there is five and a poor Delano,*
> *Myricks there is three & Collins there are six,*
> *Swains there are four and one blue gally Fitch.*
> *One Chadwick, Coggshall, Coleman there's but one,*
> *Brown, Baxter, two & Paddacks there is three,*
> *Wyer, Stanton, Starbuck, Moorse is four you see,*

> *But if for a Voyage I was to choose a Stanton,*
> *I would leave Sammy out & choose Ben Stratton.*
> *And not forget that Bocott is alive,*
> *And that long-crotch makes up the seventy-five.*
> *This is answering to the list, you see,*
> *Made up in seventeen hundred & sixty-three.*

12. Kezia Coffin's Revolutionary Rise and Fall

Crèvecoeur's references to "Aunt Kesiah" appear in the last of his five letters about Nantucket, a letter that contains several references to events that occurred after the outbreak of the Revolution. For a discussion of the time-frame contained within the *Letters*, see my "The Nantucket Sequence in Crèvecoeur's *Letters from an American Farmer*," *New England Quarterly* (September, 1991). *Miriam Coffin, or The Whale-Fishermen: A Tale* was published anonymously in 1834. See Lisa Norling's "'How Fraught with Sorrow and Heartpangs': Mariners' Wives and the Ideology of Domesticity in New England, 1790–1880," *New England Quarterly* (September, 1992), for a brief comparison of Crèvecoeur's and Hart's portrayals of Kezia Coffin. Mrs. Starbuck's reference to having torn down Kezia's country house in Quaise appears in "Personal Reminiscences of Mrs. Eliza W. Mitchell," dated November 27, 1894, NHA Collection 252.

The tradition concerning Kezia's conduct during a town meeting is recounted by George Worth in the Worth Family Papers, NHA Collection 129, Book 9. For more information about Kezia's sister Judith, see Norling's "Judith Macy and her Daybook; or, Crèvecoeur and the Wives of Sherborn," HN (Winter, 1993). Franklin's letter to Kezia appeared in NI (January 26, 1824). The reference to her in-town mansion is from George Worth; Hart also goes into a fair amount of detail about the house in *Miriam Coffin*. In a September 2, 1918, letter to Alexander Starbuck, Henry Worth (NHA Collection 144, Folder 18) recorded all references in Quaker records to Kezia and John Coffin; one entry reads: "Kezia Coffin disowned for keeping a spinet in her house and permitting her daughter to play thereon."

At some point Kezia Coffin Fanning's diaries were tragically lost; what remains are the fairly detailed notes and transcriptions made by family members in NHA Collection 2. Kezia Fanning's diary has several references to the spinet and the Quaker disciplinary committee.

The March, 1773, reference to Phineas Fanning is in the first volume of the Nantucket Court Record Book. Traditions concerning Phineas Fanning's arrival on the island are contained in "Nantucket Surnames," *The Gleaner*, New Bedford, 1847 (NHA Collection 43, Folder 4), as well as *Miriam Coffin*, in which Fanning appears as the lawyer Grimshaw. Just as Nantucketers had a natural aversion to hireling priests, they did not seem to have much use for lawyers, a tradition that may have dated back to the days when old Stephen Hussey sued the town selectmen. Even with Kezia as a client, Fanning appears to have had plenty of time on his hands, and he soon became one of the island's leading duck hunters and fishermen. In her journal, Kezia Fanning regularly recorded the day's kill; a typical entry: "P.F. shoots geese, teal, coot, duck, bluebill, redhead, broadbill." Crèvecoeur explicitly states that there was so little legal business on the island that if it were not for the fact that Fanning had married the wealthiest heiress on the island, he would have been a very poor man. Unfortunately for the Fannings, Crèvecoeur's words would prove prophetic, with Fanning serving at least one sentence in debtor's prison (see Chapter 14).

As to be expected, loyal Nantucketers of the nineteenth and twentieth centuries have tended to deny vehemently Crèvecoeur's claim concerning opium use, even though they have been perfectly willing to accept his many other, less controversial observations concerning the islanders' habits, the geography of the island, and the details of the whale fishery—all of which have withstood (to an amazing degree) the test of time. In a personal communication to the author (May, 1991), Everett and Katherine Emerson, who are at work on a definitive edition of Crèvecoeur's *Letters*, claim that they have uncovered historical evidence concerning opium use in the eighteenth century that convinces them that Crèvecoeur's observations are correct.

The information concerning the extent of the whale fishery in pre-Revolutionary Nantucket is in Byers. In his *History*, Obed Macy provides a detailed description of how interconnected the whale fishery was with the community on Nantucket. Besides Kezia Fanning's diaries and Edouard Stackpole's *Whales and Destiny: The Rivalry between America, France and Britain for Control of the Southern Whale Fishery* (Amherst,

1972), my account of what Byers calls the "combative hierarchy" among Nantucket's whaling merchants, as well as Nantucket's position just prior to and soon after the outbreak of the Revolution, is based primarily on Byers, who cites Hussey's complaint against the Rotches as well as William Rotch's comment concerning the level of "friendship" a fellow merchant can (or cannot) expect. The Boston merchant's reference to the Nantucketers' unwillingness to negotiate is also cited by Byers.

The secret of how to manufacture sperm candles came relatively late to Nantucket, the result of some high-stakes espionage work on the part of the Rotches in the early 1770s; see Macy's *History*. According to an account in NI (August 3, 1827), the Rotches' on-island monopoly of candle-making "was not to be endured," so Walter Folger, "a man of uncommon perspicacity," determined to figure out the secret himself, ultimately starting a successful candle factory with Thomas Jenkins, the man who would accuse Kezia, Rotch, and the others of treason during the Revolution; after the war Jenkins would be one of the men behind the founding of the whaling port of Hudson (see Chapter 13).

The Rotches were so savvy (and ruthless) in their manipulation of the whale oil market that not even such Boston heavyweights as the Hancocks were able to wrest control of it from them in the 1760s; see Byers.

The letter describing the arrival of the Boston refugees on Nantucket was written by Abraham Williams to Col. Nathaniel Freeman on July 20, 1775, and is in NHA Collection 197; Williams also states that there are Nantucketers who "expect to make their own fortune in the squabble, without danger to themselves"—a plan that Kezia Coffin seems to have latched onto from the very beginning of the Revolution.

Stackpole in *Nantucket in the American Revolution* (Nantucket, 1976) speaks of the confiscated whaleboats going to Lake Champlain. Rotch's reference to religious persecution appears in Byers; for an account of the still-murky circumstances surrounding the plan for a Falkland-based whale fishery see Stackpole's *The Sea-Hunters*. Besides Kezia Fanning's diaries, Macy's *History* is an excellent source of firsthand information concerning the Revolutionary period on Nantucket.

Hart provides this account of Kezia's Quaise estate in *Miriam Coffin*: "When last we saw it, time and exposure to storms had covered it with a mossy coating, and it was occupied by an industrious farmer and his family, who seemed to take pride in speaking of its origin and its peculiarities." The reference to the factual accuracy of Hart's novel appears in NI (July 16, 1834).

In the introduction to *Miriam Coffin*, Hart recounts sharing some chowder with a character obviously based on Benjamin Franklin Folger in his squalid shack in Siasconset. Hart even goes to the lengths of claiming that the actual text of the book is based on a manuscript given to him by the Folger character. Eliza Mitchell met Folger when she was a twelve-year-old girl and later recalled: "We were from that time on always the most friendly terms, and from him I learned much that to me was very interesting. But he never seemed willing to give me opportunity to write any down. He simply said, 'Your memory's good enough, and you'll remember, because you cannot forget.'" Folger recounted to Mitchell the specifics of how he discovered Kezia's secret passageway: With the help of an old farmer, who referred to it as "that old Tory's Smuggling Hole," he began digging where "I often had been told the entrance might be found." Eventually he came to what he described as "an opening," and "in a few days after the air had passed through," he crawled inside and found the "storage place" (NHA Collection 23). As is indicated in his diaries, William C. Folger, a schoolteacher, surveyor, and noted genealogist on the island, got most of his information from Franklin Folger, whom he visited on a regular basis in the 1830s and '40s.

Before the Revolution put them on opposite sides of the political fence, Timothy Folger provided his "cousin" Benjamin Franklin with information concerning the Gulf Stream that Franklin used to make an extremely accurate chart; see NP for a copy of the chart and Franklin's comments concerning the Nantucketers' familiarity with the Stream. For a description of Kezia Coffin's legal entanglements after the Revolution, see Emil Guba's *The Great Nantucket Bank Robbery Conspiracy* (Waltham, 1973).

Although William Rotch wanted no part of the Revolution, in February, 1783, his ship the *Bedford* was the first to fly the American flag in London. No matter what the political leanings of the ship's owner might have been, at least one crew member was a true patriot. According to an anecdote related by William F. Macy, one of the sailors was a hunch-back who, after being asked by a British tar what it was he had under his coat, replied, "Bunker Hill and be damned to you!"

13. The "Removals": From Jethro Coffin to William Rotch

In his *History*, Obed Macy says that Nantucketers "were so closely connected by birth, similarity of pursuits, and habits of intimacy, that in some respects they appeared and conducted as one family. Perhaps there is not another place in the world, of equal magnitude, where the inhabitants were so connected by consanguinity as in this. . . ." Godfrey in *Island of Nantucket* describes the differences between Nantucket and Martha's Vineyard speech patterns. Franklin's letter to his sister is dated August 3, 1789, and appears in NP.

My account of the Mendon settlement is based on Elizabeth Little and Margaret Morrison's "The Mendon-Nantucket Connection: 1708–1737" (NHA, 1986), in which they describe the transplanted Nantucketers as "peripheral suppliers." The Rev. Timothy White's bride, Susanna Gardner, was part of the return migration from Mendon. As Little points out, economic factors may have also contributed to the end of the settlement; by 1726 Nantucket had developed to the point that there were plenty of coastal traders willing to make the trip out to the island, reducing the need for a peripheral supply-town such as Mendon.

After expelling the French Acadians from Nova Scotia in 1758 (some of whom were sent to Nantucket before resettling elsewhere), the British were attempting to bolster the English presence on the island. For an account of the Nantucket settlement of Cape Sable, see Edouard Stackpole's "The Nantucket Migrations," HN (October, 1958).

For information on the settlement in New Garden, North Carolina, see William Macy's "Migrations of Nantucketers to the South and West," HN (1933); also Robert Frazier's "Nantucket and North Carolina," NI (October 26, 1967). Copies of removal certificates are in "Nantucket Friends Records: Testimonials of Denials, Acknowledgements, Removals, 1777–1812," NHA Collection 52, Book 21. An example: "To the Monthly Meeting at New Garden: Margaret Marshall having removed from hence to settle among you, and requesting our certificate, these are to certify that she is a member of our society and hath settled her outward affairs as far as we know to satisfaction, and is clear of marriage engagements as far as appears, as such we recommend her to your Christian care, with desires for her growth and establishment in the truth, remain your friends brethren and sisters. Signed in and by order of the above and Meeting by William Rotch, Clerk; Ruth Gardner, Clerk." An original copy of the letter from William and Phebe Stanton is in NHA Collection 36, Folder 28.

The migration from North Carolina to Indiana and Ohio is discussed not only in William Macy's article but also in Guba, who speaks of the town of Nantucket, Indiana, as well as the "commonwealth" of Nantucket. An example of a Nantucket descendant taking his "genius" into the interior of the country is provided by Levi Coffin, popularly known as the "President" of the Underground Railroad and the model for the character of Simeon Halliday in *Uncle Tom's Cabin*. In his *Reminiscences*, Coffin speaks proudly of his Nantucket heritage while describing his migration from North Carolina to Indiana; indeed, at one point in his autobiography he talks about the "Underground Railroad business" in just the same way that his ancestors spoke of the "whaling business."

A colorful account of the Hudson, New York, settlement is provided by Charles S. Clark in "Emigration from Nantucket to Hudson, N.Y.," HN (1928). Stackpole's *Whales and Destiny* also deals with Hudson while providing a blow-by-blow account of the international "chess game" between England, France, and America in the Dartmouth, Dunkirk, and Milford Haven settlements. The letter from Rotch to Samuel Rodman is cited in Stackpole, as is his reference to a "second Revolution" in France. Moses Brown's remarks concerning Rotch are quoted by Byers. Greville's three aims regarding the Milford settlement were made in a memorandum to the "Committee of South [Sea] Whalers," cited in Stackpole. Abiel Folger's diary is also cited in Stackpole.

Although it never came to fruition, plans were made for yet another Nantucket offshoot community, this time in Lima, Peru. In a letter (at the NA) dated November 10, 1799, addressed to Captain Wyer and signed "X" (but with handwriting that resembles Benjamin Tupper's), the writer claims that "I have been about 10 mo. on a project of establishing a whale fishery at Lima in Peru which I have obtained an exclusive right for 10 years free of all duties. . . . I . . . embark for N. York to put my project into effect with American ships and sailors. I shall have 10 ships of 150 to 300 tons . . . and 3 large ships of 600 tons in bringing the proceeds from Lima to Spain."

Crèvecoeur mentions Kennebec as the northern alternative to New Garden for Nantucketers wishing to remove; Nantucketers also went to Saratoga, New York, prior to the Revolution. In his daily journals (NHA Collection 96), Obed Macy also refers to early nineteenth-century removals to Kennebec; New York City is another favorite destination; interestingly, Boston is almost never mentioned.

Micajah Coffin's letter to Walter Folger, Jr., is dated November 18, 1811, and is at the NA. The 1818 letter from J. Rotch is in NHA Collection 144, Folder 81. William Rotch's reputation seems to have undergone a dramatic turnaround on Nantucket. In 1781, a traveling Quaker referred to him as "much esteemed by the people" and as "a prince of the island" (in Henry Cadbury's "An Off-Islander's Impressions, June, 1781," HN, June, 1949); by the 1790s, such was not the case.

14. A "Nest of Love" No Longer: William Coffin and the Bank, Commons, and School Wars

An article in NI (May 30, 1825) looks back to the days of the Federalist-Democrat division on Nantucket: "Every man, woman, or child could tell a Democrat from a Federalist, at the slightest glimpse.— There were a 1000 little lines, demi-lines, and sublines of character, which rendered it as impossible for a member of one party to counterfeit the marks of his opponent as for a turkey buzzard to pass for a cockroach." William Coffin's 1793 letter is to Thomas Upshur, Jr., and is in NHA Collection 150, Folder 78. The tightening of the Friends Discipline on Nantucket can be traced in the "Quaker Committee Book of Objections," NHA Collection 35, Box 4, Book 9; also see Byers. William Coffin had a direct professional connection with Kezia Coffin, deciding in her favor when asked to mediate a debt dispute, and apparently representing her in court at one point. William Coffin's portrait can be seen in the Coffin School, of which he was the first president of the trustees.

In June of 1795, just before the opening of the Nantucket Bank, the town's name was changed back from Sherburne to Nantucket; the bank (where the Lion's Paw now stands) was robbed only two weeks after opening its doors. For a detailed and thoroughly researched account of the robbery and its effect on Nantucket, see Emil Guba's *The Great Nantucket Bank Robbery Conspiracy and Solemn Aftermath or the End of Old Nantucket* (Waltham, 1973); another good account of the controversy (from a lawyer's perspective) is in Robert F. Mooney and Andre

R. Sigourney's *The Nantucket Way* (New York, 1980). As whaling vessels became larger and the voyages became longer (by this time whalers were rounding the Cape of Good Hope and Cape Horn for the Pacific), it was vital that Nantucket shipowners and merchants have access to increased capital; hence the formation of the bank.

A treasure trove of materials relating to the Nantucket Bank robbery, including letters, depositions, and other documents are in NHA Collection 91. The joke concerning the latch string is in Charles Clark's previously cited "Emigration . . . to Hudson." Nathaniel Coffin's letter is from *The Chronicle* (November 30, 1795) in NHA Collection 91, Folder 17. Silvanus Macy's letters (several of them to William Rotch) are in Collection 91, Folder 6; Coffin's correspondence is in Folder 5; the threatening notice is in Folder 17. Kezia Fanning's deposition (Folder 3) provides a very personal look into the incredible maneuvering and backstabbing involved in the controversy.

The full title of the ballad is "Siasconset Laws or The Laws of Siasconset, A Ballad, Proposed with a pipe of Tobacco as An Evenings Amusement to the Fisherman (to the tune of 'Vicar of Bray.') By a Friend of Native Simplicity." An 1845 edition of the poem is in the NA.

My account of William and Micajah Coffin's square-off owes much to Guba and Will Gardner's *The Coffin Saga* (Nantucket, 1949). Freeman's description of Nantucket's "spirit of bitterness" is in NP; in 1801 Josiah Quincy met Albert Gardner during a visit to Nantucket and commented on how the scandal had devastated him (in NP). On his deathbed in 1808, Jethro Hussey asked that several of those who had accused him of the bank robbery be brought to his bedside; he then swore that "he was an utter stranger" to the robbery (a copy of his moving address to his accusers is in Folder 3).

The irony of a "thee and thouing" Quaker such as Silvanus Macy leading a cover-up operation is made plain by a reference to "The Epistle from the Yearly Meeting held in London—1796" (in the NA), a Friends document that was printed in New Bedford and distributed throughout the island in the midst of the scandal: "In these times of worldly commotion, the concern still remains with us, that our brethren may be preserved from joining with any thing, that immediately or remotely conduces to mixing . . . with the fluctuating politics of the times."

For an account of the religious aftershocks of the scandal, see Guba and Byers. By 1823 the Methodist church that presently stands on Center Street (with a seating capacity of 1,000) was built, although the pillars that now dominate the front were not added until 1840.

Churchman's account of the proprietary is in Henry J. Cadbury's "An Off-Islander's Impressions, June, 1781," HN (1949). Josiah Quincy (in NP) made the comments about exhausting the land. Obed Macy's discussion of sheep grazing is in his *History*. Perhaps the most eloquent defense of the proprietary came from Joseph Sansom writing in 1811 (in NP): "[T]here is now a plan in agitation for dividing to each proprietor his share, in fee simple under the specious plea of putting it into the power of every man. . . . Should this operation take place, it will probably throw large tracts into particular hands, who may improve the breed of sheep, and ameliorate the soil . . . but the place would lose forever its most interesting peculiarities." For an account of the Commons War, see Guba's "The Sheep Commons Fight," HN (July, 1964). A copy of the original petition to divide the commons as well as the pamphlet "A Nest of Love" are at the NHA ("Commons Land" blue-dot file).

For an account of the Federalist-Democrat wrangling during the War of 1812, see Reginald Horsman's "Nantucket's Peace Treaty with England in 1814," *New England Quarterly* (June, 1981); Starbuck also offers a good documentary account of some of the more controversial town meetings. During the war, a bloody battle between the American privateer *Neufchatel* and British frigate *Endymion* just off the southeastern end of the island flooded the town with wounded sailors. As a five-year-old boy Frederick Sanford (Chapter 18) heard the screams of men being operated on in a tavern, something he would never forget.

Sanford also remembered Uncle Cash and the Newtown Gate, as well as the east and west sheep shearings. For those seeking to explore the arcane intricacies involved in what makes up a sheep's common (from a lawyer's perspective), there is Orrin Rosenberg's concise and readable "History of Sheep's Commons and the Proprietary," an unpublished manuscript, as well as Guba's article.

Copies of Coffin and Gardner's "Bank Narrative" are at both the NHA and NA. Obed Macy's journals are in NHA Collection 96. See Byers on the Quakers' deemphasis of education. For an overview of Nantucket schools, see W. D. Perkins's "Education," HN (January, 1960). William Coffin was part of a committee that determined in 1818 that there were hundreds of children on Nantucket without schooling. Unfortunately, after briefly instituting a fledgling school system, the town withdrew its support.

For an account of Isaac Coffin's relationship with Nantucket, see the video "Admiral Sir Isaac Coffin, Baronet: The Vicarious Nantucketer" (for which I wrote the script) in the archives of the Egan Maritime Institute, as well as Thomas C. Amory's *The Life of Admiral Sir Isaac Coffin, Baronet* (Boston, 1886). The original Coffin School was built on the corner of Lyons and Fair Streets; the current building on Winter Street was built in the 1850s.

For Samuel Jenks's account of the history of the Democrat-Federalist feud, see his previously cited editorial in NI (May 30, 1825). In the advertisement for Macy's *History* (NI, 1834–5), William Coffin, Jr., has this to say about his role as ghostwriter, "The part which it was proposed that the writer of this should perform has been readily and cheerfully undertaken, and, although he can claim no honor as a historian, and is desirous of none for the drudgery of re-writing, it gives him pleasure to anticipate that he may be the means of hastening a publication, and possibly of securing to this generation, what might otherwise have been postponed to the next."

In 1821 when Owen Chase, a survivor of one of the worst disasters to strike a whaleship (see Chapter 15), returned to the island, he certainly looked to someone else for literary help. As none other than Herman Melville observed, Chase's *Narrative* of the *Essex* (one of the chief inspirations for *Moby-Dick*) "bears obvious tokens of having been written for him; but at the same time, its whole air plainly evinces that it was carefully & conscientiously written to Owen's dictation of the facts." The empathetic eloquence displayed in both the *Bank* and *Essex* narratives has led the literary critic Thomas Farel Heffernan, in *Stove by a Whale* (Middletown, 1981), to point to William Coffin, Sr., as the only Nantucketer capable of writing what has become one of the most celebrated whaling narratives ever written. However, his son, William, Jr., must also be considered as a possibility; he was closer in age to Chase and would perform the same service for Obed Macy in 1834–5; also Macy's *History* contains a plug for Owen Chase's book, suggesting that William, Jr., may have indeed been the author. In her introduction to selections from the *Globe* narrative in the *Nantucket Journal* (Spring,

1991), Helen Winslow Chase speculates that William, Jr., was also the ghostwriter for Lay and Hussey. For a good example of his prose, see not only the *History* but also the pamphlet "Address Delivered before the Nantucket Assoc, for the Promotion of Temperance," April 1, 1833 (NHA Collection 150, Folder 79). The younger William Coffin's obituary in NI (April 28, 1838) describes him as "possessed of a remarkably philosophic mind highly improved by classical attainments." William Comstock makes the comments concerning the "depravity" of Nantucket Quakers in *The Life of Samuel Comstock* (Boston, 1840).

15. The Golden Boy and the Dark Man: Obed Starbuck and George Pollard

For accounts of Obed Starbuck's whaling career see Stackpole's *The Sea-Hunters* as well as "The Whalemen of Nantucket and their South Sea Island Discoveries," HN (1946). The *Hero* incident is recounted in the anonymous "The Unusual Career of the Whaleship *Hero* of Nantucket," HN (April, 1984); Thomas Nickerson also provides a detailed account in an appendix to *The Loss of the Ship "Essex"* (Nantucket, 1984). The account of the *Loper*'s arrival is in NI (September 11, 1830); the reference to the "glorious sight" of the *Loper* trying out its oil at the Nantucket Bar is from Obed Starbuck's obituary, written by F. C. Sanford in NI (July 1, 1882); NI (September 25, 1830) gives an account of the festivities associated with the arrival of the *Loper*. The crew's parade: "Instead of guns, the crew carried harpoons, whale-spades, lances, etc. The generalship displayed by the marshals, the correct time of the music, and the soldierly step of this little band of whalers, together with the novelty of the scene, afforded a rare treat of amusement to numerous spectators." Also of interest are the many toasts delivered after the dinner: "1.—Captain Obed Starbuck—No man living has given so much real light to the world, in the same length of time. 2.—The memory of all good whalemen—May they never want oil to smooth their way. 3.—Captain Obed Starbuck—He that keeps the best look out from the mast head, will the soonest see home [In reference to the fact that they spotted a whale as they approached the island]. 4.—Fourteen months— Long enough for a good captain and a good crew. 5.—Short voyages— He that tries hardest will try the most. 6.—The *Loper*'s bucks—Like the

American Ensign—adorned by the STAR. 7.—Whalebone and Ivory. 8.—To War: that war which causes no grief, the success of which produces no tears—war with the monsters of the deep. 9.—Black Skin—The best skin which whalemen can see. 10.—Cabin, Steerage, and Forecastle— If well filled, will secure a full hold, and between decks. 11.—The fair sex—Short voyages make sweet faces. 12.—Death to the living and long life to the killers— / Success to wives of sailors, / And greasy luck to whalers. 13.—Ship *Loper's* voyage—No good luck, but great exertion."

The most oil ever brought into Nantucket by a single ship occurred during the same year of the *Loper's* record voyage when the *Sarah* (Captain Frederick Arthur) came in with 3,497 barrels worth $89,000 after a three-year voyage (in Starbuck).

Stackpole in *The Sea-Hunters* chronicles the many islands Starbuck discovered; one of the earliest and most notable discoveries by a Nantucketer was that of Captain Mayhew Folger of the *Topaz* who stumbled across the *Bounty* colony on Pitcairn Island in 1808; his logbook is at the NHA. NI (May 23, 1825) contains the article concerning the state of the Nantucket whale fishery.

An example of the community-wide importance Nantucketers attached to promotion is found in a letter (at the NA) written by Alexander Pinkham in 1821 (which, coincidentally, was delivered to Nantucket on the *Eagle*, the same ship that carried most of the *Essex* crew home): "I have heard not without some astonishment but with a greater degree of pleasure that Franklin is out second mate of a ship. I knew he was good, and that fortune favors the brave, but that is a step seldom taken—from boatsteerer to mate, yes, but from seaman (and first voyage too) to second mate is rather unprecedented. Whilst he figures so handsomely on the ocean, Elizabeth will be no less conspicuous in society to which she must undoubtedly become a shining member. . . ."

When it comes to the story of the *Essex*, there is no better resource than Thomas Farel Heffernan's *Stove by a Whale, Owen Chase and the Essex*, which includes the complete text of Owen Chase's original account of the *Essex* published in 1821. Interestingly, soon after the publication of Heffernan's book, Thomas Nickerson's handwritten account of the *Essex* was discovered in the attic of a house in Connecticut and subsequently published in 1984. When it comes to the ordeal in the whaleboats, Nickerson clearly depended on Chase's earlier account; his version is most interesting when it deals with the events prior to and after the disaster. Henry Carlisle's novel, *The Jonah Man* (New York, 1984), provides a fascinating look at the incident from Pollard's perspective and owes much to the Nickerson account.

The anecdote about the boy harpooning his cat is in Macy's *Scrap Basket*. The island's focus on "Oil! Oil!" is described in the *Nantucket Journal* (October 26, 1826). The comments concerning the "surly importance" of the Nantucket whaleman come from William Comstock's *The Life of Samuel Comstock, The Terrible Whaleman*; Comstock continues: "You will often hear a Nantucket mother boast that her son . . . is a real spit-fire, meaning that he is a cruel tyrant, which, on that island, is considered the very acme of human perfection." One of Admiral Sir Isaac Coffin's favorite stories was of a Nantucket whaleman in Portsmouth, England, who (literally) threw a British naval officer off his ship for swearing at him, then refused to drink wine with the illustrious Admiral (calling him "a damn Englisher") even though Sir Isaac had pulled strings to keep the Nantucketer out of prison (in Amory's biography of the Admiral). Clearly, Nantucket produced strong-headed seamen. The reference to a whale as a "tub of high-income lard" is from Robert McNally's *So Remorseless a Havoc, Of Dolphins, Whales and Men* (Boston, 1981). Comstock makes the reference to the "honor" of being island-born on a Nantucket whaler; he continues, "After a crew has shipped on board a Nantucket whaler, the first step taken by the officer, is, to discover who are natives of the island, and who are strangers."

Pollard's account of Owen Coffin's death originally appeared in *Journal of Voyages and Travels by the Rev. Daniel Tyerman and George Bennett, Esq.* (London, 1831) and is reprinted in Heffernan. There is a traditional (and undoubtedly apocryphal) story about Pollard in which he is asked by a "stranger" if he ever knew a Nantucketer by the name of Owen Coffin. "Knew him?" Pollard is reputed to have replied, "Why I et him!" The reference to the gruesome condition of Pollard and Ramsdell upon their rescue is from Commodore Charles Goodwin Ridgely's *Journal*, quoted in Heffernan. Nickerson describes the reaction of Owen Coffin's mother to Captain Pollard in an 1876 letter to Leon Lewis, the author who was to use his journal as the basis for a book that was never published. Pollard's reference to lightning never striking twice is related by Charles Wilkes, who was midshipman of the *Waterwitch*, in his *Autobiography* (quoted in Heffernan); Pollard's despairing resignation to his fate is in Tyerman and Bennett.

Generations of American children would read about the *Essex* in McGuffey's *Eclectic Fourth Reader*; according to the author of a September 3, 1896, article in the *Garretsville* (Ohio) *Journal* (in the *Essex* blue-dot file at the NHA), "Such accounts as that make impressions on the minds of children that last." See Heffernan's chapter "Telling the Story" for a synopsis of how the *Essex* story has been retold throughout the centuries; Heffernan also includes a transcription of Melville's comments in his copy of Chase's *Narrative*. For an account of Melville's visit to Nantucket, see Susan Beegel's "Herman Melville: Nantucket's First Tourist?" HN (Fall, 1991). Emerson makes the comment concerning the islanders' sensitivity in his *Journals*. The reference to the *Essex* being a taboo topic on Nantucket comes from Stackpole's afterword in Nickerson.

The reference to "a spy amongst us" is from NI (April 18, 1822); Stackpole makes the claim that Nantucketers were "a superior type" in *The Sea-Hunters*, adding, "Tradition had given these men of the sea a background of religion and home which made them both Godfearing and self-respecting"; Stackpole also refers, however, to the brutal Captain Worth. For an account of David Whippey, who "lived among the cannibals" (and never left), see Ernest S. Dodge's *Islands and Empires, Western Impact on the Pacific and East Asia* (Minneapolis, 1976), as well as Stackpole. Captain Swain is described in *Wanderings and Adventures of Reuben Delano* (Boston, 1846). Samuel Comstock and the *Globe* mutiny are chronicled in Comstock, as well as Hussey and Lay's firsthand narrative of the mutiny. Interestingly, Comstock's actions were not universally condemned on Nantucket; for some he seems to have been a kind of Jesse James of the whale fishery, a good-hearted outlaw pushed to extreme measures by extreme abuses; see the highly romantic poem "The Young Mutineer," which appeared not only in NI but in Comstock as well.

Moses E. Morrell's journal, "The Whim Whams and Opinions of M. E. Morrell, Written by Himself, for his own amusement on a voyage to the South seas on board the Ship *Hero* of Nantucket, 1822–4," is in the Edouard Stackpole Collection at the NHA. Morrell makes several unflattering references to the *Hero*'s officers. When the crew is not allowed to celebrate on deck during the Fourth of July, Morrell wishes that "our officers [were] as Patriotic as they are avaricious."

For an account of the orgies and abuses that were a routine part of the Pacific whale fishery, see Dodge; the first chapter of Joan Druett's *Petticoat Whalers* (Auckland, 1991) also has some fairly lurid accounts of the whaling life. The letter concerning her grandfather Starbuck's reticence was written by Charlotte Vain in 1940 to Edouard Stackpole and is among his papers at the NHA. The record of Obed Starbuck's voyages can be traced in Starbuck's *History of the American Whale Fishery*. Starbuck's final voyage on the *Zone* was also plagued by the loss of the third mate, who was knocked overboard and drowned.

For Nantucketers, the arrival of a whaleship was of "intense interest." According to an article in NI (May 14, 1842), "It is an era in most of our lives. It breaks in upon the monotony of common life, either by gladdening our spirit with good tidings, or chastening it by sad intelligence. . . . We feel a singular blending of joy and grief on such occasions. We know not whether to smile or to weep. Our emotion at all events is much subdued." Frederick Sanford's recollection of the arrival of the *Two Brothers* and *Hero* appeared in NI (March 28, 1879).

16. Absalom Boston and Abram Quary: "Of Color" on the Grey Lady

Boston's portrait is at the NHA, while Quary's is at the NA. Grace Brown Gardner's article "Abram Quary and his Portrait" (in the blue-dot "Quary" file at the NHA) is an excellent source of information; she quotes an NI article by Benjamin Franklin Folger that describes conversations Folger had with Quary; William Crosby Bennett (also quoted by Gardner) makes a reference to Quary as "the Prince of Nantucket caterers, and without his assistance no evening entertainment was deemed quite complete" (see Epilogue). A hand-colored photograph of Quary in extreme old age is at the NHA. For information concerning Absalom Boston and New Guinea, I have relied upon Lorin Lee Cary and Francine C. Cary's "Absalom F. Boston, His Family, and Nantucket's Black Community," HN (Summer, 1977).

Stephen Hussey's will is in the Nantucket Probate Court Records and is also referred to in Starbuck. Copies of Elihu Coleman's pamphlet (reprinted several times) are at the NHA and NA. Both the Carys and Stackpole recount the incident involving Prince Boston, Swain, and

Rotch that led to the end of slavery on Nantucket. Receipts for labor and purchases between Absalom Boston and various members of the Williams family are part of NHA Collection 197. According to information provided by the NHA: "John Williams, a Portuguese, and his family were the only members of the name of Williams to settle in Nantucket."

For an insightful, nonidealized portrait of African Americans on Nantucket, see Isabel Kaldenback-Montemayor's B.A. Thesis, "Black on Grey, Negroes on Nantucket in the Nineteenth Century" (Princeton, 1983), a copy of which is at the NHA. My own "'I Will Take to the Water': Frederick Douglass, the Sea, and the Nantucket Whale Fishery," HN (Fall, 1992), deals with many of these same issues but from the perspective of Douglass's first visit to Nantucket. As I mention in that article, there were even Nantucketers who participated in the slave trade. In a letter written from Havre, France, in 1796, Benjamin Tupper wrote to his mother on Nantucket: "I have bought a large ship of 500 tons and she sails this day for the West Indies. . . . She carries 500 Negroes, if she arrives safe I shall have money enough to come home & live with my friends"; the letter is reproduced in HN (July, 1937). The 1807 reference to the submissiveness of seamen of color is made in J. Freeman's "Notes on Nantucket" in NP. The letter from Abraham Williams to Nathaniel Freeman is in NHA Collection 197. Vickers's reference to a single caste of seamen of color is in his dissertation; as early as 1723 the appointment of a constable's watch on Straight Wharf referred to "Indians, Negroes, and other suspected persons." Macy speaks of the "inebriety" of the blacks in his *History*.

See *On Our Own Ground, The Complete Writings of William Apess, A Pequot*, ed. Barry O'Connell (Amherst, 1992), for Apess's brief mention of his trip to Nantucket; later he would become involved in what came to be known as the "Mashpee Revolt" among the Indians on Cape Cod. For an account of how the "total environment" of the ship fostered relative racial equality in the early nineteenth century, see W. Jeffrey Bolster's "'To Feel Like a Man': Black Seamen in the Northern States, 1800–1860," *Journal of American History* (March, 1990). The reference to a "Guine[a]" whaler is in a journal in the "Misc. Papers, Letters, etc." file in the NA.

Anna Gardner's reference to Absalom Boston is recorded in her collection of poetry and prose, *Harvest Gleanings* (New York, 1881).

Other "volunteer toasts" delivered by African Americans during the *Loper* banquet and recorded in dialect were: "De ship *Loper* and her crew—Strong as de lion, meek as de ram, catch de whales when he can see him, who do dat?—Tune, Keep a look out there. Our Nantucket Carmen and Butchers—No more like de Boston gentleman than Aunt Philis Painter's nose like a bunch of Horse radish. Tune—Pitman's march. Misser President Jackson—No more like Misser Henry Clay than Sam. Harris fiddle like a roll of a blackball. Whale Captains of Nantucket and N. Bedford—No more like Capt. Starbuck, than horse-foot like elephant. To Woahoo—Glad he cant speak no cuckold telltale, den all our captains go by him jus like ship *Loper*" (NI, September 25, 1830).

In NI (April 18, 1822), the letter writer refers to "the few 'heathen youth' which . . . have been imported within the short period of a month." The mention of the Sandwich Islanders attending Sunday school is in NI (April 25, 1822); Stackpole quotes from the story about the "Heathen School" on Nantucket and the response it incited in NI (May 9, 1822); the reference to the tractability of the Polynesians is cited by Stackpole. According to Elmo P. Hohman in *The American Whaleman: A Study of Life and Labor in the Whaling Industry* (New York, 1928), during the period from 1800 to 1820 Nantucket whalers "contained a much higher percentage of both Negroes and Indians than in later years." In 1807 it was estimated that the average whaling crew (which ranged between sixteen and twenty-one men) contained between seven to nine blacks. In 1820, one-eighth of all Nantucket whalemen were said to be full-blooded Indians (many of them coming from the Vineyard), with two-eighths to three-eighths being of both black and Indian descent, such as Absalom Boston. Reuben Delano tells the story of his early life on Nantucket and his experiences on a series of whalers in *Wanderings and Adventures of Reuben Delano*. William Comstock's statement concerning the treatment of blacks on Nantucket whalers is from his *The Life of Samuel Comstock, The Terrible Whaleman*. Kaldenback-Montemayor also points to the fact that no African Americans made it out of the *Essex* disaster alive.

That white Nantucketers were not about to associate themselves with seamen of color is indicated by an anecdote related in Amory's biography of Admiral Sir Isaac Coffin. At one point during Coffin's meeting with the Nantucket sailors in Dartmoor Prison in 1815, an African-American

sailor claimed that his last name was Coffin, thus earning him the privileged status of belonging to a "neutral country." When the Admiral
asked him how old he was, the black sailor responded that he had just
turned thirty. Sir Isaac, who was known throughout the British Navy for
his sense of humor, shook his head and said, "Well, then, you are not one
of the Coffins, because they never turn black until they are forty."

Melville's "The 'Gees" first appeared in *Harper's New Monthly Magazine* in 1856 and is currently available in *The Piazza Tales and Other
Prose Pieces, 1839–1860* (Evanston and Chicago, 1987). In "The 'Gees"
Melville makes a scathing reference to the island that would have had,
if they had read the article, a deeply personal relevance to both Quary
and Boston: "Among the Quakers of Nantucket, there has been talk of
sending five comely 'Gees, aged sixteen, to Dartmouth College; that
venerable institution, as is well known, having been originally founded
partly with the object of finishing off wild Indians in the classics and
higher mathematics." In his *Etchings of a Whaling Cruise* (Cambridge,
1968) (of which Melville strongly approved), Browne claimed that while
on board a whaler in the 1830s he "would gladly have exchanged my
place with that of the most abject slave in Mississippi."

John Greenleaf Whittier's reference to Nantucket as a "refuge of
the free" comes from his poem "The Exiles," referred to in the Notes for
Chapter 3. Certainly some individual members of Nantucket's Quaker
community had done more than talk about their commitment to anti-
slavery. In the 1820s, two runaway slaves from Virginia, Arthur and
Mary Cooper, were successfully hidden from the authorities by several
leading Quaker citizens. And in 1841 Anna Gardner, who taught at
the African School, helped organize the first anti-slavery meeting in
which Douglass spoke. For excellent accounts of the abolitionist scene
on Nantucket in the 1840s as well as the fight to integrate the island's
school system, see Barbara White's "The Integration of Nantucket Public Schools" and Susan Beegel's "The Brotherhood of Thieves Riot of
1842" (from which the reference to David Joy's letter comes), both in
HN (Fall, 1992).

Adding an eerie sense of cultural finality to Quary's death was
the miraculous return of bluefish to island waters. The fish had virtually disappeared after the Plague of 1763 and, according to an Indian
prophecy, would not return until the death of the island's last Native

American. Although Quary was Nantucket's last "practicing" Indian, there were, of course, many people still living on the island (particularly in New Guinea) with Native American blood in their veins. Soon after Quary's death, Dorcas Honorable, an Indian domestic described by Eliza Mitchell as "6 feet tall and a noble woman of her tribe," also died.

Although some island historians have attempted to discount the Nantucketers' involvement in the degradation of the South Pacific, the evidence is to the contrary. For example, according to the First Lieutenant of the U.S. Naval ship *Vincennes*, "Your Nantucket whalemen have caused us more trouble than all other causes combined" (quoted in Delano). In an article in the *Boston Advertiser* (in "Memorial to Frederick Coleman Sanford, 1809–1890," NA), Sanford claims that "it is unjust to class the Sandwich Islanders with the Polynesians and New Zealanders as cannibals." In *Islands and Empires*, Ernest S. Dodge paints an extremely sordid picture of life in the Bay of Islands. In a fascinating study in contrasts, NI (October 29, 1822) contains a story on the Coopers's rescue from slave catchers as well as this description of a shrunken head from the Bay of Islands: "It appears to have been that of a person about 30 years of age. The skin resembles parchment, and is very curiously tattooed.—The inside of the skull is perfectly clean and smooth—the teeth in a fine state of preservation, as are the eyelids, ears, lip, nose, etc. The whole structure of the mouth and even the cartilages of the nose are plainly discoverable through the aperture at the neck. The sockets of the eyes are filled with a substance resembling sealing wax. The hair about two feet long and very black."

The reference to the effects of "civilization" on the Pacific islands is in NI (May 2, 1825). Melville's lecture on the South Seas (delivered in 1858–9) is reprinted in the *Piazza Tales* volume. For an account of how the Pacific was overrun by America and Europe, see Alan Moorehead's *The Fatal Impact, An Account of the Invasion of the South Pacific, 1767–1840* (London, 1966). Melville's reference to "pirates of the sphere" is in his long poem *Clarel*, published in 1876 (Evanston and Chicago, 1991).

17. Maria Mitchell, the Provincial Cosmopolitan

Besides the papers in the collection of the Maria Mitchell Science Library on Nantucket, the best published sources of information concerning Maria Mitchell are Phebe Mitchell Kendall's *Maria Mitchell, Life, Letters, and Journals* (Boston, 1896) and Helen Wright's *Sweeper in the Sky* (New York, 1949). Kendall, who was Maria's sister, seems to have been guilty of "editing" or expunging the more personal (and probably more interesting) portions of Maria's papers. At one point in her biography she complains that her sister "had no secretiveness, and in looking over her letters it has been almost impossible to find one which did not contain too much that was personal, either about herself or others, to make it proper." Because of Kendall's efforts, there is much about Maria Mitchell we may never know.

Jenks's article about astronomy is in NI (October 18, 1829). Maria's comment concerning women and "night work" is from William F. Macy's *Scrap Basket*. Lucretia Mott's remarks are quoted in Margaret Hope Bacon's biography *Valiant Friend* (New York, 1980). Although Mott never lost her love for the island (visiting it many times), not all of her memories were positive. As a child she was horrified by the sight of a woman being publicly whipped in front of the town hall. According to Bacon, "Seventy-five years later she led grandchildren and great-grandchildren to the spot where the whipping post had been and told them in a trembling voice how angry it had made her."

Mrs. Folger's letter, dated June 6, 1768, is at the NA and anticipates the emotions that would be expressed by whalemen's wives in the nineteenth century when three-year voyages became the norm. See Lisa Norling's "'How Fraught with Sorrow and Heartpangs': Mariners' Wives and the Ideology of Domesticity in New England, 1790–1880" for a sensitive reading of similar letters from wives in the New Bedford area.

Opium bottles were uncovered during sewer work in the 1980s; see my article on Crèvecoeur and the Nantucket letters (cited earlier). Combine the long absences of the whalemen with Quakerism's proscription against "indulgence of the grosser animal senses" (the words of the religion's founder, George Fox) and you have the makings of what we would call today unhealthy or abnormal conjugal relations. As Helen Wright points out, one of Maria's married sisters admitted that she could not bear to touch another person's skin; another proudly stated that in all her years of married life she had never seen her husband naked; yet another insisted that it was impossible for a woman to enjoy sex. There is a Nantucket tradition of a different sort that claims the whalemen helped their wives cope with the long periods of separation by providing them with what were known as "He's at Homes": porcelain sexual aids from China.

The poem referring to the proper "sphere" of a wife is contained in the "Misc. Papers, Letters, etc." file at the NA. For more information concerning William Mitchell, see Helen Wright's "William Mitchell of Nantucket," HN (1949). The story from the *Nantucket Gazette* of Walter Folger, Sr.'s independent discovery of how to make sperm candles (so as to break William Rotch's island-wide monopoly of the technology) was cited earlier. The anecdote concerning Mrs. Folger, Jr.'s comments concerning her studious husband come from the *Scrap Basket*; Wright speaks of Maria's visits with Folger, Jr., and Phoebe Folger.

One of the young people Maria deeply influenced was Alexander Starbuck, historian of both the island and whale fishery, who as a boy used to work at the Atheneum. In a letter to Starbuck dated August 24, 1859, she wrote, "My Atheneum 'boys' have turned out wonderfully well—they were good boys at the outset or I should not have employed them, and I hope they learned no evil from me" (NHA Collection 5, Folder 1).

The letter concerning the degeneration of Quakerism appeared in NI (May 31, 1844). The description of a Nantucket Quaker meeting comes from a letter dated September 2, 1849, in the NA. The Quaker Committee Book of Objections (previously cited) is at the NHA.

The reference to the beauty of Nantucket women is made by William Comstock in *The Life of Samuel Comstock*; he also describes the "very select" nature of social gatherings in *A Voyage to the Pacific, Descriptive of the Customs, Usages, and Sufferings on board of Nantucket Whale-Ships* (Boston, 1838), published, interestingly enough, by the Seamen's Journal Office. Elmo Hohman speaks of the use of chock-pins as a Nantucket status symbol in *The American Whaleman*. That Nantucket's courting rituals were an ancient part of the island's social fabric is indicated by the reported persistence of the age-old custom of "bundling" on Nantucket, in which a courting couple spent the night in bed together divided by a wooden "bundling board." According to William F. Macy, bundling was still being practiced on Nantucket long after it had been abandoned elsewhere in New England (the last recorded use of bundling on Cape Cod occurred in 1827); see Henry Reed Stiles, *Bundling, Its Origin, Progress and Decline in America* (1869; rpt. Cambridge/Watertown, 1991).

The *Scrap Basket* has several anecdotes concerning Maria's dark complexion and deep voice. The reference to Nantucket girls being blond with black eyes comes from an article written by a Dr. Hobbs for the *Boston Atlas* and reprinted in NI (August 17, 1860); Hobbs also states: "Grace of carriage may also be said to be a characteristic of the Nantucket ladies; as is likewise a good development of chest. There is little consumption among them, but much of muscle, florid cheek and ruby lip. Some of these possessions, or all of them, added to their excellent education, refined manners, and virtuous principles, account for their meeting so readily with husbands."

Audubon wrote about the limited intellectual scope of most Nantucketers in his letter to his son (previously cited). In his account of his voyage aboard the *Hero*, Moses Morrell wrote in 1822 that Nantucketers were "with few exceptions . . . avaricious, ignorant and superstitious." In a poem entitled "Nantucket Sorosis [*sic*]" included in her book *Harvest Gleanings*, Anna Gardner speaks derisively of the island's response to the formation of a "Woman's Club," while applauding women's aspirations for something "above the groveling subject life" that apparently was considered, in her own words, a "woman's only proper sphere" on Nantucket.

Mitchell's poem about Maushop, entitled "An Old Story," appears in the verse collection *Seaweeds from the Shores of Nantucket* (Boston, 1853). For a discussion of Melville's visit with Maria Mitchell and the poem he ultimately wrote, see my article "Hawthorne, Maria Mitchell, and Melville's 'After the Pleasure Party,'" *ESQ: A Journal of the American Renaissance* (December, 1991).

To the credit of island "capitalists" (despite the claims of the NI in 1846), there were other, nonwhaling businesses (from silk weaving to the manufacture of shoes and straw hats) attempted on Nantucket in the nineteenth century, none of which proved economically viable.

The best first-person account of the Fire is by William C. Macy in the second edition of Obed's *History of Nantucket*; see also Stackpole's "The Great Fire of 1846," HN (1949). Although the damage done by the Great Fire was of astounding proportions, the worst to occur on the island as far as the loss of human life happened on February 21,

1842, when the Quaise Poor Farm burned down, killing ten of the fifty-nine occupants. When the Poor Farm was rebuilt it was equipped with what may have been the island's first forced-hot-water heating system, described in the *Vineyard Gazette* (July 19, 1849) as "zinc pipes through which hot water is constantly circulating, without the danger of the house being again fired by the carelessness of imbecile persons." Jenks's report concerning the 1846 Fire is quoted in full by Hugo-Brunt in "An Historical Survey of the Physical Development of Nantucket." Emerson speaks of the post-Fire looting and the concentrated wealth of the island in his *Journals*; Wright describes how Maria destroyed her private papers soon after the Fire.

Adding to the general trauma experienced by the Nantucket community in 1846 was yet another bank scandal involving (this time) Barker Burnell, Jr. The NI (January 1, 1847) provided a recap of that "eventful" year: "First came the failure of the bank, accompanied, unavoidably, with great distress and prostration of business. . . . Men knew not whom to trust, every one, for a time looked suspiciously upon his neighbor. Mutual confidence was just beginning to be restored, and the old spirit of union and cooperation to be again manifested,—when a deluge of fire came upon us, and swept away nearly one third of the town."

Parker's reference to Nantucket women is quoted by Wright. See Will Gardner's "Nantucket Farms," HN (1947), for an account of the more than 100 farms on Nantucket in the 1850s. Anna Gardner's poem "Nantucket Agricultural Song" is in *Harvest Gleanings*. Julian Hawthorne's description of Maria is in *Nathaniel Hawthorne and his Wife* (Boston, 1884). Maria's letter stating her appreciation for Nantucket is undated and addressed to a Mrs. Crosby (NHA Collection 5, Folder 1). Anna Gardner's words concerning Lucretia Mott and Nantucket (in *Harvest Gleanings*) might also be applied to Maria Mitchell: "Though Nantucket, this little world by itself, was her native isle, it cannot properly be said of one so cosmopolitan, with so large benevolence of soul, and world-wide sympathies, that she belonged to any small locality or even to America. . . ."

18. F. C. Sanford, the Mythmaker

In his island *History*, Alexander Starbuck speaks of the "lack of cooperation" of Nantucketers when it came to developing alternatives to whaling. The reference to the island as *the* summering place is from NI (August 14, 1845). Mary Starbuck's comments concerning the islanders' pride in the past and lack of enthusiasm for summer people were made in an article entitled "A Protest from Old Nantucket" in the *Boston Evening Transcript* and reprinted in NI (undated clipping in NHA blue-dot file); see also her article "Whale Oil and Spermaceti" in *New England Magazine* (July, 1902), where she writes: "The old Nantucket is a thing of the past. . . . A new Nantucket is being evolved, but what shall be its character no prophet may yet foretell." One of the best short treatments of Nantucket at its "lowest ebb" is to be found in Marc Simpson's "Taken with a Cranberry Fit: Eastman Johnson on Nantucket," in the exhibition guide *Eastman Johnson, The Cranberry Harvest, Island of Nantucket* (San Diego, 1990). Samuel Adams Drake in *Nooks and Corners of the New England Coast* (New York, 1875) describes the emptiness of Nantucket at this time. W. B. Drake in "Nantucket," *Lippincott's Magazine* (September, 1868), speaks of Nantucket being death-like; cited by Simpson.

For information regarding F. C. Sanford, I have depended primarily on these sources: Dr. Will Gardner's "Memorial to Frederick Coleman Sanford, 1809–1890," a handsomely bound scrap book and narrative at the NA; Sanford's assorted papers, also at the NA; the NHA's green-dot file on Sanford, which contains a manuscript by Edouard Stackpole about Sanford; and George F. Worth's transcription of Sanford's articles in the NI and other newspapers, to be found in NHA Collection 129, Book 19.

Sanford speaks of Nantucket as "the Chief in the World!" in a letter dated November 10, 1875, to Alexander Starbuck who was in the midst of researching his whaling *History* (NHA Collection 144, Folder 11). Starbuck apparently came to have a less glorious view of Nantucket's whaling history than did Sanford, who wrote him a nearly continual stream of letters during this period; see Starbuck's reference to "shattered idols" in the Preface.

A traditional Nantucket anecdote concerns a Captain Manter, an islander like Captain Gardner who found himself in the jaws of a whale; when asked what he was thinking while in the whale's mouth, he replied, "Wal, I thought he'd make about sixty berril" (in E. U. Crosby's *Eastman Johnson at Nantucket*, Nantucket, 1944). In her diary, Kezia

Fanning mentions the two Cantonese merchants on the island in 1807, as does Stackpole in *The Sea-Hunters*. Sanford recorded his account of Gardner's involvement with the Chinese in his copy of Vincent Nolte's *59 Years in Both Hemispheres*, which he donated to the NA. Irene Jaynes Smith writes of Sanford's marginalia in her description of Sanford's collection, included in Gardner's "Memorial."

One of Sanford's ancestors was Peleg Sanford from Newport, whose account book is one of the best sources of information on seventeenth-century trading practices; cited in Carl Bridenbaugh's *Cities in the Wilderness* (1938; rpt. London, 1966). The tradition at the Zenas Coffin Counting House was a New England–wide practice; as early as 1665, merchants in Boston were meeting every day at 11:00 to discuss business (in Bridenbaugh). William C. Macy speaks of the Panic of 1837 in Part 3 of Obed Macy's *History*.

A total of four whalers were built at the shipyard on Brant Point: *Charles Carroll* (1832), *Lexington* ('36), *Nantucket* ('36), and *Joseph Starbuck* ('38); it seems to have been a relatively "high-tech" yard, with the *Nantucket* featuring "live-oak" and copper-fastened construction, which was state-of-the-art at the time. See Elizabeth Little's "Live Oak Whaleships," HN (October, 1971), for an interesting account of shipbuilding during and before this period. The *Charles Carroll* was built specifically for Captain Owen Chase, survivor and first mate of the *Essex*. Sanford purchased the *Rambler*, a 318-ton ship, from Aaron Mitchell in 1838; a conservative estimate places the dollar amount of oil the ship brought in for Sanford at 1.5 million over the course of its career. Providing an interesting insight into the practices of a Nantucket whaling merchant in general and Sanford in particular is this record of his "Proffits" from his various ships in 1841:

1/16 Chas. Carroll	1323.87
3/12 Lexington	268.41
1/8 Rambler	2238.94
1/12 John Adams	140.00
1/8 Ganges	820.44
1/4 Japan	5488.00
PROFFIT	$10279.76

In a letter to Alexander Starbuck (December 21, 1875), Sanford describes his trip "around the world" and to New Zealand in 1838; it was during this voyage that Sanford assembled "the first statistical sheet ever made up on the whale fishery"; he claims that he soon "gave it up to others" (NHA Collection 144, Folder 11). Gardner's "Memorial" contains a detailed analysis of the many transactions involved in Sanford's gradual acquisition of the land surrounding the Barnabas Coleman House. Sanford's agitation over what he called "Gold Mania" in California was so great that he wrote Captain Bunker three nearly identical letters in the course of a single month just to make sure he got the message (NHA Collection 3, Folder 35).

Once the bugs were worked out of the system, Ewer's camels were able to carry a whaleship across the bar in as little as four and a half hours; see H. Flint Ranney's "Whaling and Nantucket—the Decline," HN (April, 1961), for a detailed account of not only the camels but the efforts to dredge a channel across the bar. Sanford spoke of the tendency toward centralization in his November 10, 1875, letter to Alexander Starbuck, adding that in the old days, "New Bedford was nothing, nor any other port on this continent, aside of our old recovered entrepôt. I can remember when they came from every point in New England. Yes! even from the Vineyard to earn a whaling reputation." William C. Macy's comments concerning the Nantucket whaling captains' conservatism are in his addendum to Obed Macy's *History*.

Captain Charles Low's account of Sanford in San Francisco is from *Some Recollections, Captain Charles P. Low* (Boston, 1906); cited in "Memorial." After two successful runs to China, Captain Coleman returned to Nantucket, with the command of the *Houqua* going to yet another islander, William Cartwright. On Cartwright's second voyage, the ship and all hands were lost, including Henry Coleman's son.

The Nantucket waterfront seems to have been a favorite (and exceedingly dangerous) playground for children. NI (September 15, 1832) reports on the death of a seven-year-old boy while playing with some friends on a waterwheel in a blacksmith's shop; he was caught between the spokes and crushed to death.

The description of Sanford's pleasure in farming comes from an undated article by Gustav Kobe included in the "Memorial." The statistics on shipping in Nantucket Sound were assembled by William Mitchell and are included in Helen Wright's previously cited article; Samuel Drake speaks of the many sails on the Sound.

For Sanford's own account of lifesaving on Nantucket see Godfrey's 1882 guide. Sanford's hypersensitivity to Crèvecoeur's mention of opium may have been heightened by his involvement in the China trade, through which the Chinese population was ravaged by opium supplied by European and American trading vessels; see Ernest Dodge in *Islands and Empires* on the "Opium Wars" and the effects of the drug on the Chinese. Sanford's Crèvecoeur volume is at the NA, although his copy of *The Pilot* is missing; William O. Stevens in *Nantucket, the Far-Away Island* (New York, 1936) quotes Sanford's comments about Long Tom Coffin and Reuben Chase. For an account of the history of "The Nantucket Tea Party," see Guba; Sanford's signed affidavit concerning the letter is in the "Memorial," which also contains the account of the carriage ride with President Grant. Stevens says that Sanford was "often referred to as the 'King of Nantucket.'" Alcon Chadwick in a previously cited article speaks of Sanford's dignified, somewhat racy appearance. See HN (April, 1966) for a photographic record of the demolition of the F. C. Sanford House. Forman's re-creation of old Siasconset contains references to the Sanford cottage.

Epilogue

Information concerning the *Gay Head* comes from Paul C. Morris and Joseph F. Morin's *The Island Steamers* (Nantucket, 1977). Of interest is that in the early 1890s the *Gay Head*'s captain was Grafton L. Daggett, a descendant of the same Daggett who served as Thomas Macy's pilot and "boarder" in 1659.

In the *Scrap Basket*, Macy defines squantum as "the Nantucketer's name for a party outing or picnic—differing from a 'rantum scoot' in that a squantum usually implies some definite destination for the cruise." In his *History* Macy says of Siasconset: "As a summer resort, no place in the United States presents greater attractions for the invalid. . . . The village is compactly built on a level grass plat, near the edge of a steep cliff; the land rises in the rear, so as to cut off a view of the town of Nantucket, and serve as a barrier to the cares and bustle of a turbulent world.

In front, the eye rests on a broad expanse of the Atlantic, and below, the surf rolling and breaking, gives animation to the scenes by day, and lulls to repose by night."

Josiah Quincy in NP speaks of both the pond-fishing whalemen and the annual sheep shearing. Abram Quary's life as "the Prince of Nantucket caterers" is mentioned in a previously cited NI article by William Crosby Bennett; Gardner in his F. C. Sanford "Memorial" also speaks of Quary. John Steinbeck's comments concerning our tendency to "celebrate an illustrious past" we never had were made in an article entitled "This is the Monterey We Love" written for the *Monterey Peninsula Herald* in 1967; he voiced a very similar attitude concerning Sag Harbor's whaling past. (I'd like to thank Susan Shillinglaw, Director of the Steinbeck Research Center in San Jose, California, for bringing this article to my attention.) Crèvecoeur's mesmerizing encounter with the surf off Siasconset caps the five-letter Nantucket sequence in *Letters from an American Farmer*; Emerson recorded his reaction to the Nantucket surf in his *Journals*.

Acknowledgments

HAVING SPENT THE GREATER portion of a year taking up space in their often cramped and crowded quarters, I would first like to express my gratitude to the staffs of several important island institutions: the Nantucket Historical Association (especially Jacqueline K. Haring, Betsy Tyler, Michael Jehle, Maureen Dwyer, and Peter MacGlashan), the Nantucket Atheneum (Charlotte Maison, Barbara Andrews, and Lee Burne), and Jane Stroup of the Maria Mitchell Science Library. Thanks also to the staffs of the Registry of Deeds, Probate Court, Superior Court, and Town Clerk's Office in the Nantucket Town Building.

Special thanks to Albert "Bud" Egan, Jr., not only for publishing this book but also for the Brant Point bourbon; to Mimi Beman and Dwight Beman for pushing me in the right direction at an early stage; to Helen Winslow Chase for sharing her knowledge and setting me straight; to Wes Tiffney for a Sunday morning of consultation that immensely improved this book; to Susan Beegel for her support and wide-ranging input; to Peter Dunwiddie and his comments on Indians, snakes, and the environment; to Elizabeth Little for her advice on "Old Saul"; to Robert Oldale for his hunches on Jeremiah's Gutter; to Dr. Timothy Lepore for his waiting-room words on roadkill, Indians, and inbreeding; to Bruce Courson and his *Argument Settlers* on steroids"; to Amy Rockicki for all her research help; to Mike Gordon and his dream of Lily Pond; to Lisa Norling for the xeroxes and conversation; to George Dawson for bringing an important resource to my attention; to Hank Kehlenbeck and his picture of Maria's cupola; to Charly Walters and his legend of Kezia's tunnel; to Rick Blair and a legend of a different sort; to Nancy Thayer, for listening; and to Edouard Stackpole and Louise Hussey, the two sages of Old Nantucket; and to Fred and Diane Swartz for their design and production work.

The editing of this book would not have been possible without the help of many "off-island" friends and family members: Peter Gow, soulmate and editing wizard—this book is as much yours as it is mine; Elizabeth Douthart, my indexing mother-in-law from Maine; Marc Wortman, whose late-inning advice and enthusiasm kept me going; and my parents, Thomas and Marianne Philbrick, the dissertation advisors I never had. Final thanks to my wife, Melissa D. Philbrick, and to our children, Jennie and Ethan—I couldn't have done it without you.

Index